MUSIC AS
MAO'S
WEAPON

MUSIC AS MAO'S WEAPON

*Remembering the
Cultural Revolution*

Lei X. Ouyang

**UNIVERSITY OF
ILLINOIS PRESS**
Urbana, Chicago, and Springfield

Publication supported in part by the Swarthmore College
Constance Hungerford Fund and the Society for Ethnomusicology
Deborah Wong Research and Publication Award.

Library of Congress Cataloging-in-Publication Data
Names: Ouyang, Lei, author.
Title: Music as Mao's weapon : Remembering the Cultural
    Revolution / Lei X. Ouyang.
Description: Urbana : University of Illinois Press, 2021. | Includes
    bibliographical references and index.
Identifiers: LCCN 2021038212 (print) | LCCN 2021038213 (ebook) |
    ISBN 9780252044175 (cloth) | ISBN 9780252086212 (paperback)
    | ISBN 9780252053115 (ebook)
Subjects: LCSH: Music—China—Political aspects—History—20th
    century. | China—History—Cultural Revolution, 1966–1976—
    Music and the revolution. | Music and state—China.
Classification: LCC ML3917.C6 O89 2021 (print) | LCC ML3917.C6
    (ebook) | DDC 780.951—dc23
LC record available at https://lccn.loc.gov/2021038212
LC ebook record available at https://lccn.loc.gov/2021038213

For my mother, Cathy Chen Ron Ouyang 歐陽青蓉,
and my sister, Mai Ouyang Bryant Kelly 歐陽小湄,
for everything.

And for everyone who carries a memory of Mao's music.

CONTENTS

ILLUSTRATIONS

Figures

Musical Examples

Tables

ACKNOWLEDGMENTS

This project would not be possible without the willingness of every single individual who sat down to talk with me about the songs, the Cultural Revolution, or lived experiences. I am deeply grateful for every person's time and trust. I will forever appreciate your individual and collective contributions to this project.

It is a humbling moment to write out the acknowledgments for this book, as so many people played an important role (big or small, direct or indirect). It is a nearly impossible task for me to give full credit where credit is much deserved, so my sincere apologies to anyone I have inadvertently left out!

Fieldwork conducted for research was generously supported through Andrew Mellon Predoctoral Fellowships, the Asian Cultural Council, and the Asian Studies Center and Nationality Rooms at the University of Pittsburgh. During my postdoctoral fellowship at Macalester College, Jan Serie's mentorship in general was transformative, and her specific help in making the Freeman Foundation grant possible was a necessary and timely boost to my ongoing research and fieldwork. At Skidmore College my research was funded through multiple internal grants, including the Doris E. Morgan faculty development grant. I am thrilled to have recently joined the faculty at Swarthmore College, where my scholarship has already been supported in many ways, including Faculty Research Grants and through the Constance Hungerford Fund. I thank the Society for Ethnomusicology's recognition of my scholarship and this project with the Deborah Wong Research and Publication Award.

This manuscript began with fieldwork conducted during my graduate studies. My work would not have been possible without the wisdom and support of individuals at the University of Pittsburgh and the Music Research Institute of the Chinese National Academy of Arts. At Pitt, I was fortunate to have had an entire team of graduate advisors and mentors who inspired and helped to shape my research. The Department of Music and the Asian Studies Center provided tremendous funding opportunities and scholarly engagement throughout my time at Pitt. Specifically, I thank Andrew Weintraub, Wenfang Tang, Nicole Constable, Evelyn Rawski, Mathew Rosenblum, and Zhang Haihui at the University of Pittsburgh, and Yu Yueming at Carnegie Mellon University. A very special thank you goes to my incredible graduate advisor, Bell Yung, who simultaneously challenged and supported me from the very first day. My work is unquestionably stronger as a direct result of studying with him.

In Beijing at the Music Research Institute, the project would not have been possible without the generous guidance from Qiao Jianzhong, Ju Qihong, Xiao Mei, Zeng Suijin, and all of the library staff during my visits. I can never thank them enough for their assistance during the early stages of my research. Quite some time has passed since we last sat down together, and any errors in this book are fully mine. I am so grateful for their willingness to share their expertise with me. Thanks go as well to Peter and Sara He, Liang Maochun, and Maggie Shao during my time in Beijing.

It was invigorating to have the opportunity to draw into conversation the exceptional English-language scholarship on the Cultural Revolution (arts and society), most notably with Xiaomei Chen, Denise Ho, Sheldon Lu, Xing Lu, Barbara Mittler, and Guobin Yang. All of their work informs this project here, and I thank them for their scholarship.

Many thanks go to all of the responses and comments to papers presented at the national conferences of the Society for Ethnomusicology (Estes Park, 2002; Miami, 2003; Tucson, 2004; and Albuquerque, 2018), the Association for Asian Studies (San Diego, 2004), and the American Historical Association (Philadelphia, 2006). Thanks also go to the hosts for the invitation and experience to present my work at Luther College (2005), Michigan State University (2006), Hamline University (2006), Macalester College (2011), Bowdoin College (2015), and Temple University (2017). Each of these opportunities to share my research helped develop my work, and I really appreciated all of the questions, comments, and engaged listening.

Cover art for this book is a commissioned piece by artist Stephanie Shih. Her reimagining of the Cultural Revolution propaganda poster brings a contemporary resonance to this project. I appreciate the artistry, care, and intention with which she works and am so honored that she is part of this project.

A rotating team of student assistants helped with various research tasks over the years; my sincere thanks go to Clay Conley, Eva Hagan, Ni Fang, Carol Jia Lu Li, Yaomingxin Lu, Ayako Shapiro, Gillian Stone, and KunYu Tan. Librarians make everything possible, and I am indebted to the assistance of so many, including Dunglan Chen, Donna Fournier, and LF Li. Thanks also go to editors Julie Bush and Michael Needham for their careful work with my words and ideas. Thanks are due to everyone at the University of Illinois Press and especially Laurie Matheson. The book production process was expertly handled by an entire team, including Jennifer Comeau, Ellie Hinton, and Tad Ringo. Much appreciation to Elizabeth Lin for the final Chinese proofreading and to David Martinez for the index.

Navigating graduate school and three different institutions takes networks of care and support. I am grateful for so many wonderful colleagues and friends over the years. Graduate school would not have been possible without Tian Chen, Melissa Dickinson, Gilda Lyons, and Dawn Seckler. During my postdoc years, I cherish the connections with Sarita Gregory, Sejal Shah, and Cindy Wu. Thanks go to colleagues at Skidmore for seeing me through all of the ups and downs: Joel Brown, Mary Campa, Youngon Choi, Eunice Ferreira, Kristie Ford, Winston Grady-Willis, Ruben Graciani, Shelley Currans Joyce, Sue Layden, Robin Nelson, Michelle Rhee, Gordon Thompson, Amber Wiley, and Joshua Woodfork. Now at Swarthmore College, I am in the excellent company of my music colleagues Jamie Blasina, Andrew Hauze, Jon Kochavi, and Jerry Levinson. Special thanks are due to Barbara Milewski for the very close readings of portions of this manuscript and earlier drafts. My Asian studies colleagues so quickly and warmly welcomed me to campus, including Will Gardiner, Steven Hopkins, Akiko Imamura, Haili Kong, and Tyrene White. And I especially treasure my colleagues across campus Roseann Liu, Bakirathi Mani, Edwin Mayorga, and Sarah Willie-LeBreton.

Ongoing thanks go to senior scholars in Asian studies, ethnomusicology, and related disciplines: Susan Asai, Mercedes Dujunco, Tomie Hahn, Eileen Hayes, Fred Lau, Tong Soon Lee, Nancy Rao, Helen Rees, Sue Tuohy, Deborah Wong, and Su Zheng. Their wide-ranging contributions and continued support and guidance—simply knowing each of them—has made all the difference in the world to me.

I cannot imagine the year 2020 without my SEM Board colleagues Jean Kidula, Alejandro Madrid, Noriko Manabe, Sarah Morelli, Tes Slominski, and Steve Stuempfle. I learned so much from each of them and our work together.

For my own and the next generation of scholars inside and outside ethnomusicology and Asian studies, I am fortunate to be in such extraordinary company with Catherine Appert, Shalini Ayyagari, Nilanjana Bhattacharjya, Kim Chow-Morris, Eric Hung, Krystal Klingenberg, Donna Kwon, Liz Macy, Noriko Manabe, Dan Neely, Griff Rollefson, Meredith Schweig, Mike Silvers, Tes Slominski, Yun Emily Wang, and Chuen-Fung Wong. I thank each of them for their contributions to our shared research interests, for our past, present, and future collaborations, and especially for our friendships and collegiality.

I am so fortunate to have such strong, talented, and fun women in so many areas of my life. There aren't enough words to express how grateful I am for the decades of friendship with Kelly, Heather, and Rachel. And more recently, it's been such a treat to get to know and have the support of my mother-in-law, Betsy Wise.

To my mother, Cathy Chen Ron Ouyang, and my sister, Mai Ouyang Bryant Kelly, I can't ever thank you enough for your love and support, especially during my graduate years when this project was truly coming together.

Finally, thanks to Alex, Ari, and Eli for everything you provided to help me complete this book. The joy, love, and humor you bring to every minute we have together keeps me going.

NOTES ON PINYIN, SURNAMES, TRANSLITERATION, AND TRANSLATION

I use the standard Hanyu pinyin romanization system for the transliteration of Chinese language, following current scholarly practice in English language scholarship and studies of the People's Republic of China. Some exceptions include Chiang Kai-shek, KMT (Guomindang), and a few others where variations from Hanyu pinyin are well-established and recognized.

Fieldwork interviews were primarily conducted in Mandarin Chinese, English, or a combination of both. As such, English translations of references and excerpts of interviews are mine unless otherwise noted. Chen Jiebing's interviews are the exception, as most of our interviews were conducted primarily in English with some reference to Chinese terms and names.

I largely maintain the Chinese practice of surname first followed by a given name (for example, Chen Jiebing). I use the English-language convention of a given name followed by the surname for scholars and individuals based outside of the PRC who have published and are recognized as such (for example, Xiaomei Chen).

MUSIC AS MAO'S WEAPON

1

RESEARCHING THE BATTLEFIELD

When people in (or originally from) China learn that my research focus is the music of the Cultural Revolution, the most common reaction is laughter. Sometimes the laughter is nervous—this music is not a common topic of discussion—and other times it reflects the fact that these songs have often been considered the worst music in Chinese history. The art of the Cultural Revolution is often deemed unworthy of serious analysis because of its regressive politics. But when I start talking about the individual songs, a certain light comes into many respondents' eyes, the songbooks clearly sparking some memories. When I first listened to the songs in 2001, when I was a graduate student, their lyrics sounded like blatant political propaganda, devoid of any human emotion to me. I did not directly experience the Cultural Revolution myself, but as I spoke with my respondents about the songs, I started to observe patterns of deeply emotional and personal connections to the music. I was initially surprised to discover how the songs could trigger emotionally heightened memories that were completely estranged from the political campaigns that created them.

As I began to research Cultural Revolution music, an obvious starting point was the politics of the music and the context within which the music was created and disseminated. I quickly learned of one of Mao Zedong's (毛泽东) leading cultural policies informing Cultural Revolution propaganda, one in which music was to serve as a weapon in the ideological endeavor of transforming China into a socialist society. As I interviewed musicians, editors, scholars, and individuals who experienced the Cultural Revolution firsthand, two additional themes emerged: the significance of childhood and generational imprinting, set within a broader discussion of memory. Researching the Cultural Revolution decades after its end placed this work squarely within one of memory, particularly on the topic of music and its impact. This research relied almost entirely on ethnographic fieldwork and thus conversations occurring in a contemporary moment about the past. The current manuscript is organized around these three large themes: politics, childhood, and memory.

Music as Mao's Weapon ultimately considers the questions "Why music?," "Why does this matter today?," and "What can we learn?" After moving through the politics of the time period, the particular impact on individuals who experienced the Cultural Revolution as children, and the contemporary memory of the period, my attention turned to the particular combination of extremes during the Cultural Revolution. While the period is well known for the political, historical, and cultural extremes, including violence and trauma, I argue that it was also a sensory environment of historic extremes. The weaponization of music and the totalitarian dissemination of political propaganda arts was not merely a political or ideological revolution but also a revolution of the senses. Understanding the legacy of Cultural Revolution music today offers insight into the impact of exploitation and manipulation of music.

One Day at Lunch

The "Great Proletarian Cultural Revolution" (Wuchan jieji wenhua dageming 无产阶级文化大革命), or Cultural Revolution for short, is most commonly understood as a ten-year period of chaos in China that lasted from 1966 through the death of Mao Zedong in 1976. The impact of this period lingers on in contemporary China, but each individual who lived through this time remembers, reconstructs, or imagines the Cultural Revolution differently. A researcher of the Cultural Revolution must attempt to disentangle personal memories, emotions, and politics in the field while simultaneously negotiating issues of identity and one's own role as a researcher. I take inspiration from Tomie Hahn's "reflexive approach to fieldwork, analysis and writing . . . as a path to comprehend the complexity of embodying the halfie-performer-researcher and impart it to others" (2006, 94). As a multiracial Chinese American ethnomusicologist conducting fieldwork in China and the United States, I have found that my research has been shaped by the challenges that are unique to the contemporary memory of the Cultural Revolution and the post–Cultural Revolution context. As Lila Abu-Lughod writes, "Feminists and halfie anthropologists cannot easily avoid the issue of positionality. Standing on shifting ground makes it clear that every view is a view from somewhere and every act of speaking a speaking from some-where" (1991, 141). As such, I turn first to the story of my own fieldwork to make transparent the reflexive ethnographic approach.[1] I will then address the subject of my work, that is, the individual stories of musicians and artists who lived during (and after) the Cultural Revolution.[2]

I spent the summer of 2001 in Beijing, China, at the Music Research Insti-tute of the Chinese National Academy of Arts (Zhongguo yishu yanjiuyuan yinyue yanjiusuo 中国艺术研究院音乐研究所). As a visiting scholar, I met with professors regularly and explored the wealth of materials that were available in the library and archives of the institute. The main purpose of my visit was introductory research—an attempt to familiarize myself with the institute and its scholars in the hopes of designing a research topic for my doctoral dissertation. One day I was invited to lunch with some of the leading academics and administrators at the research institute and was in-troduced as the Chinese American scholar from the United States who was attempting to develop a research topic. As ideas started bouncing back and forth, one professor suddenly stopped the conversation and definitively said, "I know the perfect topic for you; nobody has dared to touch it yet, and you are the perfect person for it."

This academic proceeded to tell me about an anthology of revolutionary songs titled *New Songs of the Battlefield* (*Zhandi xinge* 战地新歌) that was published during the latter half of the Cultural Revolution. Despite the wide-spread dissemination of these songs during the Cultural Revolution, scholars had not yet focused on them. The academics at the Music Research Institute felt that I had a unique position: as an American, and someone who did not experience the Cultural Revolution, I had a political and emotional distance. Furthermore, as a Chinese American, I shared a heritage and possessed a ba-sic language fluency that could help facilitate connection, trust, and rapport with respondents about a sensitive time and topic. I could straddle the line between insider and outsider to gain access that may have been otherwise difficult to obtain. My nationality (U.S. citizen) and place of residence (the United States) provided a perceived "safe" distance from the politically sen-sitive climate in China, while my ethnicity (multiracial Chinese and white) and language skills (Mandarin Chinese) provided opportunity for a closer connection. Sure enough, these aspects of my identity (nationality, race/ ethnicity, language skills) would be brought up during every single interview that I conducted.

During the summer of 2001 and the winter of 2002–3, I began meeting with scholars in residence at the Music Research Institute, learning the basics of the five-hundred-plus songs included in the anthology. I also began learning more about the historical, political, and musical context of the songs in order to understand the lineage and processes leading up to this large and influential body of music. I returned to China during the summers of 2005 and 2007 for additional meetings with scholars and musicians who worked on the anthology as well as with individuals interested in speaking with me about their experiences during the Cultural Revolution. Since embarking on the project in 2001 I have also conducted research from the United States on the topic, including interviews with individuals who moved to the United States at some point after the end of the Cultural Revolution.

New Songs of the Battlefield

In 1942 Mao Zedong gave a speech at the Chinese Communist Party (CCP) base camp of Yan'an (a city in Shaanxi Province in north-central China) that addressed the role of the arts in revolution.[3] The historic speech, known as "Talks at the Yan'an Conference on Literature and Art" ("Zai Yan'an wenyi zuotanhui shang de jianghua" 在延安文艺座谈会上的讲话), established the guiding principles for revolutionary arts and literature in subsequent decades that would reach a climax during the Cultural Revolution. In this speech, Mao stated that the arts and literature were to serve the people and should therefore be created by and for the people. After the declaration, revolutionary workers were sent out into the countryside to live among the peasants and begin collecting their folklore.

New Songs of the Battlefield represents the realization of Mao's campaign and serves as a chronicle of historical and political processes from the first thirty years of the Communist Party's reign. The anthology was first published and released in 1972 to commemorate the thirtieth anniversary of Mao's Yan'an talks and was published annually until the end of the Cultural Revolution in 1976. The five-volume series promoted official ideologies and represented individual pockets of socialist society. Though a select number of songs included in the anthology were carried over from earlier periods of Chinese history, the majority were newly composed songs collected from amateur and professional musicians throughout the country.

Leading up to and through the early years of the Cultural Revolution, music and the arts suffered extreme censorship and criticism. Political campaigns shifted on a near daily basis, making it difficult, and at times dangerous, to create politically acceptable and relevant music and art. Furthermore, in the mid-1960s, Mao's wife, Jiang Qing (江青), began revamping traditional Chinese operas and dramas for the Cultural Revolution.

Jiang's model revolutionary works, more commonly referred to as model revolutionary operas (*yangbanxi* 样板戏), took center stage in the performing arts, and her rebukes to critics led to a screeching halt in musical production by 1969. Musicians and artists became afraid to produce any new material. The model revolutionary works were broadcast repeatedly with almost no competition. Jiang's criticism affected revolutionary songs as well, and from 1969 to 1972 the official broadcast of revolutionary songs was limited to a set of four well-established tunes: "East Is Red" ("Dongfang hong" 东方红), "Internationale" ("Guojige" 国际歌), "Three Main Rules of Discipline and Eight Points for Attention" ("San da jilu ba xiang zhuyi" 三大纪律八项注意), and "Sailing the Seas Depends on the Helmsman" ("Dahai hangxing kao duoshou" 大海航行靠舵手). Overwhelmed by the repetition, the 1972 publication of the *New Songs of the Battlefield* anthology was a breath of fresh air, and following earlier periods of heavily militaristic influence, the newly composed songs' return to traditional melodies and styles captured the public's attention.

During tutorials with the music scholars at the institute and in conversations (formal and informal) during my fieldwork, individuals would inevitably go off on tangents, recalling their youth and discussing the memories that the songs brought forth. They would speak of the heightened sense of a collective identity, how the songs were performed as a group, and how the act of coming together would stoke their excitement and sense of vitality. After conducting several interviews, I observed that their memories of group activity in the revolution years was usually contrasted with the present-day surge of individualism in contemporary Chinese society. Respondents often recalled how music served as an escape from the hardships of the period, how the political content went in one ear and out the other, and how the melodies were enjoyable and entertaining. Nearly everyone I interviewed commented on how the group activities of music making were invigorating and that no such outlets exist today. Another common critique involved concerns about the introduction of capitalism and increasing interests in money and material goods. Though my respondents did critique the politics of the songs, it was mentioned merely as an aside, and most of them were amused by their extreme revolutionary language.

As I tried to gain insight into the Cultural Revolution period through major academic and music-related journals, I found that nearly every publication had a gaping hole for the ten-year period of the Cultural Revolution. Aside from major newspapers and party journals, few publications are readily available. As the scholars at the Music Research Institute suggested, my research would depend upon firsthand accounts of people involved in the creation of the anthology as well as of individuals who lived through the Cultural Revolution themselves.

Obtaining original copies of the *New Songs of the Battlefield* songbooks along with original recordings proved to be difficult. My contacts in China attempted to assist me in acquiring original materials through official channels, to no avail. While they tried to break through one bureaucratic chain after another, a member of the Music Research Institute suggested that I might have more luck at the flea markets of Beijing and Shanghai. Over the course of two years and visits to various markets, I was able to purchase an entire original set of the five-volume series, along with a stack of original records.[4]

Figure 1.1. Original 33 1/3 rpm flexi-disc (photo by Ari Ouyang Danovitch)

Figure 1.2. Original 33 1/3 rpm flexi-discs (photo by Eli Ouyang Danovitch)

With the originals in hand, I sought to understand individuals' knowledge of and attitudes toward the songs, both then and now. Here again, I encountered a number of obstacles. Given the level of unease when discussing the Cultural Revolution, my interviews in China were largely granted by personal and professional contacts, which led to a rather narrow group of well-educated professionals, many of whom are closely involved with the Chinese Communist Party. My academic advisors encouraged me to engage multiple disciplinary methods, and with the recommendation of a social scientist I hired a Chinese marketing research company to conduct a public opinion poll to better understand the knowledge of and attitude toward the anthology, based upon an even sampling of contemporary Chinese society.[5] The survey was conducted in the spring of 2003, when I polled five hundred individuals who were evenly distributed between urban and suburban Beijing and Shanghai. The sampling was also evenly distributed among four age groups to reflect how the Cultural Revolution affected each generation in a different manner.

The survey results supported the findings from my personal interviews to a remarkable degree yet within a broader demographic pool. For example, generational trends I observed in personal interviews correlated to survey responses in a similar fashion. It was reaffirming to see how general responses in the select group of individuals personally interviewed resonated with a much broader sampling of Chinese society. Comprehensive details of the survey appear in one of my earlier works (see Bryant 2004). However, the current book focuses on ethnographic research conducted between 2001 and 2018 with select reference to the 2003 survey.

In addition to understanding the past and present individual reception of the songs, it was equally necessary to determine the compilation process, particularly the composition and editing of the anthology. This task proved to be quite difficult, as the editorial staff of the anthology is not listed anywhere in the publication. Many of the songs bear the name of an editorial committee instead of the individual or individuals who actually made revisions. The Music Research Institute scholars were tremendously and generously helpful in this area, as each of them provided me with a list of individuals they either knew or believed to be involved with the anthology.

I started researching the anthology some thirty years after it was compiled, and for every handful of names that I was given, one or two of them had already passed away and another one or two were in the hospital or at home recovering from recent hospital stays. Therefore, every eight or nine names that were given to me would result in maybe three or four possible contacts, many of whom refused to meet with me. The most common rationale was that they had nothing to say and would not be able to provide any insight. Of the individuals whom I did interview, all but one emphasized that they were meeting with me primarily out of obligation to my contacts.

One of the main reasons for their hesitation was that the anthology had been created under the direction of Premier Zhou Enlai (周恩来) and the four leaders who were later labeled the Gang of Four (Siren bang 四人帮: Jiang Qing 江青, Zhang Chunqiao 张春桥, Yao Wenyuan 姚文元, and Wang Hongwen 王洪文). Following the death of Mao and the collapse of the Gang of Four, everyone associated with the former leaders was punished to varying degrees. Many high-level editors involved in the song anthology were sentenced to prison and experienced other punishments and are understandably cautious about discussing the anthology today.

A number of interviewees doubted my intentions and grilled me with questions about how I would use the material. These suspicions suggest that the majority of investigations into the period have revolved around denouncing individuals and destroying reputations based on previous associations and involvements. The respondents usually relaxed once I explained that I would be publishing my work in English in the United States for academic purposes and that I was not looking to point fingers or study the political bureaucracy behind the compilation. After conducting a few of these interviews, I soon realized that, although respondents spoke under the condition of anonymity, every conversation began with extreme and persistent curiosity about whom I had already spoken with and what others had to say. I proceeded with caution and was mindful of the political and other sensitivities involved.

A number of the interviews I conducted with those who were deeply involved in the anthology resulted in lengthy accounts of the political bureaucracy that was associated with the compilation process. These accounts focused on identifying exactly where directions and orders came from—how some were explicit and others required a subtle and well-tuned sense of deduction—and on pinpointing exact origins of the anthology's perceived successes and failures. A common consensus I have observed, both inside and outside China, is that the urge to identify the political bureaucracy of the anthology is a habit left over from the Cultural Revolution; the behavior, though not absent from Chinese society in other periods, reached a peak during the Cultural Revolution. The challenge at hand was to piece together bits of information while recognizing that the puzzle would never be complete and that a so-called completed puzzle was not my goal as ethnographer. Moreover, the pieces of information shared with me must be considered and interpreted with extreme sensitivity, as they were inherently shaped and colored by the political and emotional subjectivities of my sources.

I often consider how another researcher of this music might produce completely different results. My research interests and the direction of my analysis are in opposition to those of many scholars in China, and a researcher of a different race, ethnicity, gender, nationality, and place of residence would certainly have had a much different experience when obtaining and collecting information. These subtleties may appear to be fairly commonplace, but the highly emotional and political nature of the Cultural Revolution complicates the seemingly obvious. Furthermore, the simultaneous insider/outsider status in my work as a multiracial and transnational woman is inescapable. Referencing her own biracial identity and multiple identities, Tomie Hahn writes, "The explanation of my identity can be a daily performance—embodiment of biracial performativity is full-time" (2007, 169). Hahn continues on to explain how "multiracial individuals complicate and confuse the constructs of race. We do not easily fit into statistic census categories in an orderly manner. Marginalized by the mainstream and by the marginalized themselves, living double enforces a continual critical perspective of the 'politics of difference' (West 1993) and a lived flexible (flexed?) sensibility of agency. . . . I have a strong sense that biraciality is in itself a haunting performance that disrupts discrete racial boundaries for others" (169–70).

When I present accounts and analysis of my research, both formally and informally, I am constantly met with curiosity regarding the details of my work. This curiosity led me to present my fieldwork, and the story behind it, as this introduction to my research. I aim to illustrate some of the issues involved in following this line of inquiry in twenty-first-century China. Some of them are indicative of general fieldwork practices; others are particular to the complexities of researching the Cultural Revolution, contemporary Chinese society, and my own multiracial Chinese American identity.

Understanding the Past through the Present

I have often thought about my own "field site" and what it looks like. Is it the Music Research Institute in Beijing, where my inquiries began? Is it in the various dormitories and hotel rooms across Shanghai and Beijing where I was based during extended fieldwork trips in 2003, 2005, and 2007? Is it the personal residences I visited across different boroughs of New York City? Is the field site my office in upstate New York, where I interviewed a handful of visiting Chinese musicians and Chinese students? My new office in Pennsylvania, where I wrote these words? Or the faculty apartment in Taipei where I am proofreading the final stages of this book? While these are all important locations, the field site itself really exists in the memories of my interviewees. My site is the perfect combination of time and place when someone takes me back to the Cultural Revolution through their own memories. My site includes the moments when interviewees break into song, recollecting lyrics and melodies from their childhood. For me, going "to the field" is the privilege of accompanying an individual down memory lane.

One can go about studying the music of the Cultural Revolution in countless ways. As an ethnomusicologist, I am interested in how the songs trigger powerfully emotional memories of a different time and place. These memories can be lying dormant and unexplored until awoken by a familiar melody or a lyric. I am interested in how, for many who came of age during the Cultural Revolution, the songs and the memories they evoke are distinctly separated from the overtly political content and function of propaganda music. As such, I aim to share what Lila Abu-Lughod describes as the "ethnographies of the particular" (1991, 138) through conversations with individuals who experienced the Cultural Revolution firsthand. Abu-Lughod's discussions on the challenges of location (2000) offer important questions for this historical, ethnographic account of music, politics, and memory. In understanding music of the Cultural Revolution, I aim to give voice to a handful of stories and histories through song in an attempt to better understand the ethnomusicological past—and present—of the Chinese Cultural Revolution.

Writing on nostalgia in contemporary China, Sheldon Hsiao-peng Lu identifies a change in contemporary reflections on the Cultural Revolution era as depicted in cinema and other media. After the initial representation of hardship, struggle, and politics, he sees a shift toward the everyday, the mundane, and the "lives of ordinary citizens" (2007, 133). He writes that this results in a "strategy of storytelling that depoliticizes and humanizes socialism, and brings down grand ideologies to the level of the lives of ordinary people. It is the everyday, the quotidian, that structures the existence and aspirations of hundreds of millions of Chinese citizens in decades of socialist nation building" (133). Remembering times past is an important process for modern Chinese citizens, especially as the generation that came of age during the Cultural Revolution started to reach their middle age in the 1990s. Lu continues, "The socialist past becomes a matter of the private history of each and every individual who lived through those years. As a result, there is no one monolithic grand history of the socialist state, but there do exist countless small stories of individual Chinese citizens" (148). It is my intention to include some of these stories of individual Chinese citizens in this account of Cultural Revolution music. By doing so, I employ a methodology of "listening to witnesses," as proposed by Martin Daughtry in *Listening to War* (2015, 15). Daughtry's field sites of violence, trauma, and memory overlap with my field site where I study the music of the Cultural Revolution. As such, the focus on testimony proves useful as a historical account of violence and trauma and provides a moment for survivors to process their experiences through the retelling of their stories. Daughtry writes, "Their desire to speak from the subject position of the bereaved witness can be understood both in terms of publicizing tragedy to avoid its repetition—the logic of 'never again'—but it also participates in the recuperative process of speaking (testimony) in the face of the unspeakable (trauma)" (15).

Giving voice to the historic period of the Cultural Revolution requires a negotiation of shifting sites, methodologies, and approaches. Researching the past requires the researcher to understand the human experience *with* the historical subject, or as Regula Qureshi writes, to "restor[e] . . . the human relationships that produce it" (1995, 336). Moreover, in this English-language and U.S.-based representation of Cultural Revolution experiences, I seek to identify moments of agency, individuality, and humanity. My work also aims to resist overwhelmingly negative and monolithic media generalizations of Communist China to provide insight into the lived experience of a historic period when music was weaponized for ideological transformation.

Understanding Cultural Revolution Culture

There is a long history around the world of individuals and groups utilizing music to unite people and influence behaviors, yet this was taken to new extremes during the Cultural Revolution as music was viewed as a weapon to "attack and annihilate the enemy" while also attempting to create solidarity among the people (McDougall 1980, 58). What happens, then, to the role of music in one's life as it is exploited to such extremes? What happens when music is used as an ideological weapon? What does this look, sound, and feel like? What does it take for individuals and groups to engage with such music? And ultimately, what is its impact over time? In this book, I explore these questions with music and people at the center. I aim to share histories, stories, testimonies, and experiences of and with the *New Songs of the Battlefield* anthology as one path to examine the intersections of music and politics, childhood, and memory.

The politicization of music in particular, and propaganda arts in general, offers insight into historical and political moments in time as well as into the human lived experience of these moments. As Xiaomei Chen writes on propaganda theater performance in the People's Republic of China (PRC),

> propaganda can be studied as a complex, dialogic, and dialectical process in which multiple voices and opposing views collide, negotiate, and compromise in forming what looks like a mainstream ideology—and indeed functions as such—to legitimize the powerful state and its right to rule. At the same time, propaganda also insinuates itself in the form of commercial culture, star culture, youth culture, and the cyber sphere to give popular appeal. Most important, propaganda is, to a large extent, deeply lodged in personal memories and the nostalgia for a bygone past among vast numbers of individuals. (2017, 1)

The continued impact of Cultural Revolution propaganda arts has been explored from a wide range of perspectives with different subject matters, such as the work of Denise Ho (2018) and Richard King (2010) within visual arts; Xiaomei Chen's discussions on theater (2002, 2017); and Emily Wilcox's *Revolutionary Bodies: Chinese Dance and the Socialist Legacy* (2018). Interdisciplinary studies of cultural production such as the rich volume *Red*

Legacies in China, edited by Jie Li and Enhua Zhang (2016), and Paul Clark's *Chinese Cultural Revolution: A History* (2008) similarly offer new discussions on the continued legacy of Cultural Revolution culture. Du Yang (2019); Fu Xiaoyu (2012); Wei Jun (2007); Wang Guixia, Liu Yunyan, and Li Xiaowei (2008); and Wei Jianbin (2011) each speak to the impact and significance of the *New Songs of the Battlefield* anthology in the context of twentieth-century music and culture as well as to its long-lasting impact into the twenty-first century. I have enjoyed reviewing these Chinese-language examinations of the anthology from the past decade or so and anticipate that even more studies will emerge with time. Additionally, scholars such as Ren Weixin (2020) and Gao Hong (2010) are beginning to chronicle specific stories, songs, and composers of the Cultural Revolution with new detail and attention.

One of the first English-language collections of case studies with music clearly in focus was Bonnie S. McDougall's 1984 edited volume, *Popular Chinese Literature and Performing Arts in the People's Republic of China, 1949–1979*, which includes a chapter by Isabel Wong on revolutionary songs and a chapter by Bell Yung on model revolutionary opera. Paul Clark, Laikwan Pang, and Tsan-huang Tsai's 2016 volume, *Listening to China's Cultural Revolution: Music, Politics, and Cultural Continuities*, offers a noteworthy continuation of McDougall's collection, though the book focuses almost entirely on model revolutionary operas and films with no exclusive attention to revolutionary songs. Vivian Wagner's work on Red Guard songs (2001) and Levi S. Gibbs's work with singer Wang Xiangrong (2018) are valuable contributions to our understanding of music and songs leading into, during, and after the Cultural Revolution. And Barbara Mittler's work (2008, 2010, 2012, 2016)—most prominently *A Continuous Revolution: Making Sense of Cultural Revolution Culture* (2012)—has been incredibly informative in my own exploration of revolutionary songs, with her comprehensive and meticulous interrogation of music within a broader study of culture. Chinese-language scholarship since 2000—including Zhou Yun (2012); Wei Jun (2007); Wang Guixia, Liu Yunyan, and Li Xiaowei (2008); and Zhang Juan (2018)—provides important new contributions to the study of *New Songs of the Battlefield* and music of the Cultural Revolution, each work citing in its own way the significance of the anthology in its time, its historical legacy, and its contemporary impact. Specifically, Wang Haiyuan (2011) discusses the impact on *erhu* (two-stringed bowed fiddle) compositions and Wei Jianbin (2011) on the impact of *New Songs of the Battlefield* on *dizi* (flute) compositions.

My work on *New Songs of the Battlefield* sits at an intersection of interdisciplinary work, bringing work from such fields as anthropology, communications, comparative literature, dance, ethnomusicology, history, philosophy, psychology, rhetoric, and theater into conversation with music at the center. In the recent volumes *Listening to China's Cultural Revolution* and *Red Legacies in China,* the editors open with an explanation of how scholars have been approaching the study of the Chinese Cultural Revolution from different perspectives and with different goals and point out that these differences are often aligned by language, nationality, and discipline. Clark, Pang, and Tsai explain this as a division between "historical correction and accuracy" (Chinese language scholarship) and "careful textual analysis of more famous works" (English language scholarship) (2016, 4) with a lack of discussion between the two groups. And Li mentions the focus of social scientists in particular, who aim to analyze and explain what happened and why through "larger political and social patterns" that "privilege taxonomies, statistics, and scientific periodizations" (2016, 6). Similarly, Mittler introduces her work as giving attention to "both the material evidence and the lived experience of the Cultural Revolution" (2012, 5).

My work also seeks to focus on the individual lived experience with and through Cultural Revolution music to gain a deeper understanding of what happens when music is politicized and weaponized, particularly during one's youth. When I began fieldwork examining *New Songs of the Battlefield,* I was met with mixed responses, including, as previously mentioned, resistance and reluctance. In the years since, I have enjoyed meeting and seeking out individuals interested in sharing their own stories and memories of life during and after the Cultural Revolution. For the current book, I selected individual stories that speak to these larger questions of the impact of politicized music, the experience of propaganda arts during one's childhood, and contemporary memories. Two individuals who stand out are musicians Chen Jiebing and Wang Guowei. Our conversations have spanned many years and locations and offer personal insight into the impact of Cultural Revolution music, particularly as their early years with music during the Cultural Revolution laid the foundation for their professional careers long after the turbulent decade. Furthermore, both were quite young during the Cultural Revolution, and their stories shed light into the lived experience of coming of age surrounded by, and participating in, a social, political, and cultural environment of extreme control and manipulation. Additional individuals I feature include Chen Xiaojie, for a unique look at the contrasting experience in a rural countryside and as someone who did not benefit at all from the Cultural Revolution but instead was negatively impacted as a result of her class background, and the three women I feature in the "Memories of the Battlefield" sections, who speak to the impact of propaganda arts from a range of backgrounds, mostly without any specialized musical or artistic perspective. Two of these women I personally interviewed in the United States: Zhang Haihui shared memories of being a young child in Beijing, and Jin Laoshi recalled being a young adult beginning her career in Shanghai. The other woman featured, from an interview transcript from the CR/10 Cultural Revolution project,[6] is a professor's daughter who moved from urban Beijing to rural Hunan Province to attend elementary school.

In her contribution to *Listening to China's Cultural Revolution*, Nancy Yunhwa Rao takes percussion in *yangbanxi* model opera (样板戏) as her focus. Before delving into the specifics of the case study, Rao emphasizes the perils of studying propaganda art simply as a detached "product of the state" and therefore the necessity of attention to "the human beings . . . and their performances" (214–15). Taking an all-encompassing view of the human environment surrounding *yangbanxi*, Rao writes that "a fuller understanding of both the daily practice of *yangbanxi*, and the social, cultural, and musical context of the sonority of music hybridity, as well as the creative impulse that lies at the core of contemporary musical work . . . , offers a window for understanding the sonority of the post-Cultural Revolution era" (216). This simultaneous attention to humans, context, and sound underscores my work with songs and memories of the Cultural Revolution. The individuals whose stories I feature thus provide ethnographic insights into the lived experience to deepen our understanding of the impact of politicized music at a time of extremes.

An Environment of Extremes

When discussing the devastation of the Cultural Revolution, scholars often address the number of individuals who were killed or tortured or who endured other types of suffering. The disruption to the country's infrastructure and society are also commonly noted. The consequences of Mao's political failures fell directly on the individual, which in turn led to catastrophic outcomes on the larger stage of society in general. Harry Harding suggests that Mao misinterpreted the country's problems, which led to massive failures (1997, 233); the tragedy of Mao's errors became a "tragedy for the nation" (149).

At the end of the twentieth century, the Communist Party of China acknowledged the Cultural Revolution period as a "serious mistake," and a 1994 English edition of the party's official summary reads as follows:[7]

> The "Cultural Revolution" was the consequence of going astray in the effort to explore China's own road in building socialism; it was an incorrect practice carried out under the guidance of an incorrect theory. It fully revealed, in

very stark forms, the defects of our Party and state, both in respect to their work and structure. It also presented profound lessons to be learned so that a serious mistake like another "Cultural Revolution" or any similar disastrous upheavals would never be repeated. A scientific summing up of the lessons of the "Cultural Revolution" will help us to find the correct road to build socialism with Chinese characteristics and march triumphantly along this road. (S. Hu 1994, 716)

Scholars continue to unravel the complex sequence of events that led into and throughout the Cultural Revolution. Most insert sweeping statements about the extremes of the movement. Harding describes the period as "one of the most extraordinary events of this century" (1997, 148) and John King Fairbank cites it as "China's ten lost years" and "from any point of view one of the most bizarre events in history" (1987, 316), while Jiaqi Yan and Gao Gao depict a more somber tone in their generalization of the period as "a colossal catastrophe" (1996, 529). The common themes that frequently surface in historical critiques of the period include the overall experience, devastation, and failures.

The overall experience refers to an emphasis on the lived experience of the era. Though time continues forward, the memory of the period remains in the minds and bodies of those who survived. Fairbank comments, "Statistics alone cannot convey the 'experience' of the revolution" (1987, 335–37); Maurice Meisner asserts, "Besides the dead, millions of Chinese limped away from the battles and repression of the Cultural Revolution physically and psychologically scarred" (1986, 372); and the "experience" is emphasized in Harding's words: "the images of the Cultural Revolution remain vivid" (1997, 148). Clearly, the continual reference to the individual's lived "experience" demonstrates the deeply personal impact of the Cultural Revolution. An overwhelming outpouring of personal memoirs, beginning in the 1980s and continuing today, in both Chinese- and English-language publications, validates the profound mark that the Cultural Revolution has left upon Chinese society.[8]

Cultural Revolution propaganda arts, such as revolutionary songs, help us understand more about this experience and require simultaneous attention to the environment. As Barbara Mittler argues, "Understanding the aural experience that was the Cultural Revolution may help us explain its social lives and continuing vibrant repercussions in the present" (2016, 250). I am indebted to Mittler's rich work on the aural experience and bring this inquiry in line with Ban Wang's attention to the aesthetic experience: "our perceptual, sensory, sensuous, emotional, and bodily experience. Although nurtured by the culture into unconscious habits, unthinking reflexes and expectations, this experience actively animates cultural forms with a sense of the agreeable, the beautiful, the sublime, or the ugly" (1997, 7). Attention to the aesthetic experience helps to capture the aural, embodied, and sensory environment that is particular to Cultural Revolution propaganda arts, a unique environment that also served as the backdrop for an entire generation of children and youth. Rao also illuminates the required attention to the experience and environment when she claims, "It was, however, through the significant 'everydayness' that the aesthetics of the *yangbanxi* achieved the greatest potential. While they were not often conceptualized as such, the *yangbanxi* constituted a significant everyday cultural practice for many" (2016, 217).

Considering the body and the senses, the lived experience and the memories, my work seeks to give attention to a sensory environment of historic extremes that was the Cultural Revolution. This requires an interdisciplinary exploration, as Wang explains: "A focus on this experience raises questions that cannot be adequately dealt with through historical, economic, political, or anthropological analyses. These approaches tend to treat a series of historical events as an impersonal process propelled by certain objective factors. Human beings are active in this process only as socially and culturally conditioned beings, with conscious motivations and rational designs to make things happen the way they did" (1997, 199).

The focus on human beings can be seen in other works on music and conflict, such as Lisa Gilman's dynamic exploration of musical listening during and after military service in her 2016 monograph, *My Music, My War: The Listening Habits of U.S. Troops in Iraq and Afghanistan*. While the differences between our studies are many, what our work shares is the musical listening during times of conflict, the emotions and meanings that are created in and embedded to music, and the intersection of music and memory. Underlying my work are the questions, Why did Mao and the Chinese Communist Party focus their ideological efforts on music, and why does this deserve our attention? Gilman's related work helps amplify the attention that music both deserves and offers:

> The emotional connections that both producers and consumers can form
> to music are vast, thus making music a vital resource for both articulating
> and processing emotion. People can listen to music as a form of self-therapy
> that they associate with a particular psychological state, as a way to express

or fully feel that emotion, and they can listen to music to evoke a particular affect, or alternately, to try to avoid or escape an affective state. Furthermore, because people often do not have control over the music that is playing in their environments, music can operate affectively in ways outside the control of the listener. (2016, 13)

In another historic moment of extreme, Polish political prisoner Aleksander Kulisiewicz used songs and music that "helped inmates cope with their hunger and despair, raised morale, and sustained hope of survival" (Milewski 2014, 143) while imprisoned at the Sachsenhausen concentration camp. As Barbara Milewski writes of the musical life in concentration camps during the Holocaust, "Kulisiewicz's songs, and those of others, gave him a sense of purpose, a reason to endure" (143).[9]

Focusing on Cultural Revolution music, my work centers the politicization of music, its impact on individuals, and the contemporary memories of the revolutionary songs. Through an examination of politics, childhood, and memory, we can begin to find answers to the questions Why music? Why does this matter today? And ultimately, what can we learn from this case study on music as Mao's weapon?

Reimagining Fields and Fieldwork

Music as Mao's Weapon is based on fieldwork conducted in the People's Republic of China and the United States beginning in the summer of 2001. In the first stage of research, I focused primarily on learning about the *New Songs of the Battlefield* anthology and situating it within its historical, cultural, musical, and political context. This work resulted in my doctoral dissertation (Bryant 2004) and subsequent articles (Bryant 2005, 2007). Primary research in the PRC resumed in the fall of 2002 through the spring of 2003 and again in the summers of 2005 and 2007. In between fieldwork trips to the PRC, I continued to research propaganda arts of the Cultural Revolution and synthesize my research within interdisciplinary discussions of music, politics, childhood, and memory. Throughout these years, I continued to teach undergraduate courses on the topics and write about Cultural Revolution music, leading to two additional publications (Bryant 2018a, 2018b). As a scholar, educator, professional, and mother of young children based in the United States, I focused my ethnographic interviews during the second stage of my research (2010–18) with individuals who lived through the Cultural Revolution and who are currently based in the United States.

My research on *New Songs of the Battlefield* spans nearly two decades, and thus the particulars of my own professional and personal life have impacted the directions, possibilities, and limitations of my research, writing, and publication. Over the years I have imagined the different permutations of this project and realized how the realities of my professional and personal life are often misaligned with certain circulating expectations for fieldwork and ethnography. Some of these misalignments are rooted in divergent disciplinary orientations, changes in academic fields over time, and other distinctions. Yet others are rooted in histories and presents of racism, sexism, and colonialism in ethnomusicology and Asian studies. As I completed this book amid a global pandemic, the recent "Manifesto for Patchwork Ethnography" (Günel, Varma, and Watanabe 2020) strongly resonated with the ideas that had been in my mind over the past decade or so when I imagined the introduction to what would eventually become my first book. With the pervasiveness of COVID-19 there is increased concern about the impact on fieldwork, yet anthropologists Gökçe Günel, Saibel Varma, and Chika Watanabe argue that the concern predates the pandemic. While the limitations and concerns brought about by COVID-19 are real and undoubtedly long-lasting, the need for reimagining fieldwork is not new to this moment. They call for a reconceptualization of "home" and "field" in order to build upon innovations of "long-held feminist and decolonial theorizations of the intertwining of the personal and professional, the theoretical and the methodological in research" (2020). The scholars propose a new approach: "*Patchwork ethnography* . . . refer[s] to ethnographic processes and protocols designed around short-term field visits, using fragmentary yet rigorous data, and other innovations that resist the fixity, holism, and certainty demanded in the publication process" (2020).

In addition to reimagining "home" and "field," patchwork ethnography also allows for a reimagining of temporalization as new realities shift our concept of ethnographic processes. The calls for rethinking the possibilities for fieldwork and the ethnographic process align with the reality of my own research on *New Songs of the Battlefield*, as I began the project as a graduate student and the publication of this book has culminated some twenty years later. I now have my degree and fifteen years of teaching experience at three different teaching intensive institutions. I have received tenure twice (two different schools). I am the mother of twins and a cancer survivor. Because of these (and other) life events, extended fieldwork in the PRC was not an option after graduate school and particularly after the birth of my twin sons. The writing and publication process took as long as it did because of my professional and personal realities. The choices I made in continuing my work were thus reimaginings of the ethnographic process, choices that were in line with my own professional and personal realities.

Music as Mao's Weapon is a synthesis of various stages of research that first began in the PRC and then shifted to research based in the United States about the PRC. Ethnographic snapshots from individuals currently based in the United States appear as the first (Zhang Haihui) and third (Jin Laoshi) "Memories of the Battlefield" interludes. Additional ethnographic moments appear in chapters 3 and 4 as "The Past and the Present" (Chen Jiebing, Wang Guowei, and Chen Xiaojie). Finally, one interview from the oral history project *China's Cultural Revolution in Memories: The CR/10 Project* appears as the second "Memories of the Battlefield" interlude. All of these reflections are thus coming from individuals now based in the United States who are still very much engaged with twenty-first-century China, yet from a distance. As such, their accounts, and my analysis of twenty-first-century China, are unquestionably from our perspectives and positions in the United States and as part of the Chinese diaspora.

As an ethnomusicological pursuit of a historical subject, and one that has little to no English-language documentation, I aim to bring together a wide range of materials, discussion, and analysis into conversation. That is, at times I introduce the anthology or a song, in careful detail, in order to provide original documentation of the subject on hand. Elsewhere I rely on ethnographic fieldwork to provide firsthand accounts of or with the music. Finally, I draw from scholarship across multiple fields throughout the manuscript for synthesis and analysis and to center the topic of Mao's music within these interdisciplinary conversations.

Music as Mao's Weapon begins here in chapter 1 with this description of the fieldwork process and a brief overview of the subject and the methodological framework as related to the fields of ethnomusicology and related disciplines. It details the core field site for my research, which lies in the minds and memories of individuals who survived the Cultural Revolution. The sites, methodologies, and approaches are all shifting and require attention to the present moment from which individuals remember the past.

Chapter 2 examines the politicization of music during the Chinese Cultural Revolution. The chapter begins with an overview of the "Great Proletarian Cultural Revolution" to situate the political history of the *New Songs of the Battlefield* anthology. I look at cultural policies and performing arts from the time period as examples of how Mao's visions were implemented in the specific political and cultural period of the Cultural Revolution. The chapter serves as an introduction to the *New Songs of the Battlefield* anthology, beginning with a brief history of the anthology, including the compilation process, and a look at the musical and political context in which it was published. It then provides a summary of the anthology's basic musical features, followed by select musical examples to illustrate the types of songs that are included in it. The chapter continues with a detailed discussion of the language and rhetoric of Cultural Revolution propaganda through consideration of musical lyrics and the work of rhetoric scholar Xing Lu (2004, 2017).

Inspired by Martin Daughtry's framework from *Listening to War* (2015), I include three interviews—"Memories of the Battlefield"—as interludes in between the more focused discussions of music. The interviews capture life during the Cultural Revolution in the individuals' own words. These interludes help to personalize the lived experience and provide firsthand accounts of the context of the Cultural Revolution. The first interlude, "It's in Your Bones, It's in Your Blood," is an interview with Zhang Haihui. Her story includes a childhood in Beijing amid the backdrop of the Cultural Revolution and present-day work as a public historian and librarian seeking to collect and share memories of the Cultural Revolution.

By representing the people in content, form, and style, Mao sought an ideological transformation of the role of the arts in Chinese society. Chapter 3 explains the impact of children's songs, addressing the gap in current literature that Patricia Shehan Campbell and Trevor Wiggins identify as the "darker side of music by and for children" (2013, 19), by analyzing the impact of political propaganda music on children and youth. The chapter then turns to the story of a young *erhu* musician, Chen Jiebing, who came of age during the Cultural Revolution. It concludes with detailed analysis of youth and children's songs to illustrate the political mobilization of youth through music.

An interview from the CR/10 collection appears in between the discussions of childhood and memory. "Learning Music to Avoid Going 'Up to the Mountains and Down to the Countryside'" makes visible some of the distinctions between the urban and rural experiences of the Cultural Revolution.

Chapter 4 begins with an ethnographic account of two Chinese émigrés who reflect in the present about their interactions with music during the Chinese Cultural Revolution. The chapter then analyzes music and memory through a three-part discussion. First, it situates this case study within contemporary discourse on music and memory, including the influential works of Svetlana Boym (2001) and Christine Yano (2002). It then describes the processes of memory and remembering to understand general concepts of collective memory and generational imprinting (Schuman and Scott 1989). Finally, it engages general concepts of memory through research on nostalgia and reminiscence (Jansari and Parkin 1996; Janssen, Chessa, and Murre 2005; Glück and Bluck 2007) to illustrate processes of remembering and nostalgia within the Cultural Revolution generation.

"You Hear These Songs and You Are Inspired" appears between chapters 4 and 5. This final "Memories of the Battlefield" interlude features the story of Jin Laoshi, a new faculty member in Shanghai at the beginning of the Cultural Revolution.

Chapter 5 concludes the book by analyzing the impacts of Mao's weaponization of music, including a sensory environment of historic extremes. The chapter begins by speaking to how Cultural Revolution music continues to resonate today in contemporary Chinese societies through recent events such as President Xi Jinping's 2014 speech on the role of the arts in China, the CCP's 2018 ban of hip-hop culture and tattoos, and Xi Jinping's 2018 address to mark the two hundredth birthday of Marx. These contemporary moments illustrate why this study of music, politics, childhood, and memory continues to matter both inside and outside of China.

The chapter presents an analysis of three points. The first explains how understanding the songs of the Cultural Revolution requires a simultaneous perspective of the past and the present in twenty-first-century China and that certain aspects of contemporary memory contradict the propaganda's original goals. Symptomatic of life in twenty-first-century China, these processes resonate with other discussions on memory and nostalgia, as shown in Sheldon Lu's work on Chinese cinema (2007). Second, I argue that the Cultural Revolution was a sensory environment of the extreme. It requires a comprehensive examination beyond the music itself, as the messages were amplified through sonic dimensions of nationalism (Tuohy 2001) and attention to the senses (Hahn 2007). Third, I discuss how the music of the Cultural Revolution, and its contemporary memories, requires attention to the violence and trauma with which it can never be separated.

2

MUSIC AND POLITICS

In my childhood diary, I quoted Mao's sayings ad infinitum,
and I criticized myself for any thoughts or actions that devi-
ated from Mao's teachings. In addition I would think of Mao's
words when faced with challenging situations. I attended public
rituals dedicated to the worship of Mao, and there we would
dance and sing songs to worship him. I was ready to defend
and fight for Mao; I would do whatever he asked the Chinese
people to do, even if it meant sacrificing my life. I grew up
in Mao's political and rhetorical culture, having inherited his
romantic idealism, his speech, and his ways of thinking.

—Xing Lu, *The Rhetoric of Mao Zedong:*
Transforming China and Its People

Overview of the Cultural Revolution

Scholars today are still attempting to unravel the complex political and historical accounts of the Chinese Cultural Revolution and continue to debate
what exactly prompted the ten years of chaos. Appendix A provides a brief
introduction to the historical context of the Cultural Revolution, including
significant political events preceding the period. In order to understand the
specific context of the *New Songs of the Battlefield* and the lived experiences
of individuals during the time of the anthology, it is useful to begin with an
overview of the Cultural Revolution period itself and official cultural policies preceding and during the historic decade. In this chapter, I examine how
music was employed as part of an official CCP cultural policy that aimed
to transform the content and function of music in order to serve a specific
political agenda. Music was politicized—or in the language of the Chinese
Cultural Revolution, revolutionized—to advance the efforts of specific political campaigns. The chapter begins with an introduction to the historic period
known as the "Great Proletarian Cultural Revolution" and follows with the

history and development of revolutionary music (including official cultural policies dating back to the foundation of the People's Republic of China in 1949). I then turn to an introduction to the *New Songs of the Battlefield* anthology, beginning with the political and historical context of the anthology and continuing through the processes of editing and compiling. Six musical examples serve as representative samplings to illustrate the basic musical characteristics of the anthology. Last, I engage Xing Lu's work on the rhetoric of the Chinese Cultural Revolution (2004, 2017) to analyze language and song lyrics as a means to understand *how* music was politicized and to recognize the powers of language when set to music.

The details of the compilation of the anthology, including composition and editing, remain an extremely sensitive and controversial topic. The sensitivity and controversy are inevitable with any attempt to write about Cultural Revolution history and are not exclusively limited to accounts of Cultural Revolution music. Important works addressing the historical accounts are valuable and ongoing (see X. Chen 2017 and Perry 2012 as examples); however, the approach taken and its objectives are not the focus of my ethnographic scholarship and inquiries at present. Interviews with government workers, composers, and editors reveal great discrepancies in the history of the anthology, and large gaps of information will inevitably remain for quite some time.[1] Many of the chief editors and composers who worked on *New Songs of the Battlefield* suffered professional and personal hardship (including years of house arrest) following the Cultural Revolution for their involvement with the anthology. The particular individuals I spoke with during fieldwork in 2001–3 were all eventually rehabilitated back into professional careers. However, the impact of the Cultural Revolution and its aftermath continued to be painful and politically charged. The overview of the anthology here is based upon my own fieldwork, including interviews with leading composers and editors of the anthology.

The "Great Proletarian Cultural Revolution"

At the Eleventh Plenum of the Eighth Central Committee in 1966, Chairman Mao received the support of the party's Central Committee to launch the "Great Proletarian Cultural Revolution"[2] (Harding 1997, 150). In the sixteen-point decision of the Eleventh Plenum, Mao established the guiding principles emphasizing continual revolution, education of the masses, and adherence to the party line (Hinton 1980, 1565–69).

While building the socialist economy, Mao sought to attack the "revisionists" and prevent the return of capitalism. Moreover, Mao utilized the arts, literature, and educational institutions to transform the "ideological realm" of the masses (MacFarquhar 1993, 248). Though a Central Cultural Revolution Group was established in 1964 to carry out the revolution in literature and the arts,[3] the group submitted a report in February 1966 that was rejected by the Central Committee. This led to the establishment of a new Cultural Revolution Group that was led by Chen Boda and included advisor Kang Sheng; vice directors Jiang Qing (Mao's wife), Wang Renzhong, Liu Zhijian, and Zhang Chunqiao; and members Xie Tangzhong, Yin Da, Wang Li, Guan Feng, Qi Benyu, Mu Xin, and Yao Wenyuan.

In August 1966, the Central Committee gave the group the "authority responsible for the Proletarian Cultural Revolution" and renamed Jiang Qing as acting director during Chen Boda's absence (K.-S. Li 1995, 584). The group took over the duties of the Political Bureau and Secretariat and exerted great power throughout the Cultural Revolution by establishing cultural revolutionary groups, committees, and congresses at all levels (583–84).

In addition to the Cultural Revolution Group, the spirited youth played a major role, particularly in the early years of the Cultural Revolution. The "Red Guards," as they became known, answered Mao's call to "Smash the Four Olds" (Po si jiu 破四旧): old customs (jiu fengsu 旧风俗), old habits (jiu xiguan 旧习惯), old culture (jiu wenhua 旧文化), and old thinking (jiu sixiang 旧思想) (Spence 1999, 575). Also known as the "revolutionary successors" or "revolutionary rebels," the energetic youth overwhelmed the nation through acts of violence and chaos as they carried out Mao's directives.

As the revolution continued on, Mao reordered his directive regarding the structure for seizing power, known as the "Three-in-One Alliance" (Sanjiehe 三结合). The directive called for all revolutionary committees to include representation from each of the three groups: the revolutionary cadres, the revolutionary masses, and delegates from the People's Liberation Army (PLA). The factional feuding within and between the various groups escalated, particularly among the Red Guards. By mid-1968 the conflicts had spiraled out of control; Mao ordered the PLA to intervene and restore order, and the Red Guards were reprimanded.

The Cultural Revolution was declared victorious and officially over at the Ninth Party Congress (April 1969). At the same time, significant changes began in both the appointed leadership and within the general structure of the party and government. Mao was unanimously voted chairman of the party and the Central Committee, and Lin Biao was appointed sole vice chairman (Hsu 1995, 702). The shift to a new centralized leadership was most significant in that the constitutional provision appointing a sole vice chairman designated a successor in central leadership (MacFarquhar 1993, 228). Additionally, military membership in the Central Committee nearly doubled following the meeting of the Ninth Party Congress (249–50).

The years following the Ninth Party Congress created an intense escalation of power struggles within the Chinese leadership. Despite the official declaration marking the end of the Cultural Revolution, many of Mao's radical policies continued to be carried out by the military and other members of his faction, the majority of which led back to Jiang Qing and the Gang of Four. By 1969, Mao had begun to criticize Lin Biao, and a power struggle continued over the next two years. Mao was not pleased with Lin's support of increased military involvement, and the two men disagreed about foreign affairs. Rumors of a planned military coup began to surface, and in September 1971 Lin Biao and his family died in a plane crash during an alleged attempt to escape the country. Known as the "Lin Biao incident," the details of Lin Biao's final days remain murky due to contradictory accounts and the "dramatic nature of the events" (MacFarquhar and Schoenhals 2006, 335).

After Lin Biao's death, Mao felt pressure to find a new successor who would lead China after his own passing. The successor was expected to be chosen from one of three groups surrounding Mao, whom Roderick MacFarquhar refers to as the "radicals," the "survivors," and the "beneficiaries of the Cultural Revolution" (1993, 364). The radicals consisted of Jiang Qing along with the other three members of the Gang of Four (Zhang Chunqiao, Yao Wenyuan, and Wang Hongwen), who were making a noticeable attempt to succeed Mao and continuing to carry out the radical policies that fueled the Cultural Revolution. The "survivors" were senior officials, including Premier Zhou Enlai, who, despite opposing much of the Cultural Revolution, remained faithful in their support of Mao. The "beneficiaries of the Cultural Revolution" included many military figures who had risen due to the downfall of their superiors.

In 1973 Mao surprised everyone by overlooking all of those around him and introducing a young worker, Wang Hongwen, to the Politburo and, months later, appointing him third in line after Mao and Zhou Enlai (MacFarquhar 1993, 280–81). Wang Hongwen was an ideal model and representative of Cultural Revolution ideology and had worked his way up from the bottom in terms of power and status. As Wang Hongwen joined the ranks, Premier Zhou Enlai headed a number of policies to "stabilize administration and encourage production" (282). The policies attempted to restore order in industry and agriculture so that these areas could recover from the devastation of extreme leftist actions of the Cultural Revolution. Furthermore, Zhou attempted to promote stability in the educational system and in scientific research.

Zhou's anti-leftist policies infuriated the radical Gang of Four and, in 1974, Jiang Qing launched the "Campaign to Criticize Lin Biao and Confucius" (Pi Lin pi Kong yundong 批林批孔运动) as a vehicle to criticize Zhou Enlai. The campaign was similar to the "Smash the Four Olds" campaign of the early Cultural Revolution years, during which cultural targets were harassed and criticized and "the damage done to Chinese culture was unprecedented" (K.-S. Li 1995, 427). In the "Campaign to Criticize Lin Biao and Confucius," Jiang Qing also criticized senior official Zhou Enlai and fostered support for herself to become Mao's successor.

Leading up to the campaign, Zhou had fallen gravely ill with cancer, and his health was quickly deteriorating. Mao was forced to remove Zhou from the daily operations of the party and, to the dismay of the radicals, appointed Deng Xiaoping to take the position of first vice premier. Deng had been targeted as a traitor for following the capitalist road at the onset of the Cultural Revolution but had since been "rehabilitated." As Mao attempted to weaken the military's involvement in politics, Deng emerged as a strong leader with military support. But Deng's appointment outraged the Gang of Four, and the foursome's hopes to take control upon Mao's death began to crumble (MacFarquhar 1993, 288–92).

Even with Mao's support, Deng's rational policies soon left him out of favor with Chinese leadership once again. In late 1975, an ideological battle between Deng and Mao resulted in the second round of criticism against Deng. At Qinghua University, some radical followers stalled Deng's attempts to restore the educational system. As word traveled to government officials, the incident developed into what Mao perceived as a threat of division within Chinese leadership and criticism of the Cultural Revolution (MacFarquhar 1993, 292–96).

Mao was required to make a decision regarding his successor when Zhou Enlai passed away on January 8, 1976. Clearly, Deng was no longer a candidate, as it appeared that he would not continue to carry forth Mao's ideologies. On the other hand, any leader chosen among the radicals would create an unstable succession of power. Mao turned to a longtime reliable beneficiary of the Cultural Revolution, Hua Guofeng, which further outraged the Gang of Four.

At the time of Zhou's death, the Gang of Four maintained strict control of the media. Public mourning for the popular leader was banned, and the Gang of Four attacked the late premier's policies as the "Tomb Sweeping Festival" (an annual holiday to pay respect to ancestors) approached. Students, workers, and soldiers all began to place wreaths and other objects in commemoration of the late premier at the foot of the Heroes' Monument in Tiananmen Square. The outpouring of public support for Zhou made Mao's supporters, both radicals and beneficiaries of the Cultural Revolution, extremely nervous. The Gang of Four quickly ordered all of the objects to be removed, and observers who arrived the day after the holiday were met with soldiers and police guarding a closed-off square (MacFarquhar 1993, 304). Crowds gathered and riots ensued; though most individuals followed orders to disperse, those who remained into the evening were attacked when troops marched in at 9:35 p.m. Ten minutes later the confrontation ended, and individuals were taken away for questioning (304–5).

The year 1976 was a devastating one for China. Another veteran soldier and recognized founder of the People's Liberation Army, Zhu De, passed away in July, and a destructive earthquake hit Northern China a month later. Agricultural and industrial production fell dramatically, and the country was in a state of disarray. The Gang of Four and beneficiaries of the Cultural Revolution quickly began plotting against each other. Immediately following Mao's death on September 9, 1976, Jiang Qing and the Gang of Four began presenting themselves as the successors to Mao's ideological crusade and initiated their attempt to seize power. The Gang of Four had military support of the Shanghai militia but could not stand up against the beneficiaries' support and control of the People's Liberation Army. As the Gang of Four's plan for a forceful takeover of power became increasingly apparent, the beneficiaries, advised by Hua Guofeng, Deng Xiaoping, and Ye Jianying, agreed to stop the attempted coup and arrested the Gang of Four on October 6, 1976, which marked the end of the Cultural Revolution.[4]

History and Development of Revolutionary Music: Official Cultural Policies

Using music as a political tool certainly predates Mao and the Communist Party of China; however, Mao's use of music represented a watershed in modern Chinese history. The use of music as a political tool in educating the masses is a long-standing practice that was advocated in the earliest classics. Confucius looked to music as a political tool, believing that music could "induce desirable behavior" if the correct lyrics and melodies were used (X. Lu 2004, 98). As Isabel K. F. Wong carefully chronicles, the practice has been documented, from the Taiping Rebellion of the 1850s and 1860s up to the founding of the People's Republic of China in 1949 (1984, 113–18).

Songs used to educate the masses were generally simple tunes with texts that pursued educational and political ends (I. Wong 1984). Revolutionary songs[5] since the nineteenth century were typically based on a combination of foreign music and traditional Chinese folk music and were sung at political rallies and public assemblies to promote support of the state and specific political movements, directives, and policies (112). During the Taiping Rebellion, Protestant hymns were adapted for the dissemination of political campaigns. Following the 1911 Nationalist Revolution, songs with sociopolitical messages were incorporated into both primary and middle school curricula (115–16). Over the next decade, intellectuals began to look toward the Russian Revolution, Marxism, and Leninism; in 1926, the CCP published a collection of songs for the revolution that included both Russian and Chinese revolutionary songs (121).

One of Mao's earliest cultural policies was introduced at the 1929 Gutian Conference (Fujian Province in southeastern China), where he ordered the incorporation of songs into the training curriculum and established committees to collect and compose songs for the revolution (I. Wong 1984, 122). At the conference, Mao and other party members outlined the two main objectives for effective propaganda as "time quality" (*shijian xing* 时间性) and "local quality" (*difang xing* 地方性). "Time quality" recognized the annual cultural and agricultural cycles and events for individual regions, and "local quality" referred to the placement of propaganda within terms familiar to local issues and customs, as well as the utilization of local dialects and other cultural markers. Mao believed that the masses would be more apt to identify with the national messages if they were presented in regionally and culturally specific styles (Holm 1984, 6–7). The direct emphasis on "local quality" initiated the focus of targeting specific sections of the population by utilizing their regional/local forms (6–7). During the 1937–45 War of Resistance against Japan, the political use of songs was developed further through war films and demonstrations (I. Wong 1984, 124). The songs composed during this period were full of revolutionary spirit and aimed to inspire a sense of unity.

Mao Zedong's 1942 "Talks at the Yan'an Conference on Literature and Art" (later published in 1943) is perhaps one of the biggest influences in the development of revolutionary songs (*geming gequ* 革命歌曲), also referred to as mass songs (I. Wong 1984). In his speech, Mao established guiding principles for promoting literature and art as part of the "cultural army" (McDougall 1980, 59) for the revolution: "Our meeting today is to ensure that literature and art become a component part of the whole revolutionary machinery, so they can act as a powerful weapon in uniting and educating the people while attacking and annihilating the enemy, and help the people achieve solidarity in their struggle against the enemy" (McDougall 1980, 58).[6]

Here Mao set in motion an ideology that mobilized the content and function of literature and art in terms of combat and warfare. In order to implement the use of literature and art as a weapon (*wuqi* 武器), Mao definitively stated that art and literature were to serve and be utilized by the masses—specifically workers, peasants, and soldiers (McDougall 1980, 59–60). Expanding upon the Gutian Conference's emphasis on "local quality" and "time quality," Mao continued to promote the investigation of local and regional forms so that they could be reformatted into propaganda. Mao instructed composers to collect regional folk songs and to experience and understand the daily lives of the masses (60). The composers and musical workers labored and lived with the masses during the agricultural drive, including the Great Leap Forward of the late 1950s, and throughout the Cultural Revolution (I. Wong 1984, 130–31). The principles established in Mao's "Talks at the Yan'an Conference on Literature and Art" were implemented throughout subsequent decades; however, they were ultimately taken to radical extremes during the Cultural Revolution.

In August 1963, Premier Zhou Enlai presented an audience of musicians and artists with a new policy to be applied to all socialist music, dance, and art. The policy expanded Mao's outline for the new democratization of culture published in his 1954 text *On New Democracy* (*Xin minzhuzhuyilun* 新民主主义论), in which he described how culture should be scientific, national, and popular (among the masses) (*kexuede, minzude, dazhongde* 科学的, 民族的, 大众的) (Ju 1993, 73). Zhou applied Mao's policy directly to the arts and presented "Three Processes of Transformation" (Sanhua 三化), a three-part scientific summary of characteristics for socialist artistic forms. The processes may be roughly translated as "revolutionize" (*geminghua* 革命化), "nationalize" (*minzuhua* 民族化),[7] and "popularize" (*qunzhonghua* 群众化).

These points of transformation would combine to form a fundamental principle or guiding policy in socialist culture. The first process, "revolutionize," is reminiscent of Mao's Yan'an talks, in which he stated, "What we demand, therefore, is a unity of politics and art, a unity of content and form, a unity of revolutionary political content and the highest artistic form possible"

(McDougall 1980, 78). From the foundation of the Chinese Communist Party and continuing throughout the Cultural Revolution, Mao promoted the use of music and the arts as part of the "cultural army" to serve the revolution. Inherent in the process to "revolutionize" was an attempt to change the function of music so that it served the revolution, a goal that was carried out by continuing the tradition of politicizing music. In addition to the transformation of the *function* of music was the transformation of the *content* of music; by "revolutionizing" music, all music was to contain a revolutionary message presented in a revolutionary spirit.

The second process, "nationalize," addressed Mao's emphasis on making music *of* the people; in his 1942 Yan'an talks, Mao encouraged the use of existing forms familiar to the masses to serve the revolution: "we must use what belongs to workers, peasants, and soldiers themselves" (McDougall 1980, 68–69). Mao favored a return to "Chinese," as opposed to foreign, musical styles; in this way, the music would truly represent the people in content, form, and style. "Nationalizing" music also allowed additional opportunities to strategically promote images of the model socialist society. For example, the PRC officially recognizes fifty-six ethnic groups in China. The dominant majority ethnic group, Han, makes up over 90 percent of the population, followed by fifty-five ethnic minority groups. Many ethnic minorities speak different languages and maintain distinctly different cultural traditions from the Han majority, therefore creating distance and tension between the majority and minority populations.[8] Tensions between the Han majority (represented in contemporary times by the CCP) and ethnic minority groups have been a source of conflict throughout China's history and continue on in the twenty-first century. The Han oppression (political, social, and cultural) of ethnic minorities has been a troubling practice over many different historical and political eras in China's history; thus, the CCP's promotion of ethnic minorities as being "Chinese" during the Cultural Revolution period strategically placed the ethnic minorities within the CCP's concept of the "nation." As a result, "nationalizing" music utilized existing musical forms familiar to the masses while simultaneously providing identity markers for various ethnic minorities as model citizens.

The third process, "popularize," placed emphasis on music that was truly representative of the masses, as opposed to music of the elite or intellectual classes. In terms of the implementation, music was to be simple in composition and form in order for the workers, peasants, and soldiers (the three pillars of a socialist society) to be able to learn, sing, and perform them. This process may also be translated as "to make (music) *of* the masses," emphasizing the popularization of music in the context of representation rather than focusing merely on widespread dissemination.

PRC scholars frequently mention the "Three Processes of Transformation" when discussing the *New Songs of the Battlefield* anthology, yet little to no focused attention has been paid to clearly defining the individual processes.[9] Wei Jun cites the three processes as "a standard" for the anthology but does not provide any further explanation (2000, 16). Liang Maochun cites the Sanhua policy as producing "great influence upon song composition of this (Cultural Revolution) time" (1993, 14). Liang explains that the policy resulted in a great number of composers studying folk music and incorporating the traditional styles into their music because of the effort to "nationalize." However, the process "revolutionize" was taken to such an extreme that the content and form of music became narrowly defined to the point where all music sang in praise of the leader, the party, and other symbols (14). Similarly, Ju Qihong cites the Sanhua policy as promoting the prosperous development of Chinese music and art composition, though it allowed some deviation in the application and execution of the policy (1993, 74).

While the "Three Processes of Transformation" provided a direction for the role, function, and content of music, the principles may have been derived from critiques of what music ought not to be. For example, music should be for the revolution and not for entertainment; music should be Chinese and not foreign; and music should be for the masses and not just for the elite.

Music of the Cultural Revolution

Music was one part of the "cultural army" that capitalized on symbolism, totalitarianism, and the use of Chinese traditions. Writing on Cultural Revolution drama troupes, Brian James DeMare concludes that, "in using cultural performance to inform military and political action, the Communists relied heavily on the precedents of Chinese traditions" (2015, 239). Similarly, Denise Y. Ho explains how art exhibitions from the Cultural Revolution were "both mass education and mass mobilization" (2018, 1). Ho makes clear the agency of individuals when she writes, "If culture is not only a product but also a practice, then political culture includes rituals, such as the Mao-era form of personal narrative, 'recalling bitterness and reflecting on sweetness' (*yiku sitian* [忆苦思甜]) and 'comparing past and present' (*huiyi duibi* [回忆对比])" (16). Furthermore, Ho cites a propaganda handbook that explains how "'every exhibition object . . . has in and of itself a life and the ability to persuade'" (1). DeMare and Ho are but two examples of many scholars who emphasize that the CCP relied upon continuing traditions and rituals from the pre–Cultural Revolution era as a means to educate and mobilize the masses during the Cultural Revolution.

The music of the Cultural Revolution carried forth the ideology of Mao's 1942 talks as well as the systematic structure of the 1963 policy to "revolution-ize, nationalize, and popularize." Both amateurs and professionals who were appointed by the Communist Party of China worked to develop revolution-ary music in various forms and styles. Though earlier practices continued, the resulting revolutionary music from the Cultural Revolution ultimately developed a unique place in China's musical history. Chinese music scholars generally characterize the music of the Cultural Revolution as being indicative of the particular political, social, and historical context.[10] As such, the music of the Cultural Revolution is often divided into three stages that follow the main political shifts during the Cultural Revolution: 1966–69, 1969–72, and 1972–76 (Liang 1993, 17).[11]

1966–69: THE EARLY YEARS

Leading up to the Cultural Revolution, Chairman Mao's wife, Jiang Qing, began reworking traditional plays and operas in service of the Cultural Revo-lution. A former Shanghai actress, Jiang Qing presented a speech at the 1964 Festival of Peking Opera on Contemporary Themes, where she proceeded to criticize the present state of theater: "The theatre is a place for educating the people, but nowadays all we get on the stage is emperors and kings, generals and prime ministers, talented scholars and beautiful young ladies, all a load of feudalistic stuff, all a load of bourgeois stuff. Such conditions cannot pro-vide protection for the basis of our economy, but may on the contrary serve to destroy the basis of our economy" (qtd. in Dolby 1976, 252).

In the same year, the song and dance production *East Is Red* (*Dongfang hong* 东方红) set the stage for Cultural Revolution arts. Premier Zhou Enlai directed some seventy musical workers and over three thousand performers to pull off the large-scale production. The show consisted of music, dance, and theatrical sketches that summarized the history of the Communist Party of China since 1921.[12] The production was a commemoration in celebration of the fifteenth year of the establishment of the Communist Party of China and focused largely on traditional music and dance. Revolutionary history songs from previous periods were also included, along with ten newly composed songs that were more "reflective" of the Cultural Revolution period. The show promoted an ideology of China and the Communist Party of China, having overcome great hardship through numerous battles and invasions, emerging victorious, and triumphantly moving forward (Ju 1993, 76), as shown in the thematic sketch of the original titles for the various scenes depicted in the *East Is Red* production:

I. "Dawn in the East":
"East Is Red," "Old China," "October Winds from the North," "The Peasant's Song," and "Worker, Peasant and Army Unite!"

II. "A Single Spark Can Set a Prairie Fire":
"The Blood of Revolutionaries," "The Autumn Harvest Uprising," and "Three Rules of Discipline and Eight Rules of Attention"

III. "Crossing Thousands of Mountains and Rivers":
"The Red Army Soldiers Miss Chairman Mao," "The Red Sun Shines Over Tsunyi," "Taking the Tatu River," and "Crossing the Snow Mountain"

IV. "The War of Resistance against Japan":
"To Resist or Not," "Arise," "Yan'an—Shrine of Revolution," "The Graduation Song," "The Song of the Guerrilla," and "Inside the Liberated Area"

V. "Bury the Chiang Kai-Shek Dynasty":
"Unity Is Strength," "The Decisive Battle," "The March of the Chinese Peoples' Liberation Army," "Crossing the Yangtze," and "A Day in the Liberated Area"

VI. "The Chinese People Stand Up":
"The Chinese People Have Stood Up!," "Without the Communist Party, There Would Be No New China," "National Minorities Celebrate," and "Song of the Motherland"[13]

The production begins during the early days of the Communist Party of China and continues through the development of the party, including the War of Resistance against Japan and the civil war against Chiang Kai-shek's Nationalist Party (1927–37, 1946–49, also referred to in the PRC as the War of Liberation).[14] The final chapter of the production is a suite designed to inspire and promote the strength of the Chinese people, the Chinese people's dedication to the party, the promotion of ethnic minorities, and allegiance to the nation.

The revolutionary history song "East Is Red" provides the title for the epic theatrical production and, as Levi S. Gibbs writes, is "one of the songs that perhaps best epitomizes the transition from local to regional (and on to national)" (2018, 121). The song, originally a peasant folk song, was adapted with a revolutionary story to serve the socialist revolution (121–25). The significant emphasis here is on a connection between an individual peasant, Mao, and the nation, and similarly between local and Chinese musical aesthetics within a socialist (and heavily Soviet realist) aesthetic. The production provided a clear foundation establishing a cult of Mao and, as Xiaomei Chen indicates, "showcased some of the best talents in performing arts in the first seventeen years after the founding of the PRC" (2017, 24). The long-lasting memory of the individual song, and the entire song and dance production, continues to live on today, as can be seen in the work of scholars such as Chen (2017) and Gibbs (2018).

By 1967, Jiang Qing had established eight model works, including five "model revolutionary operas," two "revolutionary model ballets," and one symphony (Ju 1993). The model operas (*yangbanxi*) were *Taking Tiger Mountain by Strategy*, *Sea Harbour*, *Raid on the White Tiger Regiment*, *Shajiabang*, and *Red Lantern*; the two ballets were *Red Detachment of Women* and *White-Haired Girl*; and the symphony was *Shajiabang* (Dolby 1976, 252–53). By the end of the Cultural Revolution there were a total of eighteen model works (see Mittler 2010, 378; Yung 1984; Clark 2008; and Clark, Pang, and Tsai 2014).

The plays and ballets maintained many traditional elements such as gestures, acrobatics, and musical/percussive accompaniment for dramatic effect, but the models contained many new additions. The elaborate sets were a drastic departure from the sparse set of traditional Chinese opera. Costumes, themes, and characters were all modernized to portray obvious, contemporary images of extreme heroism or evil. The characters themselves were dressed in either bright or dark colors (for heroes or villains, respectively), enhanced by lighting and staging effects; heroes appeared in bright lights and villains lurked in the shadows. A Western European orchestra played alongside a traditional Chinese orchestra.[15]

The propagandistic language and tone is apparent in this official English-language synopsis of one of the most popular model revolutionary operas, *Taking Tiger Mountain by Strategy* (*Zhiqu Weihushan* 智取威虎山), which is also known as *Taking the Bandits' Stronghold*:

> It is winter, 1946, in the Mutankiang area in China's Northeast, during the early period of the War of Liberation. Our army has won brilliant victories on the battlefield. A group of Kuomintang-organized armed bandits, routed by our army, flee into the dense mountain forests to make a last stand. They go about harassing our rear area. Burning, killing, and looting, they arouse the deep hatred of the local inhabitants. A Chinese People's Liberation Army detachment of 36 men, acting on **Chairman Mao's instruction to "build stable base areas in the Northeast,"** penetrates into the snowy forests, mobilizes the masses, wipes out the bandits and consolidates the rear area, so as to coordinate with the field army in smashing the U.S.-Chiang attacks.

The opera provides a vivid account of the struggle in which the detachment, fearing no sacrifice and surmounting every difficulty, succeeds in taking Tiger Mountain (the bandits' den) and wiping out the Eagle [nickname of the bandit chief] gang. . . . The opera is a tribute to the great strategic thinking of Chairman Mao on people's war. (*Taking Tiger Mountain by Strategy* 1972; original emphasis)

The eight model works, of which the model revolutionary operas were most prominent, broadcast continuously throughout the Cultural Revolution and were circulated in a wide variety of scores, books, posters, and other media (Dolby 1976, 255–56). Similar to other literature and arts of the Cultural Revolution, the model works extended earlier practice and traditions to the new political context. As Xiaomei Chen writes, "Theatrical reform did not start with the Cultural Revolution, nor was it a mere concern for the revolutionary agenda of the PRC period. Its themes can indeed be traced back to the late Qing period" (2017, 75). The initial eight model works offered recounting of past revolutions in order to set the stage for the next revolution, the Great Proletarian Cultural Revolution (75).

Meanwhile, revolutionary music was developed along the political and ideological lines of the Cultural Revolution. The writings of Chairman Mao were set to music and disseminated throughout the country; these "quotation songs" (*yulu ge* 语录歌) appeared at the early stage of the Cultural Revolution (1966–69), when Lin Biao was promoting the personality cult of Chairman Mao. The "Read Every Day" campaign (Tiantian du 天天读) ordered the masses to set aside time every day to study Mao Zedong's thought (K.-S. Li 1995, 447–48), and the quotation songs were often employed in this fashion. Lin Biao had collected Mao's quotations to create the well-known *Red Treasure Book* (*Hongbaoshu* 红宝书, commonly known as the *Little Red Book*) (see Cook 2014), and Lin himself stated, "One of Chairman Mao's words is more valuable than 10,000 of others" (Deng, Ma, and Wu 1997, 63).

On September 30, 1966, the nation's newspaper, the *People's Daily* (*Renmin ribao* 人民日报), dedicated the entire edition to quotation songs, with the editor's note that "the songs and quotes of Mao will resonate all over the country" (Deng, Ma, and Wu 1997, 63). The popularization of the quotation songs escalated rapidly as newspapers and broadcasts spread them throughout the nation; for the next three years, all of Mao's important speeches and quotes were quickly constructed into quotation songs (Liang 1993, 18).

Since the quotation songs emphasized political doctrines, the artistic form was usually rather simple and often rudimentary (Liang 1993, 18). The tunes were frequently coarse, with a rigid rhythm and jumbled syntax. In reference to the aesthetics and artistic quality of these songs, Chinese music scholar Liang Maochun notes that the songs were "an exact reflection of the time" (18) and reveal a true picture of the social atmosphere during the Cultural Revolution. And Andrew Jones writes in detail of the songs as a form of popular music, designed for portability and circulation (2014, 43–45).

Music example 2.1 shows one of the most well-known quotation songs, "The Force at the Core Leading Our Cause Forward Is the Communist Party of China" ("Lingdao women shiye de hexin liliang shi Zhongguo Gongchandang" 领导我们事业的核心力量是中国共产党), composed by Li Jiefu (1913–76) and published in the *People's Daily* newspaper on September 30, 1966 (A. Jones 2014, 48). Numerous composers wrote the quotation songs, though the Chinese composer Li Jiefu is credited as the individual composer for the majority of them (Liang 1993, 8). The first two lines are a direct quotation from Mao's opening address at the First Session of the First National People's Congress of the People's Republic of China on September 15, 1954; the last three lines are popular slogans chanted at public rallies and other events.

领导我们事业的核心力量是中国共产党

THE FORCE AT THE CORE LEADING OUR CAUSE FORWARD IS THE COMMUNIST PARTY OF CHINA

领导我们事业的核心力量是中国共产党，

The force at the core leading our cause forward is the Communist Party
of China,

指导我们思想的理论基础是马克思列宁主义。

The theoretical basis guiding our thinking is Marxism-Leninism.

Example 2.1. "The Force at the Core Leading Our Cause Forward Is the Communist Party of China" (Liang 2003, 48)

共产党万岁! 毛主席万岁!
Long live the Communist Party! Long live Chairman Mao!
共产党万岁! 毛主席万岁!
Long live the Communist Party! Long live Chairman Mao!
万岁，万岁! 万万岁!
Long life, long life! Long, long life!

In addition to the quotation songs, the CCP disseminated a number of highly aggressive and militaristic songs either in praise of Chairman Mao and the party or in opposition to their enemies. At the same time, the Red Guards began to compose their own revolutionary songs that borrowed from historic and popular revolutionary songs.

Many of the Red Guard songs drew from quotation songs, military songs, and other revolutionary music. One of the most characteristic types of these songs was folk songs (*geyao* 歌谣) that included the singing or chanting of political slogans. These songs were particularly vulgar and rude and utilized exaggerated styles and metaphors. The following lyrics are typical of an extremely violent Red Guard song:

反帝必反修
ANTI-IMPERIALISM REQUIRES ANTI-REVISIONISM
砸烂苏修狗头
Smash the dog's heads of Soviet revisionists
踏着一只脚
Step on them with one foot
让它永世不得翻身!
Never let them free themselves!

刘少奇你算老几
Liu Shaoqi, who cares about you[16]
今天老子要揪你!
Today I will seize you!
抽你的筋
I'll make your muscles cramp
剥你的皮
Take off your skin
把你的脑壳当球踢!
Play soccer with your skull! (Wagner 2001, 6)

The main task of the Red Guards in the countryside was to disseminate political news and orders while providing general agitation (Wagner 2001,

7), and songs were one of their main tools. Scholar Vivian Wagner notes the lack of the main humanistic concepts of friendship, comradeship, and freedom in the songs and cites a former Red Guard: "Singing was the most important method of propaganda, a propaganda team would take a bunch of kids, teach them a song and then ask them to spread it further—snowball effect! Without any further assistance of the team, propaganda would work by itself!" (7).

When Mao introduced the concept of using music as a weapon in his famous 1942 Yan'an talks, the target of the cultural army was a foreign enemy. However, by the time of the Cultural Revolution, the enemy was no longer foreign; the battle had shifted from focusing on foreign invaders to aiming at internal offenders (largely, those individuals and groups targeted by the CCP).

1969–72: SILENCE

The violent and crude language of the Red Guard songs was met with great disapproval. In 1969, Jiang Qing criticized the state of revolutionary songs for being obscene and inappropriate, resulting in an abrupt halt to most music production. In a number of speeches, Jiang Qing specifically cited the vulgarity of the Red Guards and referred to the quotation songs as "obscene and decadent," stating that they relied too heavily upon slogans (Deng, Ma, and Wu 1997, 64). For the next two years, the publication and dissemination of revolutionary songs were limited to the *yangbanxi* (model works) and four revolutionary history songs: "East Is Red," "Sailing the Seas Depends on the Helmsman," "Three Main Rules of Discipline and Eight Points for Attention," and "Internationale" (Liang 1993, 19). Private, and especially rural, exceptions existed where music making and dissemination continued without interruption; yet the official CCP restriction and silence is notable in CCP publications, scholarship, and individual accounts.[17]

1972–76: RETURN TO TRADITION

In 1971, Mao turned over the central daily work of the CCP to Premier Zhou Enlai, who immediately criticized the harsh and abrasive qualities of slogan-based music. Zhou called for a return to traditional melodies and softer musical tones. Government workers began to collect traditional music that was more lyrical (Deng, Ma, and Wu 1997), and Zhou began working on a compilation of these new revolutionary songs that was published in 1972 as *New Songs of the Battlefield*. The success of the first volume resulted in annual publication through the remainder of the Cultural Revolution.[18]

NEW SONGS OF THE BATTLEFIELD

New Songs of the Battlefield was published in commemoration of the thirtieth anniversary of Mao Zedong's Yan'an talks. The songbook included over a hundred new revolutionary songs that were officially approved by Zhou Enlai and the Chinese Communist Party. For many people who lived through this era, the release of the anthology provided a breath of fresh air for musicians, composers, and the general public after a period of musical instability, extreme censorship, and a lack of attention to musical aesthetics in propaganda music. The anthology is cited by scholars such as Ren Weixin (2020), Gao Hong (2010), and Fu Xiaoyu (2012) for the shift in attention to lyrical aesthetics in contrast to the earlier rigid structures. The sheer number and diversity of songs, along with the use of traditional styles, is cited as the collection's main appeal. A "sequel" was published in 1973, followed by volume 3 (1974), volume 4 (1975), and volume 5 (1976). In 1977, the Chinese Communist Party published *October Battle Songs* [*Shiyue zhange*] a collection of revolutionary songs commemorating the thirty-fifth anniversary of Mao Zedong's Yan'an talks. Du Yang (2019) and Jiang Zhiwei (2008) both refer to the 1977 songbook as a potential "sixth" book in the *New Songs of the Battlefield* series despite the different title. However, my own research and fieldwork have focused exclusively on the five songbooks under the *New Songs of the Battlefield* title (1972–76), and so I look forward to continued and future scholarship on the connections with the 1977 songbook.

Figure 2.1. Original songbook cover: *New Songs of the Battlefield*, volume 1 (1972) (photo by author)

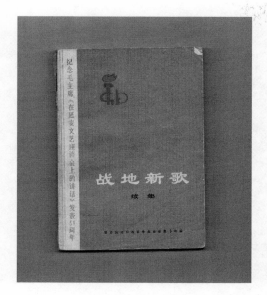

Figure 2.2. Original songbook cover: *New Songs of the Battlefield*, volume 2 (1973) (photo by author)

Excluding a few repeated songs, each of the five volumes of *New Songs of the Battlefield* presents a new set of roughly one hundred songs. Moreover, the volumes are nearly identical in format and organization with only slight variations from year to year.

Songs from *New Songs of the Battlefield* were disseminated extensively throughout China and were published regularly in daily newspapers (such as *People's Daily*), broadcast on radio and television programming, and performed by traveling arts troupes. The songs were sung and heard throughout the day, such as at the beginning and end of public meetings and rallies; LPs were available for purchase for those who could afford them. With the wide influence of the government-controlled media, *New Songs of the Battlefield* reached essentially all but the most rural parts of the country. Although the anthology was compiled and published as a collection of songs, many of the songs were disseminated independently without referencing the anthology title. As a result, numerous individuals may be familiar with several songs without knowing that they originated from the thirty-year anniversary of the Yan'an talks.

In preparation for the commemorative activities celebrating the talks, a call went out across the country to collect revolutionary songs of the workers, peasants, and soldiers. Songs were composed by individual composers, work groups, military units, and others and then submitted to their regional district; they were then promoted to the provincial level and finally presented to the central editorial board in Beijing. The background of the amateur

Figure 2.3. Original songbook cover: *New Songs of the Battlefield*, volume 3 (1974) (photo by author)

Figure 2.4. Original songbook cover: *New Songs of the Battlefield*, volume 4 (1975) (photo by author)

Figure 2.5. Original songbook cover:
New Songs of the Battlefield, volume 5
(1976) (photo by author)

musicians could vary widely; some were novices with no musical background, while others were highly skilled musicians with strong local reputations. Professional musicians were largely conservatory-trained individuals placed within the CCP as government workers, although some of them may have been untrained and appointed solely for their political merit.

The exact criteria for selecting the songs remain unclear, but the anthology was clearly intended to focus on songs from the workers, peasants, and soldiers, with representation of all provinces and of as many of the officially recognized ethnic minorities as possible. The preface to the 1972 volume outlines the origins and content of the anthology and briefly mentions the collection and editing processes:

> In commemoration of the thirty-year anniversary of the publication of the great leader Chairman Mao's "Talks at the Yan'an Conference on Literature and Art," we offer to the broad masses of the workers, peasants, and soldiers this selection of songs composed since the Great Proletarian Cultural Revolution—*New Songs of the Battlefield*.
>
> This book has selected revolutionary songs newly composed and newly revised since the Great Proletarian Cultural Revolution, ten revolutionary history songs and five revolutionary folk songs.
>
> **Yellow flowers on the battlefield are especially fragrant.** Since the Great Proletarian Cultural Revolution, amateur composers of the broad masses of

workers, peasants, and soldiers, along with revolutionary art workers, guided in line with Chairman Mao's revolutionary thought on art and literature and illuminated by the "Yan'an talks," take as model the model revolutionary works and persist in working to serve the workers, peasants, and soldiers and the proletariat politics. They have composed and produced a great quantity of outstanding revolutionary songs. This anthology of songs attempts to show the great achievements in the composition of revolutionary songs since the Great Proletarian Cultural Revolution; to take the promotion of revolutionary song composition a step further and to vigorously develop the singing activities of the masses to satisfy the needs of the broad masses of workers, peasants, and soldiers.

The compilation of the song anthology has been carried out under the energetic assistance and enthusiastic support of the broad masses of workers, peasants, and soldiers and all ranks of leaders. The broad masses and leaders recommended to us outstanding revolutionary songs created, circulated, and sung in their own areas. As a result, after selection [people in] all places can use the songs for meetings and various circumstances to mobilize the broad masses to participate in the process of selecting songs [and] to carefully listen, review, and revise to put forward more and better suggestions. This selection of works can triumph as a prerequisite.

The song anthology is composed in accordance with Chairman Mao's teachings in regard to "**political standards first, artistic standards second**" and "**strive for the unity between revolutionary political content in the perfect artistic form**." In subject matter, there are songs in praise of the Communist Party, in praise of Chairman Mao, and in praise of our socialist country; there are songs which reflect the battles and life of workers, peasants, and soldiers on different battlefields of socialist revolution and construction; there are also songs that reflect the youth and the children growing up strong under the shining illumination of Chairman Mao's thought; as well as songs that reflect the people of China and every country's people's revolutionary friendship and unity in combat. In form, the songs are of various forms that are well accepted by the broad masses including chorus, solo song, performance songs,[19] etc. Chairman Mao's revolutionary line has been achieved in all of these songs, from each and every side of the greatest victory and the battlefronts since the Great Proletarian Cultural Revolution. (*Zhandi xinge* 1972; original emphasis)

According to the preface, the songs were selected for their "political standards first" and "artistic standards second"; furthermore, the songs were to "strive for the unity between revolutionary political content in the perfect artistic form," using direct quotations from Mao Zedong. "Revolutionary" here refers to the Chinese term for revolution, *geming* (革命), which indicates music and art that are specifically related to political revolutions. Du Yang identifies the Mao quotation "Yellow flowers on the battlefield are especially fragrant" (*zhandi huanghua fenwai xiang* 战地黄花分外香) as originating in 1929 from a time when Mao, while recovering from malaria in a rural area, started and led a local agrarian revolution struggle. Mao's poetic line is thus an observation of the wild yellow chrysanthemums still thriving on the battlefield amid the brisk autumn wind and frost (2019, 58).

On collecting the songs from the provinces, the central editorial board in Beijing identified geographic areas, ethnic groups, political themes, and musical forms that were necessary to complete the anthology and assigned CCP composers and lyricists to fill in any gaps. The individual names of composers, lyricists, and editors rarely appear, and during my fieldwork I learned that many of the CCP composers representing ethnic minority groups throughout China had never actually traveled to their representative areas. Interviews also revealed that many songs credited to specific groups or units of workers, peasants, and soldiers were extensively revised in Beijing with no consultation whatsoever with the original composers.

As discussed in chapter 1, scholars examine the Chinese Cultural Revolution with a variety of approaches. Some attempt historical accounts, especially with names, as a way of documenting processes. Others focus on close readings of texts. And still others pursue an examination of the lived experience. A detailed and precise account of the editorial committees has not been the focus of my research and deserves further study. The frequency with which the subject has been raised by either individuals connected to the anthology or scholars interested in the topic demonstrates their particular desire for facts, accuracy, and documentation. I believe this to be, in part, a remnant of the political scrutiny, tension, and bureaucracy of the time period and also a genuine objective of certain scholars. Yet other individuals and scholars, like myself, do not focus our efforts on this pursuit; rather, we center our work on the lived experience as well as on interdisciplinary analysis into what the impact of arts was from this time. Furthermore, it would be difficult, if not impossible, to identify all of the individual contributions to the anthology, in part because three different editorial committees are listed over the span of five volumes.

The editorial committee cited in the first two volumes is the Revolutionary Song Collection Task Force, Cultural Affairs Office under the State Council (Guowuyuan wenhuazu geming gequ zhengji xiaozu 国务院文化组革命歌曲征集小组). The committee's name is replaced in volume 3 with "Literary and Artistic Creation Leadership Task Force, Cultural Affairs Office under the State Council" (Guowuyuan wenhuazu wenyi chuangzuo lingdao xiaozu国务院文化组文艺创作领导小组), despite numerous accounts that report that the composition of the editorial staff never changed. The editorial committee cited for the fourth and fifth volumes appears as "*New Songs of the Battlefield* Editorial Committee" (*Zhandi xinge* bianxuan xiaozu 战地新歌编选小组), although I have collected conflicting reports on the exact personnel change for the final two volumes.[20]

The preface to the original 1972 volume essentially classifies the songs into four main categories: songs in praise of the CCP, Mao, and China; songs of the workers, peasants, and soldiers; songs of the youth and children; and songs of the people of China and revolutionary friendships with people outside of China. In addition to the newly composed revolutionary songs, the 1972 volume includes ten folk songs on revolutionary history and songs from earlier historical periods of the CCP. To represent the diversity of songs included in the anthology, I expand the classifications to the following six categories:

1. CCP classics
2. Songs in praise of the CCP, Mao, and China
3. Songs of the workers, peasants, and soldiers
4. Songs of the youth and children
5. Songs of ethnic minorities
6. Songs of international relations

The six categories correspond to the song list in the table of contents, although the distinction or naming of categories is not explicitly stated in the preface.[21] Songs from the Cultural Revolution characteristically touch on multiple themes simultaneously, and my distinctions are based on the primary focus of the song for analysis and discussion. A great diversity of characteristics such as lyrics, musical form, and historical lineage appear in each of the categories, though some general features and trends are evident.

The following section includes an overview of basic musical features, including instrumentation, arrangements, and recordings. Seven musical examples are used to illustrate the variety in subject, musical form, arrangement, and historical lineage across the six categories.[22]

Basic Musical Features

The *New Songs of the Battlefield* anthology presents songs in cipher notation, a common format in which the numbers 1 through 7 represent the seven scale degrees. The notation is considered both accessible and familiar to general readers, as it would have been used in schools and earlier political campaigns preceding the Cultural Revolution. Time signatures, key signatures, and musical expressions are like those used in five-line staff notation, and their dynamics and articulations are virtually identical; yet the cipher notation is considered a more simplified notation system requiring less formal instruction or training to understand.[23] Because the songs were intended for the masses, the general musical characteristics of the songs are also rather basic. Mode, meter, and rhythm are all relatively simple and easy to learn. With some exceptions (usually in songs that were written for solo voices), the phrasing and general musical form are straightforward and repetitive to aid in memorization. Over three-quarters of the songs are in 2/4 time; the remaining songs are mostly in 4/4 time, with a few instances of 3/4, 6/8, and 3/8 time. Around a dozen songs have no time signature; they are free and lyrical solo pieces. In general, the songs fall into either upbeat marching or work songs or free and slow-tempo ballads. Most often,

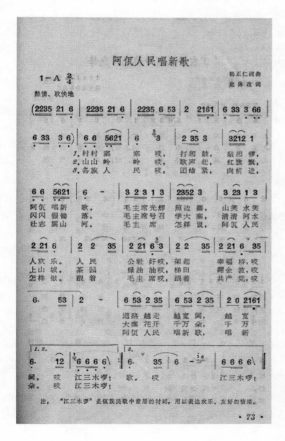

Figure 2.6. Original score: "Awa People Sing a New Song" (from *New Songs of the Battlefield*, volume 1) (photo by author)

a musical expression—such as "lively" or "staunchly"—is printed to indicate the style of song.

The key signatures listed in the printed anthology all suggest Western European scales, though at times these may be Western European scalar approximations to a folk or regional practice of Chinese origin. The songs are within a comfortable singing range for the average untrained voice. Accidentals, or pitches not belonging to the key signature, are used infrequently, though a considerable amount of ornamentation appears in the songs that replicate more traditional Chinese folk music styles.

Though the majority of songs in the *New Songs of the Battlefield* anthology were published for vocalists, they were usually recorded with instrumental accompaniment,[24] and everyday performance of the songs frequently included instrumentation as well. Several songs in the anthology include a few measures of instrumental overture or accompaniment, but only as an introduction or during an interlude. Songbooks in mass circulation were thus designed exclusively for singers, and while I have not encountered any instrumental scores for accompaniment, they certainly must have existed for performance troupes, professionals for recordings, and so forth.

Nearly half of the songs designate a particular vocal arrangement, either by gender or age, such as women's or men's voices or child's voice, or by number of voices, such as solo, duet, or small chorus. The overwhelming majority of these specific arrangements are for women's voices or solo voice. The breakdown for the 209 songs that designate a particular arrangement are found in tables 2.1–2.4.

The CCP often centered women in its revolutionary messaging, and women's voices may have been used as a symbol of the motherland. This preference for women's voices, however, is initially curious, given that the promotion of gender equity during the Cultural Revolution often resulted in defeminizing

Table 2.1. Arrangements for women's voices in *New Songs of the Battlefield*

woman's solo	*nüsheng duchang*	46
women's small chorus	*nüsheng xiaohechang*	26
women's chorus	*nüsheng hechang*	11
women's performance song	*nüsheng biaoyanchang*	9
women's soprano solo	*nü gaoyin duchang*	4
women's chorus in unison	*nüsheng qichang*	2
woman/women play (an instrument) and sing	*nüsheng tanchang*	1
	Total	99

Table 2.2. Arrangements for men's voices in *New Songs of the Battlefield*

man's solo	nansheng duchang	18
men's small chorus	nansheng xiaohechang	11
men's chorus	nansheng hechang	6
men's performance song	nansheng biaoyanchang	1
men's baritone solo	nan zhongyin duchang	1
	Total	37

Table 2.3. Arrangements for children's voices in *New Songs of the Battlefield*

girl's song	nüsheng ertong chang	4
boy's song	nansheng ertong chang	1
children's song	ertong gequ, ertong chang, or tongsheng ertong chang	13
children's performance song	ertong biaoyanchang	2
children's duet	ertong duichang	1
boy and girl song	nannü ertong chang	5
	Total	26

Table 2.4. Arrangements for mixed and other designated voices in *New Songs of the Battlefield*

solo	duchang	36
performance song	biaoyanchang	4
small chorus	xiaohechang	2
duet (man and woman)	nannüsheng duichang	2
duet	duichang	1
mountain song duet	shange duichang	1
mixed small chorus	nannü xiaohechang	1
	Total	47

and desexualizing women.[25] Yet it can be understood through what Meng Yue describes as the "double play" of women in socialist society in which the CCP employs images of women as "special agents" (Yue 1993, 118). Put simply, depicting women could offer the CCP a way into the personal lives of the masses, utilizing women as cultural signifiers of love and family while simultaneously making public and politicizing the personal. Importantly, as Yue writes, the

desexualizing and politicizing of subjectivity, of course, does not mean anything like the existence of woman-dominant discourses, nor does it prove that sexist ideology has disappeared in Chinese literature. On the contrary, although it left no room for male desire or subjectivity, the discourse itself is still a masculinist one. Both its narrative focus and its implied reader-audience do not in any way include women as a gender. There is only one respect in which socialist narratives are different from previously male-dominant discourse. The topic of discourse is no longer how to dominate women but rather how to subject oneself in every possible way to the Party and to the Party's discourse. The unique female images employed in socialist narrative were used to create the dominated men of contemporary Chinese literature and ideology. (135)

Yue's discussion of literature offers important and relevant parallels in music—that is, the shift of focus to the CCP and its ideology. Moreover, the desexualizing, defeminizing, and politicizing did not undo gender inequities in Chinese society (pre–Cultural Revolution or during the Cultural Revolution) but rather displaced the focus from gender and the personal to the nation and the CCP.

Instrumentation, Arrangements, and Recordings

The scores that appear in the *New Songs of the Battlefield* anthology were intended both for individual voices and for group voices. Predictably, the songs were performed in a variety of settings, greatly influencing the instrumentation and arrangement. New arrangements based on the published scores utilized the expertise of amateur and professional musicians alike. In the recordings, instrumentation and additional arrangements include a combination of Chinese and Western European musical accompaniment and instrumental ensembles. The following selection of musical recordings surveyed illustrates the multiple combinations of arrangements and instrumentation. The recordings have no publication dates. However, it is my understanding that they were produced and distributed during the Cultural Revolution.

Many songs were recorded and released in a variety of arrangements, with varying instrumentation. For example, "Song in Praise of Beijing" was recorded by the Central Broadcasting Cultural Workers' Troupe Orchestra (Zhongyang guangbo wengongtuan guanxianyuetuan 中央广播文工团管弦乐团) both as an arrangement for orchestra (*guanxianyue* 管弦乐) (China Record BM-75/20016) and for women's soprano solo (*nü gaoyin duchang* 女高音独唱) (China Record BM-33/73129). Chinese instrumental ensembles were most commonly heard in the songs of ethnic minorities and songs that were associated with a specific geocultural region within China.[26]

Table 2.5. Examples of musical recordings of songs from *New Songs of the Battlefield*

Song title	Arrangement	Instrumentation
"Song in Praise of Beijing"	Instrumental	Western European orchestra
"I Love Beijing's Tiananmen"	Children's chorus	Western European orchestra
"Workers and Peasants Are All One Family"	Mixed chorus	Western European orchestra
"The Song of Emancipation"	Female solo	Chinese instrumental ensemble
"Strike the Tanks"	Male chorus	Accordion
"The Heart of the Dazhai People is Toward the Red Sun"	Female chorus	Chinese instrumental ensemble
"Song of the Tractor Drivers"	Male solo	Western European orchestra
"Red Guards on the Grasslands Have Met Chairman Mao"	Instrumental	Chinese instrumental ensemble
"The Railways Are Built Up to the Miao Village"	Mixed chorus	Chinese instrumental ensemble

Chinese Communist Party Classics

The thirty-four CCP classics published in the *New Songs of the Battlefield* anthology fall into three subdivisions: revolutionary history songs (*geming lishi gequ* 革命历史歌曲), revolutionary folk songs (*geming minge* 革命民歌), and Mao poetry songs (the poetry of Chairman Mao set to music) (*wei Maozhuxici puqu* 为毛主席词谱曲) (see Bryant 2004 for additional information). The story behind the CCP classics is representative of the complex processes and debates regarding the editing and compilation of the anthology. The anthology was created under the premise of promoting newly composed songs for the Cultural Revolution, but the editorial committee decided to include ten older revolutionary folk songs. The chief editors of the anthology admitted to me that they were pressured to include revolutionary history songs and Mao poetry songs. The balance of old and new was extensively debated, and a chief editor told me that the song "Sailing the Seas Depends on the Helmsman" was a last-minute insertion after Zhou Enlai commented that the song was integral to any compilation of revolutionary songs. The song was glued by hand in the first printed edition so that it would be released on time.

Composed during earlier periods in CCP history, the CCP classics are not representative of the *New Songs of the Battlefield* anthology, nor are they the focus of my study. Although they were placed prominently in the first volume of the anthology as the first thirty-four songs, which illustrates their outstanding legacy, thematically and musically they are mentioned here primarily to compare with other songs. A leading example of these classics is the Red Army

Example 2.2. "Three Main Rules of Discipline and Eight Points for Attention"

song "Three Main Rules of Discipline and Eight Points for Attention" (music example 2.2), which is a military song but is based on a folk song. It is listed in the anthology simply as a "Red Army song" (*Hongjun gequ* 红军歌曲), though composer Cheng Tan (程坦) originally set the quotation to music (Zhongguo yishu yanjiuyuan 1984, 329). In 1928, Mao Zedong announced the "Three Main Disciplines and Six Points of Attention" for the Red Guards; in 1929 he revised this to "Three Main Rules of Discipline and Eight Points for Attention." By 1935, Mao's directives were set to music and the song was popularized throughout the War of Resistance against Japan as well as during the War of Liberation (1927–50). The song appears in both volumes 1 (1972) and 3 (1974) of the *New Songs of the Battlefield*.

三大纪律八项注意
THREE MAIN RULES OF DISCIPLINE AND EIGHT POINTS FOR ATTENTION [FIRST VERSE]
革命军人个个要牢记,
Soldiers of the revolution must each be disciplined,
三大纪律八项注意:
Three main rules of discipline and eight points for attention:
第一一切行动听指挥,
First, obey orders in all of your actions,
步调一致才能得胜利;
Consistency in every step is the only way to victory

The song has eight verses that are repeated to the same eight-bar melody, which list all eight points for attention and three main rules. The melody consists of two phrases of four bars each, in a simple AB pattern. The entire song does not go beyond the range of one octave and maintains simple rhythmic contour; both of these factors result in a song that is easy for soldiers to sing. These types of songs emphasize the lyrics, which aided in memorization for political campaigns, and were quickly disseminated throughout the country.

Newly Composed Songs

Newly composed songs may be classified into five categories: songs in praise of the CCP, Mao, and China; songs of the workers, peasants, and soldiers; songs of the youth and children; songs of ethnic minorities; and songs of international relations. The following six examples present staff notation, transliteration, English translation of lyrics (first verse only), and general musical characteristics of newly composed songs based on the five categorizations.

The first two examples of newly composed songs praise the CCP, Mao, and China. Individuals (inside and outside of the scholarly community) frequently cite both examples, one for its extreme popularity and artistic merit and the other for its apparent lack thereof. "Song in Praise of Beijing" ("Beijing songge" 北京颂歌) (music example 2.3) was published in volume 2 of the *New Songs of the Battlefield* anthology. It was composed by professional musicians Tian Guang and Fu Jing with lyrics by Hong Yuan; it was extremely popular during the Cultural Revolution and is still popular today. The song is more demanding than many others in the anthology. It includes an instrumental introduction and requires a vocal range of nearly two octaves; a skilled singer is needed to effectively and artistically produce the melodic ornamentations. As a solo piece (*duchang* 独唱), the song allows for dramatic and lyrical expression on the part of the singer and includes the printed musical expression of "stately, solemnly" (*zhuangyan di* 庄严地). "Song in Praise of Beijing," like many other praise songs, simultaneously promotes a number of political ideologies. Although the title suggests a song about Beijing, the complete lyrics refer to a number of other topics such as Mao, the motherland, unity, victory, Daqing (model in industry 大庆), and Dazhai (model in agriculture 大寨).

北京颂歌
SONG IN PRAISE OF BEIJING

灿烂的朝霞，升起在金色的北京，
Magnificent rosy dawn rises upon gold colored Beijing,
庄严的乐曲，报导着祖国的黎明。
Stately music announces the dawn of our motherland.

啊! 北京啊北京! 祖国的心脏，团结的象征，
Ah! Beijing, ah Beijing! The heart of our motherland, the symbol of
  unity,
人民的骄傲， 胜利的保证。
The pride of the people, the guarantee for victory.
各族人民把你赞颂, 你是我们心中一颗明亮的星。
People of all ethnic groups extol you; you are the shining star in our hearts.

Example 2.3. "Song in Praise of Beijing"

In contrast, "The Great Proletarian Cultural Revolution Is Indeed Good" ("Wuchanjieji wenhua dageming jiu shi hao" 无产阶级文化大革命就是好) was composed by an amateur group; its lyrics and music are credited to the "Literature and Art Study Class, City of Shanghai Workers' Cultural Palace" (Shanghaishi gongren wenhuagong wenyi xuexiban 上海市工人文化宫文艺学习班).[27] The vocal range is just over an octave, with an uncomplicated melody and rhythm resulting in a song that can be sung loudly and forcefully

Example 2.3. *Continued.*

by large groups of people. For example, the song includes a middle section in measures 36–39 where the phrase "The Cultural Revolution is indeed good" is shouted twice. The musical expressions listed are "enthusiastically" or "warmly" (*relie* 热烈), "lively" or "happily" (*huankuai* 欢快), and "staunchly" or "firm and strong" (*jianding youli* 坚定有力). The title phrase is sung an additional two times with the embedded phrase of "indeed good" appearing ten times. The repetition is enhanced in the final line as the melodic line swells up to an F (dominant) an octave above the starting note before moving back down to rest on the tonic (B-flat). The song is then repeated again for a second verse.

无产阶级文化大革命就是好

THE GREAT PROLETARIAN CULTURAL REVOLUTION IS INDEED GOOD

无产阶级文化大革命（嗨！）就是好！

The Great Proletarian Cultural Revolution (hey!) is indeed good!

就是好呀 就是好，就是好！

Indeed good yeah indeed good, and indeed good!

Example 2.4. "The Great Proletarian Cultural Revolution Is Indeed Good"

马列主义大普及，上层建筑红旗飘，
Marxism-Leninism is widely popularized, red flags flutter in the
    construction of a higher formation,
革命大字报,(嗨！) 烈火遍地烧，
Revolutionary big-character posters, (hey!) spread like raging fires,
誓把修根铲除掉，七亿人民团结战斗，
Vowing to eradicate the roots, seven hundred million people unite in
    the fight,
红色江山牢又牢。
The red landscape grows more and more resolute.

文化大革命好！文化大革命好!
The Cultural Revolution is good! The Cultural Revolution is good!
无产阶级文化大革命就是好!
The Great Proletarian Cultural Revolution is indeed good!
就是好! 就是好! 就是好!
Indeed good! Indeed good! Indeed good!

"The Great Proletarian Cultural Revolution Is Indeed Good" is often cited as representative of Cultural Revolution culture, dominated primarily by political content and an inherent lack of musical complexity.[28] This style aligns with earlier periods that were influenced by military and political songs for the masses such as quotation songs ("The Force at the Core Leading Our Cause Forward Is the Communist Party of China") and CCP classics ("Three Main Rules of Discipline and Eight Points for Attention"). Alternatively, "Song in Praise of Beijing" is often cited as one of the highlights of the *New Songs of the Battlefield* anthology and a popular example of the newly composed songs. Both praise songs demonstrate a primary focus on political standards with simple lyrics that extol the CCP, China, Mao in general, and Beijing and the Cultural Revolution in particular. Yet a varied approach in artistic standards appears in the music and lyrics. "Song in Praise of Beijing" includes poetically warm lyrics such as "magnificent rosy dawn" and musical phrases full of ornaments and melismatic passages. In contrast, the lyrics of "The Great Proletarian Cultural Revolution Is Indeed Good" are more militaristic and speak of raging fires, fighting, and eradicating roots. Its musical phrases are short and punctuated by chanting and shouting.

Songs of the workers, peasants, and soldiers similarly vary in musical composition and approaches to political and artistic standards. "Strike the Tanks" ("Da tanke" 打坦克) is a newly composed soldiers' song composed by Shen Yawei with lyrics by He Zhaohua. The soldiers' song is representative of songs written for workers, peasants, and soldiers in its short and repetitive form, making it ideal for the masses. It is simple, rousing, and repetitive and designed to inspire and encourage morale and perhaps to facilitate in manual labor or marching. The song has a rousing/energetic (*fenfa* 奋发), upbeat tempo (*shao kuai* 稍快, or "a little fast") that reflects the song's title and lyrics.

打坦克
STRIKE THE TANKS

嗨! 哎, 嗨! 哎嗨, 嗨嗨! 打坦克, 劲头大。
Hey! Ah, hey, ah hey, hey hey! Strike the tanks, with great strength.
肩扛爆破筒, 手雷腰里插。
The demolition gun rests on the shoulder, an anti-tank grenade at the
　　waist.
革命战士浑身胆,
Soldiers of the revolution are brave from head to toe,
老虎嘴里敢拔牙。
We dare to pull a tooth from inside the tiger's mouth.

冲上去, 靠近打。
Forcefully advancing, fighting up close.
炸履带, 轰油箱。
Exploding in its tracks, [we] strike the fuel tanks.
挖好了陷坑我等着它!
After digging out the trap [we] wait in the pit for them!

来一辆, 打一辆!
If a unit [of tanks] comes by, [we'll] attack the unit!
来一群, 打一群!
If a pack [of soldiers] comes by, [we'll] attack the pack!
来一辆, 打一辆!
If a unit [of tanks] comes by, [we'll] attack the unit!

来一群, 打一群!
If a pack [of soldiers] comes by, [we'll] attack the pack!
谁敢来进犯, 就坚决粉碎它!
Whoever dares to intrude, indeed [we] will firmly crush them![29]

"I Love Beijing's Tiananmen" ("Wo ai Beijing Tiananmen" 我爱北京天安门), with lyrics by Jin Guolin and music by Jin Yueling, is a newly composed song for children. Similar to songs in the other thematic categories, it is aesthetically simplistic. "I Love Beijing's Tiananmen" has a simple ABA pattern; musical expressions listed are "enthusiastically" (*reqing* 热情)

Example 2.5. "Strike the Tanks"

and "vivaciously" or "lively" (*huopo* 活泼); and the song is categorized as a children's song (*ertong gequ* 儿童歌曲). The lyrics are simple—two lines are repeated three times:[30] "I Love Beijing's Tiananmen, the sun rises over Tiananmen, / Our great leader, Chairman Mao, guides us forward." Once again Tiananmen, the sun, and Mao are all utilized as imagery of the CCP, here in quite simplistic form. In fact, its lack of reference to specific political campaigns has led to its continued promotion in the present day.

我爱北京天安门

I LOVE BEIJING'S TIANANMEN

我爱北京天安门，天安门上太阳开，
I love Beijing's Tiananmen, the sun rises over Tiananmen,
伟大领袖毛主席，指引我们向前进。
Our great leader, Chairman Mao, guides us forward.

我爱北京天安门，天安门上太阳开，
I love Beijing's Tiananmen, the sun rises over Tiananmen,
伟大领袖毛主席，指引我们向前进。
Our great leader, Chairman Mao, guides us forward.

我爱北京天安门，天安门上太阳开，
I love Beijing's Tiananmen, the sun rises over Tiananmen,
伟大领袖毛主席，指引我们向前进。
Our great leader, Chairman Mao, guides us forward.

Many of the songs of ethnic minority groups are identifiable and perceived as such through lyrics, instrumental arrangement, and performance. Lyrics may specifically mention terms or geographical landmarks that are

Example 2.6. "I Love Beijing's Tiananmen"

stereotypically identified as belonging to a particular ethnic group, and instrumental arrangements commonly featured instruments that were associated with that group. The newly composed "Red Guards on the Grasslands Have Met Chairman Mao" ("Caoyuan shang de hongweibing jian daole Mao zhuxi" 草原上的红卫兵见到了毛主席) is a musical example of the songs of ethnic minorities. The song was composed by Gao Shiheng, with lyrics by Li Dequan, and identifies the Red Guards from the grasslands, a familiar reference to Mongolia.[31] In the lyrics, markers of Mao and the CCP (such as Tiananmen and the revolution) are connected to markers of Mongolian peoples and culture (such as the grasslands and the clouds).

"Red Guards on the Grasslands Have Met Chairman Mao" reinforces stereotypical identity markers of Mongolians in multiple ways. Ethnomusicologist Charlotte D'Evelyn emphasizes how "the grasslands were and continue to be a ubiquitous and iconic symbol to evoke the region" and mentions that the grasslands are a symbol that still holds a lot of power "both for local Mongols and in Han stereotyped images" (personal communication, September 2020).

草原上的红卫兵见到了毛主席
RED GUARDS ON THE GRASSLANDS HAVE MET CHAIRMAN MAO

我们是毛主席的红卫兵，
We are the Red Guards of Chairman Mao,
从草原来到天安门。
We come to Tiananmen from the grasslands.
无边的旗海红似火，
Boundless seas of banners red as fire,
战斗的歌声响如云。
The voice of the revolution enters toward the clouds.
伟大的领袖毛主席，领导我们闹革命。
Great leader Chairman Mao, leading us to make revolution.

啊嗬咳 啊嗬咳 敬爱的毛主席，
Ah-ha-he ah-ha-he respected and beloved Chairman Mao,
不落的红太阳，
The red sun that will never set,
草原上人民热爱您，
The people of the grasslands are loyal to you,
永远革命志不移。
Forever our revolutionary spirit will not be altered.

The upbeat song begins with an instrumental introduction; no musical expression is listed, but the tempo marking is "a little fast" (*shao kuai*). Like

Example 2.7. "Red Guards on the Grasslands Have Met Chairman Mao"

many of the other songs, the final melodic line emphasizes the lyrics as the highest B-flat appears (with a fermata) on the word "Mao" in the third to last measure. Additional musical analysis and comparative research is necessary to identify whether any trademark or characteristic "Mongolian" styles appear within the music itself, but the instrumentation, lyrics, and additional performance practices intentionally present stereotypical symbols of Mongolia. D'Evelyn observes that the piece features "arching melodies in a pentatonic minor mode characteristic of many Mongolian folk songs" and suggests that the fiddle techniques may be derived from traditions of Northern China

2

Example 2.7. *Continued.*

(including both contemporary Shaanxi and Inner Mongolia) that became sonic icons of the grasslands in twentieth-century repertoire (personal communication, September 2020).

An undated recording of the song (but understood to be of the Cultural Revolution era) includes both a vocal and an instrumental arrangement that features the *erhu* (二胡), the two-stringed bowed fiddle introduced to Han Chinese from nomadic peoples of central and northern Asia and integrated into common practice during the Qing dynasty (1644–1911) (T. Liu 2001, 214). In addition to the *erhu*, other musical features in the song include the percussive woodblocks imitating galloping horses, animals that are central in Mongolian culture and commonly used as representation, often stereotypically or superficially, of an ethnic minority group. In "Representing the Minority Other in Chinese Music," ethnomusicologist Chuen-Fung Wong writes how "China and its majority Han ethnicity have had a long and well-documented history of exoticizing practices for representing their various 'Others.' Yet it was not until the Communist takeover in 1949 did such exoticism become systematized as a state-sponsored enterprise often with explicit sociopolitical ends" (2010, 121). Wong continues on to emphasize the distinction between folklorism and the very political "minority exoticism" of the CCP through "representation[s] of minority otherness" (140).

The final example is the newly composed song of international relations "Albania, My Dear Comrade and Brother" ("Aerbaniya, wo qinmi de tong-zhi he dixiong" 阿尔巴尼亚，我亲密的同志和弟兄). The song was composed by the "Composition Committee, Central Political Propaganda Team" (Zongzheng xuanchuan dui chuangzuo zu 总政宣传队创作组), most likely a group of government workers of varied musical backgrounds. Similar to the songs of ethnic minorities, "Albania, My Dear Comrade and Brother" also utilizes a combination of lyrics, music, and performance to enforce its identification as a song of international relations. The lyrics speak to the unity of China and Albania in their united fight through metaphors of bravery and

Example 2.8. "Albania, My Dear Comrade and Brother"

2

50

tong zhi he xiong di._____ di.

Lie huo chui lian le wo men de you yi, wo men jin mi tuan jie zhan wu bu

sheng. Wei le gong tong fan dui di, xiu, fan, wo men qu jin xing wei da de dou__

zheng. Guangrong Mao Ze dong, En Wei 'er! Guangrong En Wei 'er, Mao Ze dong.__

Example 2.8. *Continued.*

commitment versus natural and ideological forces. The lyrics specifically identify the Adriatic Sea, and the final lines praise the leaders of the two countries, Mao Zedong and Enver Hoxha.[32]

阿尔巴尼亚，我亲密的同志和弟兄
ALBANIA, MY DEAR COMRADE AND BROTHER

迎着阳光，穿过云层，
The welcoming sunlight, passes through the layers of clouds,
有一只矫健勇敢的山鹰。
There is an agile and brave mountain eagle.
它不怕天塌地倾，它不怕海啸山崩，
It is not afraid of a landslide, it is not afraid of a tsunami,
高高地飞翔在亚得里亚海上空。
High above it circles in the air above the Adriatic Sea.

啊英雄的阿尔巴尼亚，我亲密的同志和弟兄。
Ah heroic Albania, my dear comrade and brother.
天地越动志越坚，
The more changeable the world, the more resolute the will,
山海越险心越红，
The more perilous the mountains and seas, the redder the heart,
我亲密的同志和弟兄。
My dear comrade and brother.

为了共同反对帝，修，反，
Because of our common fight against imperialism, revisionism, and
    counter-revolutionaries,
我们去进行伟大的斗争。
We will advance in the greatest struggle.
光荣，毛泽东，恩维尔！
Glorious, Mao Zedong, Enver Hoxha!
光荣，恩维尔，毛泽东！
Glorious, Enver Hoxha, Mao Zedong!

The tune's complexity, relative to the songs for the masses, reflects the musicianship of the composer and demands a vocalist with musical training to grasp the extended vocal range and lilting melody. The song is marked "bright and clear" (*minglang* 明朗) and "affectionately" (*qinqie di* 亲切地). Though not labeled specifically as a solo, "Albania, My Dear Comrade and Brother" contrasts with the other revolutionary songs with its expressive melody, poetic lyrics, and smooth rhythmic contour.

The writers and editors of the anthology blended different musical styles into even the heavily militaristic CCP classics, which would be sung in unison with a primary attention to lyrics and a secondary attention to musical aesthetics. They were originally composed for the untrained voice, maintain a simple melodic line, and have a rather narrow melodic range. However, the committee attempted to incorporate traditional elements and more lyrical and artistic styles.

The "newly composed songs" such as "Strike the Tanks" and "I Love Beijing's Tiananmen" do not appear to be all that new in their simple revolutionary form and content. However, many of the newly composed songs—"Song in Praise of Beijing," "Red Guards on the Grasslands Have Met Chairman Mao," and "Albania, My Dear Comrade and Brother"—demand advanced musicianship of the vocalist and stray from the simple form and style of general revolutionary songs designed for the masses without musical training. My interviewees told me that, after soliciting songs from the masses across all of the Chinese provinces, the editorial team asked the professional musicians to compose a handful of different songs to balance out the anthology. These more technically demanding numbers covered politically significant themes like Beijing, ethnic minorities, and international relations. On the other end of the spectrum, the *New Songs of the Battlefield* anthology is also known for its compositions that were clearly chosen solely for their political content. Songs such as "The Great Proletarian Cultural Revolution Is Indeed

Good" were often composed by amateur musicians, in this case, a group of workers from Shanghai.

The examples uncover a number of key points in regard to the musical characteristics of the *New Songs of the Battlefield*. First, the historical lineage of the CCP classics illustrates the development of revolutionary songs from the early twentieth century up through the Cultural Revolution period. Many revolutionary songs have been revised and have reappeared throughout different historical periods, thus becoming known as "revolutionary history songs" or "revolutionary history folk songs." Second, many of the newly composed songs continue in a similar musical fashion and are constructed largely as revolutionary songs for groups of specific individuals (workers, peasants, soldiers, youth, and the like). The songs maintain a simple musical form and utilize didactic language to promote political campaigns and ideologies. Third, some of the songs reach beyond the simple form of most revolutionary songs; they are longer and have greater musical complexity in terms of tempo, rhythm, vocal range, and overall form. Compositionally the songs add a new layer to the revolutionary songs, although their political message remains the primary focus.

Conclusions

Music was used as a weapon under the direction of politicizing the arts, as outlined by the Sanhua policy ("Three Processes of Transformation"). The first of the three parts, "to revolutionize," was an attempt to transform both the function and content of music. As indicated in the dedication to the *New Songs of the Battlefield* anthology, Mao's directive was explicit in its primary attention to politics, with art in a secondary role. Thus, revolutionizing music began with a transformation of lyrical content to exclusively political rhetoric. The music then supported this transformation, first with militaristic and inspiring aesthetics to energize and mobilize the masses and later, with *New Songs of the Battlefield*, more lyrical and culturally meaningful aesthetic choices.

Revolutionary songs, specifically the transformation of lyrical content, was just one application of political rhetoric during the Chinese Cultural Revolution. The CCP understood not only the power of language and its ability to transform the way people think but also how this transformation could also impact one's actions.[33] Communications scholar Xing Lu offers sharp analysis into the CCP's political strategies when she writes, "Polarized language leads to polarized thinking; the rhetoric of agitation leads to fanaticism and violence, as evidenced in human history. Moreover, violent actions and human atrocities are justified by moralistic rhetoric and the dehumanization of perceived enemies. This is exactly what occurred during the Chinese proletarian Cultural Revolution (1966–1976), one of the most catastrophic mass movements and political upheavals of the twentieth century" (2004, xi). Lu explains how Mao's rhetoric was successful in part because it extended cultural traditions that had been long established in Chinese history. For example, Confucius "recognized the power of language in maintaining social order and political control" (31), and "for Confucius, words served as an impetus and catalyst for social transformation and behavior change: new words and concepts called for new ways of acting and perceiving reality as well as for organization strategies regarding cultural and political meanings" (32). Mao skillfully took advantage of this established cultural practice and applied it in a new social and political era. (Ironically, in a group of songs discussed in chapter 3, Confucius was targeted as one of the "Four Olds" that needed to be destroyed.)

Efforts to "revolutionize" began with a transformation of lyrical content that would focus exclusively on disseminating political ideology. As Xing Lu writes, "It has been the Chinese Communist belief that 'thought determines action'; thus, correct thought (adherence to Marxist-Maoist ideology) would bring about correct action (acting in line with Mao's directives and the party's dogma)" (2004, 42). In other words, the goal of revolutionizing music was to transform both thought and action in support of Cultural Revolution politics.

Political slogans are the focus of most CCP classics, and they continue to appear throughout the newly composed songs as well. The environment in which the slogans appeared during the Cultural Revolution was intense, pervasive, and exclusive: slogans surrounded individuals at every corner and were reinforced through multiple senses, including sight, sound, and touch. "Political slogans permeated every aspect of Chinese culture during the Cultural Revolution. They were the primary rhetorical symbols used to justify violent behavior, dehumanize class enemies, encourage anti-traditional acts, and elevate the cult of Mao" (X. Lu 2004, 53). Political slogans, which educated the masses as to the specific political campaign of the moment, were reinforced in all aspects of one's daily life and ultimately transformed how individuals were thinking; all of this then impacted their actions and behaviors (53). Conversations with individuals who are not familiar with the Cultural Revolution almost always include questions about why and how individuals would believe the political slogans and, similarly, whether anyone challenged or questioned these campaigns. As Xing Lu explains, "During the

Cultural Revolution in particular the worldview of the Chinese people was locked into a language system that indoctrinated their minds and allowed only one version of the truth to filter through" (35). The isolation of language and repetitive dissemination created an environment that is difficult to imagine in most other modern contexts. While some exceptions did occur and there surely was not only one unilateral or monolithic response to political propaganda, the extensive and isolated dissemination of sharply focused political propaganda is a historic characteristic of the Cultural Revolution.

The CCP classics offered musical accompaniment to lyrics that were almost exclusively tied to political campaigns and were full of direct quotations. Songs such as "Three Main Rules of Discipline and Eight Points for Attention" were set to marchlike melodies with stiff and unremarkable attention to musical aesthetics. Even so, the songs often inspired marching or other group activities.[34] The music provided a means to support the political lyrics, instilling a sense of group identity and commitment to Mao, the CCP, and the nation. Xing Lu writes of how her mother was sent away to a labor camp and "each morning after a simple, coarse meal they lined up, sang a revolutionary song, and marched to the field to do intense labor" (2004, 21). She describes the camps as a place where people suffered great detriments to both their bodies and their minds. Lu's mother would come home about once a month and teach her children a new revolutionary song to lift their spirits. Lu's reflection of the experience illustrates the impact of the revolutionary songs: "Mother did not have a good singing voice, and the song was not aesthetically appealing; however, its marching quality and connection to Mao's teaching stirred our spirits and drew us closer to Mother. Ironically, this was the only time I can remember Mother spending time with us. She never complained about her hardships but instead was proud of herself and always in good spirits" (22). Lu specifically mentions how the upbeat tempo and rhythms lent themselves to lifting their spirits. But the lyrics alone cannot account for the impact of this moment of singing. The content of the lyrics was inspiring and hopeful, and the moment together was precious and dear. Multiple senses were engaged, despite the fact that the song "was not aesthetically appealing." In my own ethnographic fieldwork, nearly every individual has mentioned how the revolutionary songs were inspiring and motivating and effectively reinforced political campaigns.

The newly composed songs, on the other hand, built upon this history and practice of revolutionary songs and extended their capacity in a manner that was consistent with the changing political climate of the second half of the Cultural Revolution (1972–76). The poetic line "yellow flowers on the battlefield are especially fragrant" from the *New Songs of the Battlefield* preface suggests a more nuanced and lyrical expression of the revolutionization of music. No longer black and white but perhaps something in between, the *New Songs of the Battlefield* offered the same politicization of music, and revolutionary content, but packaged in a slightly different manner. Of course, politics remained first, but the attention to musical aesthetics became a much closer second.

Zhou Enlai's extension of Mao Zedong's original cultural policies directed revolutionary music to serve the revolution and to be revolutionary in content. "To revolutionize" music, the first of his three-part policy, allowed the CCP to transform both the content and the function of music. *New Songs of the Battlefield* presented new songs for the revolution, all completely dedicated to the revolution in content and function. This was achieved first and foremost through the attention to correct political standards and through the explicit and direct politicization of lyrics, followed by an increasing development of musical forms that engaged with the political lyrics. The notes on a yellowed page of a songbook purchased at a flea market in Beijing may appear insignificant, but the songs take on new meaning in light of ideological and artistic efforts. The anthology is an important collection that offers insight into a historic period when musical works were considered "more fragrant" by planting them firmly within the fertile soil of an ideological "battlefield" to be nurtured by the sunlight and waters of a distinct political line.

Memories of the Battlefield

"It's in Your Bones, It's in Your Blood"

"How would I describe it [the Cultural Revolution] now? It depends on who you talk to. If you talk to someone my age, or someone older, we do not even have to describe it. Because they understand, they know. But to explain to someone else, you really have to think about how to say this. You have to think about their capacity to understand. And what is their background? Did they grow up in China? Did they grow up in the United States? *Bu yiyang* [different ("It's not the same") 不一样]" (Zhang Haihui 2018, personal interview).

While historical overviews and political analyses can provide valuable insight into what happened in China during the Cultural Revolution at a structural level, how can we understand what the period was like for someone who lived through the tumultuous time in China's history? Experiences varied tremendously based on a number of factors, including age, location, and social and political status. In early 2018 I sat down to speak with two women who lived through the Cultural Revolution.

I first met Zhang Haihui and Jin Laoshi when I was a graduate student and began speaking with academics at various universities across the United States, consulting different individuals with ties to the Cultural Revolution to ask for their expertise and assistance in accessing sources, translating and transliterating source materials, and contextualizing my fieldwork. As these two women and I worked together, we would inevitably have our own separate conversations, and many of these "side" conversations led to personal accounts of their time during the Cultural Revolution. Nearly fifteen years after completing my PhD I sat down to interview them about their personal experiences during the Cultural Revolution and to revisit some of our earlier conversations about the impact of the time period on contemporary China. Like Martin Daughtry in *Listening to War* (2015), I include excerpts of these two interviews as interludes in between the more focused discussions of music in order to capture life during the Cultural Revolution and to contextualize and personalize the lived experience.

Before starting to write about the *New Songs of the Battlefield* anthology, I reconnected with Zhang Haihui, whom I had interviewed after I began my initial research in 2001. Zhang is the head of the East Asian Library at the University of Pittsburgh and has always been a tremendous resource to me and to other scholars who research East Asia.

In 2016 Zhang Haihui launched an online oral history project through the University of Pittsburgh's library system called *China's Cultural Revolution in Memories*, or "CR/10" for short (see the several East Asian Library, University Library System [ULS], University of Pittsburgh entries in the bibliography). Zhang was interested in collecting the stories of everyday people who had lived through the Cultural Revolution. As a historian, Zhang wanted to create a space to collect and share the memories of the aging generations who had directly experienced the Cultural Revolution. She felt that much of the scholarship on the Cultural Revolution focused on the celebrities, "the people who have recognition either in politics or tragedy" (2018, personal interview), and wanted to provide an alternative.[1] As Zhang shared, "Every person is a story . . . every person has their own memory . . . and each of them has their own worth." Her qualitative approach informs the project, wherein Zhang herself, along with other trained interviewers, ask people to talk for ten minutes about the Cultural Revolution.[2] The ten-minute limit is intentional in design; as Zhang explained, "People could talk for days and days, hours and hours," but if they are asked to talk for only ten minutes, it requires them to filter and go right to the most powerful or memorable moment. Additionally, Zhang noted that with long and open-ended interviews, the researcher gets to decide what to share and what to omit. Using her method, the interviewees choose what is included in the project. As of April 2021, over one hundred interviews have been uploaded and are available for viewing.

How does Zhang describe the Cultural Revolution today? To those who grew up in China after the Cultural Revolution, "We need to tell them that these ten years"—Zhang sighed and continued—"we need to tell them to be extremely reluctant to allow [this] to happen in China again, to experience again, this ten-year period. A ten-year period that we cannot allow to be experienced ever again."

Zhang's tone shifted when she turned to talk about generations younger than hers who grew up in the United States. "Like my son. There is no way they can understand what happened. They also do not have any interest in it, and this is a problem. . . . I do not even have the experience of a younger person asking me this question. I do not even have the opportunity to explain." Zhang spoke about how many of the students working in her office have such a limited knowledge of the Cultural Revolution and believe that it has nothing to do with their lives. Zhang shifted back to our current conversation and said that, for us, for our conversation, these ten years were *taikepa* (太可怕)—so horrible, so frightening. She stopped herself and clarified that this was her own experience in Beijing and should not necessarily be extended to everyone who came of age during the era. "Now that I have been working on CR/10, I am not sure if everyone had this experience. People in the countryside, in a factory, they would not have had the same experience. So you have to see where people were [because the] experiences will be different."

Zhang Haihui's interest in the Cultural Revolution stems from her own experience growing up as a young child in urban Beijing amid the political chaos leading up to the Cultural Revolution and later spending time in rural Shaanxi Province during the Cultural Revolution. From her work on the CR/10 project she has learned in more nuanced ways how one's experience is directly linked to age, location, and family background. In her own lived experience she witnessed firsthand how one's positioning impacted an individual's or family's outcome during the Cultural Revolution. For example, she shared with me (and in her own CR/10 interview) how her father was labeled a rightist (*youpai* 右派) in the 1950s and sent to Dongbei (northeastern China). "So my mother was protecting me and divorced him." Her mother remarried before the start of the Cultural Revolution, and because Zhang Haihui's stepfather was in the military, their new family was protected during the Cultural Revolution. Zhang could participate in the activities of the Little Red Guards (Hongxiaobing 红小兵), and their family was free from criticism because of their military background. However, Zhang had schoolmates who shared her father's rightist background, and those children suffered tremendously. Once denounced, they were targets of much violence and criticism and were not allowed to participate in as many activities. Thus Zhang's fate, and her family's, was transformed because of her stepfather's military affiliation.

Zhang Haihui appears in the CR/10 collection with her own story as told to a research assistant. The first thing she shares is her memory of when the Cultural Revolution started: "We must have been in third grade, I think. One day, we were in the middle of class with our teacher, who was about 40 years old and surnamed Liu. Suddenly the door was kicked open, and several older students came in. They pointed at our teacher and said, 'You can't teach anymore.' Then, they told us, 'Go on, go home! There's no more class.' So if you ask me when my understanding of the Cultural Revolution started, it began on that day" (East Asian Library, ULS, University of Pittsburgh 2016b).

This short story is insightful but not necessarily historically nuanced or complex. Zhang chose to start with a historical account of when the revolution began in her life, but in the context of memory, violence, and trauma, the story (or the memory) can be understood with more depth. This day was a defining moment. With traumatic events there is commonly an association of life "before" and life "after."

In her CR/10 interview, Zhang continues to discuss how she and her classmates were so young that it was difficult for them to fully understand the Cultural Revolution. What they did understand was that violence suddenly surrounded them in "unnatural" ways. She shared with me in our interview how "I witnessed a lot. I witnessed suicides, witnessed criticism of teachers, witnessed fighting . . . anyhow, the Cultural Revolution, most of it I witnessed." She relived the horror of these suicides and families being separated and not understanding exactly why they were happening. One thing was clear: "only revolutionary relationships were okay . . . personal, human, relationships were all deemed not right." Exhausted, Zhang Haihui paused: "I don't really know how to say all of these things, you ask me [another question]."

So I shifted our focus to music. I asked, "When you were young, did you hear these songs from *New Songs of the Battlefield*? Where did you sing them? Where did you hear them?" Animated again, she responded with a quick, "Oh yes!" and continued to say how they were so easy to remember. "They picked songs that were easy to sing. Also there weren't that many other activities, so we would just sing these songs." Zhang explained how they would sing the songs at school and at other meetings. "And the loud speakers. During the Cultural Revolution these were too loud. You think about it, anywhere you would walk you would hear the loud speakers. All day and every day." She mentioned the model revolutionary operas (*yangbanxi*) and how everyone learned them simply by hearing them day in and day out. In fact, in recent years Zhang was attending a live performance of a model revolutionary opera with others her age. The singer slipped and missed a line, and the entire audience chimed in and kept the music going. "Shows you how this whole generation is familiar with them. It's in your bones, it's in your blood. If we have Alzheimer's we probably still would not forget these. How could it have such a lasting impression?" The sights and sounds are deeply embedded in an entire generation.

I recall Zhang's CR/10 interview where she goes into detail about the suicides—how "one jumped from a high building; one jumped from a chimney. If you say 'Cultural Revolution,' these scenes definitely come to mind" (East Asian Library, ULS, University of Pittsburgh, 2016b). The sounds and images, and their associated emotions, are all a part of these memories. "Entertainment was never like those ten years, even today. . . . Entertainment was at its peak during the Cultural Revolution in the countryside. . . . At that time, in the countryside, peasants were singing and dancing, singing contests on stage. Everyone went on the stage." Entertainment was at its peak, as was violence; the concurrent intensity of propaganda arts and violence became impossible to separate.

3

MUSIC AND CHILDHOOD

Music is, for children, a port in the storm, a resting spot,
a retreat from the madding crowd and their hectic lives.
It is their safety valve, an appropriate release of energy at
those times when no other channel seems possible.

—Patricia Shehan Campbell and Carol Scott-Kassner,
Music in Childhood

For many, music is a vehicle for the expression of artistry and human emotion, but it can also be a comforting part of one's childhood. What happens when children's music is politicized? What happens when the storm of a political and cultural revolution is directly connected to children's everyday lives? What happens when music is no longer a safe escape from the adult world?

In Mao Zedong's policy for revolutionary culture, presented in 1942 (and discussed in chapter 2), he detailed how the arts could act as a "powerful weapon" in uniting and educating the masses, "attacking and annihilating the enemy," and simultaneously foster solidarity in the struggle (McDougall 1980, 58). Accordingly, revolutionary music, this policy proclaimed, should focus on the three pillars of socialist society: workers, peasants, and soldiers. Thus, many children's songs were composed and disseminated in attempts to educate the next generation of the Chinese socialist society. Seemingly opposing forces came together in these children's songs as music was utilized as a weapon for the revolution. If we understand propaganda as biased and at times evil, and indoctrination as a process of teaching a group to accept a set of beliefs uncritically, then how can we understand the line between enculturation and indoctrination? Between patriotism and propaganda? In this chapter, I introduce select examples of children's songs from the *New Songs of the Battlefield* anthology and the cultural policies that informed them to explain the techniques used to politicize children's music and transform the content and function of music into Cultural Revolution propaganda. I then turn to a firsthand account of a childhood immersed in musical propaganda with an ethnographic account of Chen Jiebing, who entered the Chinese Navy orchestra at age nine and retired as major at the age of twenty-two. Finally, my analysis will consider how children's songs are a dangerous and extreme example of the exploitation of music.

Children's Songs in *New Songs of the Battlefield*

The *New Songs of the Battlefield* anthology was directed toward the three pillars of socialist society: workers, peasants, and soldiers. The editors aimed to provide a means for members of the new socialist society to find representation of themselves in the songs' messages, images, and music. Thus, the editors explicitly placed children and youth directly within the purview of their political ideology in order to bring the next generation into the revolution while highlighting the promise of future generations in China's socialist society. Zhang Juan underscores the significance of songs for youth with a call for a focused examination of songs for the *zhishi qingnian* (知识青年), "educated youth" or "sent-down youth" (2018). And the use of music to educate children and the children's songs themselves are not unique to the Cultural Revolution, as can be seen in Zou Xia's overview of children's songs during the twentieth century (2015). The songs, in their intended function and lyrical and melodic content, are not exclusive to the Cultural Revolution; instead, as Feng Zhiping (2004), Li Cheng (2010), and Liu Jing (2014) each write, the songs are part of a gradual historical process that peaked during the intensity of the Cultural Revolution. As such, children's songs from the Cultural Revolution form a significant musical chapter in the history of children's songs in China.

The widespread dissemination, censorship, and political and physical punishment for counter-revolutionary culture created a unique context for the *New Songs of the Battlefield* during the Cultural Revolution.[1] During the Cultural Revolution, children's songs of the anthology were essentially the *only* approved songs for the generation that came of age when the CCP strictly censored all music and arts. While some individuals or families may have resisted by playing other music in private, the punishments for doing so were so severe that individuals, by and large, would not dare sing anything but revolutionary songs, even behind closed doors.[2] With some exceptions, particularly in rural and remote areas, children would encounter revolutionary songs on a daily and repeated basis during the Cultural Revolution. Loudspeakers wired in neighborhood districts played revolutionary music throughout the day, often as announcements to signal the beginning and end of the day, lunch, work group gatherings, and the like. Groups, for work or study, met repeatedly throughout the day and often started and ended with everyone singing revolutionary songs. As a result, the songs became the soundscape for those who came of age during the Chinese Cultural Revolution.

Over the five volumes of the *New Songs of the Battlefield* anthology, ninety-two songs are directed at children or youth; they typically appear toward the end of a volume in a group and either are explicitly stated as such (for example, "children's song," *ertong gequ* [儿童歌曲]) or mention youth in the title or lyrics (for example, "Marching Song of the Revolutionary Youth," "Geming qingnian jinxingqu" [革命青年进行曲]). At times, a song may not be explicitly labeled as a children's song, but fieldwork, including multiple interviews with editors, composers, and individuals who interacted with the songs, confirms that particular pieces were still commonly understood as children's songs, either through their placement in the anthology (appearing alongside titles that were labeled as children's songs) or through lyrics that discussed children or children's activities. Songs for children or youth make up roughly 17 percent of the anthology; this is a combination of roughly 5 percent songs for youth and roughly 12 percent (sixty-five songs) specifically children's songs targeting elementary-age children and younger.[3] Characteristic of the time, the children's songs often reference China's history of struggles through the lens of the CCP, ethnic minority songs, and folk songs (Feng 2004, 81–83). Over half of the songs are one page or less (roughly thirty to forty bars of music) in length, and 74 percent (forty-eight songs) are under two pages. The children's songs are all in major keys, with the majority in C major, D major, or G major. While key signatures from Western European musical systems are used, Li Cheng explains that the children's songs typically follow traditional Chinese systems of pentatonic scales (2010, 35–36).[4] Nearly one-third of the songs (twenty-one of them) include a tempo marking with a preference for more upbeat and uptempo songs. The songs are predominantly monosyllabic and often match linguistic tonal contour with melodic contour, as is common in children's songs of other eras as well as other musical traditions.[5]

Table 3.1. Children's songs by key signature in *New Songs of the Battlefield*

Key signature	Number of songs	Percentage
C major	24	37%
D major	10	15%
G major	9	14%
E major	7	11%
F major	7	11%
B-flat major	5	8%
E-flat major	3	5%

Table 3.2. Children's songs by time signature in *New Songs of the Battlefield*

Time signature	Number of songs	Percentage
2/4	61	94.0%
combination of 2/4 and 4/4	1	1.5%
4/4	1	1.5%
3/4	1	1.5%
3/8	1	1.5%

Table 3.3. Tempo markings in children's songs in *New Songs of the Battlefield*

Tempo marking	Translation	Number of songs
稍快 (*shao kuai*)	a little fast (upbeat tempo)	11
中速 (*zhong su*)	medium speed (tempo)	7
进行速度 (*jinxing sudu*)	march speed (tempo)	2
慢速 (*man su*)	slow speed (tempo)	2

Li Cheng describes the children's songs as "stable, bright, and strong . . . positive, lively and optimistic in spirit" (2010, 35–36). Such tones are evident in the musical expressions provided for 71 percent of the songs (forty-six songs in total), with some including more than one expression. The most frequently listed musical expressions include *happily, enthusiastically, lively,* and *delightfully.*

A classic example of a children's song is "I Love Beijing's Tiananmen" (see discussion in previous chapter). The song is labeled as a children's song with the markings "enthusiastically" and "vivaciously." The song is in 2/4 time in the key of C major, and the lyrics include two simple lines that are each

Table 3.4. Common musical expressions in children's songs in *New Songs of the Battlefield*

Musical expression	English translation	Number of appearances
欢快地 (*huankuai di*)	lively or happily	18
活泼地 (*huopo di*)	vivaciously or lively	8
热情地 (*reqing di*)	enthusiastically or passionately	6
喜悦地 (*xiyue di*)	delightfully or joyfully	4
亲切地 (*qinqie di*)	affectionately	4
朝气蓬勃地 (*zhaoqi pengbo di*)	vibrantly	3
自由地 (*ziyou di*)	freely	3

Note: Some songs include more than one expression. The character 地 after an adjective creates an adverb in Chinese. Musical expressions primarily, but not exclusively, use the adverb form—for example, 活泼地 (*huopo di*) or 活泼 (*huopo*).

repeated three times in the published score (though more repetitions appear in recordings). The song consists of a simple ABA pattern with an upbeat and playful rhythmic contour in the A section and a slightly more lyrical and elongated melodic line for the B section. Among my interviewees, this song is the most frequently identified and recognized across multiple generations. Furthermore, because the lyrics lack any specific reference to the Cultural Revolution or any political campaign, the song continues to be circulated today. Indeed, the Chinese international students who were born between 1988 and 1993 and studied at Skidmore College in New York whom I interviewed are all familiar with the song, despite having no direct experience with the Cultural Revolution.[6] This song is somewhat atypical in that, to my knowledge, it is the only one with such wide recognition across generations and historical time periods. Beijing, Tiananmen Square, and Chairman Mao remain today as symbols to promote the Communist Party and China as a nation, and thus the simple lyrics still resonate decades beyond the composition's original release.

Children's songs represent one of six thematic categories in the entire *New Songs of the Battlefield* anthology and maintain similarities to the other five categories such as promoting unity and praising Mao and the Communist Party. Some songs about international relations are dedicated to children, some songs of ethnic minorities specifically identify children, and so forth. This overlap is evident in Liu Jing's (2014) identification of five thematic categories within children's songs of the "New Songs of the Battlefield" anthology:

1. Songs of praise (*songge* 颂歌)
2. (Songs of) political activities (*zhengzhi huodong* 政治活动)
3. (Songs of) children's activities (*ertong shenghuo* 儿童生活)
4. International diplomatic relations (*guoji waijiao guanxi* 国际外交关系) and cross-strait relations (*liang'an guanxi* 两岸关系)
5. Voices of children of all ethnic groups (*ge zu ertong xinsheng* 各族儿童心声) (125)

Liu Jing's five categories reinforce the earlier understanding of the types of songs within the anthology. Specifically within the children's songs, I take Liu Jing's analysis one step further to observe three defining characteristics that help illustrate some of the primary techniques that were employed to create revolutionary music for children during the Cultural Revolution. These are politically explicit songs, action songs, and "little" songs.

Table 3.5. Politically explicit children's songs in *New Songs of the Battlefield* (selected examples)

Year	Title	Composer/lyricist
1972	"Study Well and Make Progress Every Day"	Zhang Zoya/Zhang Lansheng
1973	"Grow Up to Be a Good Member of the Commune"	Liu Delun/Chen Guanxuan
1974	"Lin Biao and Confucius Are Both Bad Things"	Ru Yinhe/Xiao Fengdeng
1975	"On the '5.7' [May 7 Directive] Road We Quickly Run Forward"	Wu Zuqiang/Zhang Yibin
1976	"Grow Up to Be a New Peasant"	Li Zhigang/Li Caiyong

POLITICALLY EXPLICIT SONGS

Songs containing overt political content and language make up the majority of children's songs in the *New Songs of the Battlefield* anthology. See table 3.5 for examples. In these songs, music is utilized as a weapon for the revolution by bringing explicit political ideology and revolutionary language (including references to struggle, weapons, and violence) into a child's musical world.

While the song "Study Well and Make Progress Every Day" (music example 3.1) continues the general practice of utilizing songs to educate children on topics of morality, like studying every day, reading, and the like, it also includes overt and explicit directives for instilling patriotism and a commitment to communism and the Chinese Communist Party. Musically the song is played in the style of a march (*jinxingqu* 进行曲) and shares many characteristics with the other overwhelmingly short, didactic songs found in the anthology. Furthermore, the song places children directly within the revolution and the politics of the day, thereby providing an image of children as recognized members of the political society that surrounded them. Songs such as "Grow Up to Be a Good Member of the Commune" and "Grow Up to Be a New Peasant" likewise emphasize these children's future place in China's socialist society.

好好学习天天向上
STUDY WELL AND MAKE PROGRESS EVERY DAY
红小兵心最红，忠于人民忠于党。
Little Red Guards' hearts are most red, loyal to the people loyal to the party.
好好学习，天天向上，认真读书为革命。
Study well, make progress every day, study hard for the revolution.
好好学习，天天向上，长大要当工农兵。
Study well, make progress every day, grow up to become the workers, peasants, and soldiers.

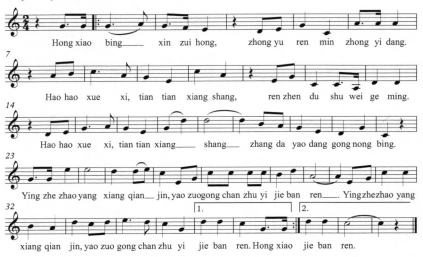

Example 3.1. "Study Well and Make Progress Every Day"

迎著朝阳向前进，要做共产主义接班人。
Facing the sun to move forward, we must become the successors of
    communism.
迎著朝阳向前进，要做共产主义接班人。
Facing the sun to move forward, we must become the successors of
    communism.

While the general practice of educating the masses through song predates Communist China, the strategy was taken to new ends during the Cultural Revolution (I. Wong 1984, 112). Political indoctrination was more extreme in the children's songs of the Cultural Revolution, which contain explicit and overt propagandistic lyrics. A noteworthy example is "Lin Biao and Confucius Are Both Bad Things":

林彪，孔老二都是坏东西
LIN BIAO AND CONFUCIUS ARE BOTH BAD THINGS
叛徒林彪，孔老二，都是坏东西。
Traitor Lin Biao, and Confucius, are both bad things.
嘴上讲"仁义"，肚里藏诡计，
Mouthing "justice," while concealing deception in their belly,

a little fast

Pan tu Lin_ Biao, Kong lao_ er dou shi huai dong_ xi.

Zui shang jiang "ren yi_____ ." Du li_ can gui ji,

gu__ chui "ke ji fu__ li," yi xin_ xiang fu__ bi. Pei!

Hong xiao bing qi__shang_ zhen, da jia dou lai hen hen_ pi!

Hong xiao bing qi_ shang_ zhen, da jia dou lai hen hen_ pi! Hai!

Example 3.2. "Lin Biao and Confucius Are Both Bad Things"

鼓吹"克己复礼"，一心想复辟。呸！
Advocating "restrain oneself and observe the rites," while at heart
    staging a comeback. Bah!
红小兵齐上陣，大家都來狠狠批！
Little Red Guards are all ready to go into battle, everyone come
    ruthlessly criticize!
红小兵齐上陣，大家都來狠狠批！咳！
Little Red Guards are all ready to go into battle, everyone come
    ruthlessly criticize! Hey!

    Musically, the song is rather simple and bland. In the key of D major and
with a 2/4 time signature, the tempo marking indicates "a little fast" (*shao kuai*
稍快) (similar to "allegro"). It has a militaristic tone that is more reminiscent
of earlier revolutionary songs as opposed to the more lyrical and upbeat
characteristic of many children's tunes in the *New Songs of the Battlefield*
anthology. The song title references a political slogan, and the lyrics serve as
the focal point for the song. Explicit lyrics identifying "traitor" Lin Biao and
Confucius as two "bad things" provide a clear and precise message of right
and wrong according to the politics of the Cultural Revolution. The polar-
ization of good and evil is what Xing Lu refers to as "radicalization," which

she explores in her rhetorical analysis of political slogans from the Cultural Revolution (2004, 67).

In this designated children's song, *ertong gequ*, the lyrics identify children as the "Little Red Guards" (Hongxiaobing 红小兵), a reference to the mobilized generation of youth who fueled the Cultural Revolution known as "Red Guards" (Hongweibing 红卫兵). The term itself, as well as the propaganda that used it, placed young children as the next generation to struggle and fight for revolution. The lyrics call the children to join the battle of the Cultural Revolution by disparaging Lin Biao and Confucius—for "everyone [to] come ruthlessly criticize" (*hen pi* 狠批). By pulling children into the fray, the message alienates those who do not participate. "Alienation" is another rhetorical theme Xing Lu identifies in her analysis of Cultural Revolution rhetoric (2004, 68).

ACTION SONGS

Action songs place children directly in some type of socialist engagement. I consider this technique to be a type of musical application of the CCP's use of socialist realism. Just as monuments and other visual arts represent members of a socialist society as eternally in motion (for example, moving forward in a lunge), here children are depicted as musically in motion, in activities that benefit the socialist society.[7] While this occurs in songs throughout the anthology, six consecutive songs in the second volume (1973) have explicit wording in their title that emphasize a specific action.

In this set of songs, lyrics reference everyday activities of farmers and peasants such as planting flowers and trees, feeding animals, and delivering feed. But they also depict children's everyday activities of play, like riding a rocking horse and playing telephone. Embedded in these everyday activities are the implications of connecting ordinary life with the abstract concept of the socialist revolution, such as the promise of growth and prosperity through agriculture.

Table 3.6. Children's action songs in *New Songs of the Battlefield* (selected examples)

Year	Title	Composer/lyricist
1973	"Plant Sunflowers"	Wuhan Central No. 8 Creative Team/Wang Zhongnong
1973	"Plant Tree Seedlings"	Jie Jiaping/Dan Bao
1973	"Delivering Feed"	Luo Ruding/Tang Yaohui
1973	"Feeding the Chickens"	Wang Jian/Wang Zhi'an
1973	"Ride the Little Rocking Horse"	Xiang Zhiqi
1973	"Calling on the Telephone"	Kang Shouxin/Zhang Zhongliang

The six songs appear in succession toward the end of volume 2 and all refer to children, though only "Calling on the Telephone" is listed as a "children's song." Once again, though the songs are not all explicitly labeled as children's songs, they are commonly understood as such because of their placement in the anthology, their child-related themes such as children's play, or their imagery of youth and growth. For example, in the second volume, this set of songs appears near the end of the table of contents with only three songs of international relations that follow. As such, they can be understood as a group of children's songs, which were typically grouped together at the end of a volume. Continuing the practice from the previous two categories of children's songs, political campaigns of the Cultural Revolution are explicitly placed within a child's everyday play:

打电话

CALLING ON THE TELEPHONE

(甲) 你站这儿，我站那儿，

(A) You stand here, I stand there,

乙) 拉根线，打电话。

(B) Pull the wire, and make a call.

Example 3.3. "Calling on the Telephone"

甲) 喂，喂，你要哪儿?
(A) Hello, hello, where do you want to call?
乙) 我要挂到亚、非、拉。
(B) I want to connect to Asia, Africa, and Latin America.

(合) 向各国小朋友问个好，我们的朋友遍天下。
(Together) To greet the children of many countries, we have friends all
over the world.
世界人民团结紧，把帝、修、反全打垮，全打垮。
People of the world unite in solidarity, to fully defeat imperialists,
revisionists, and counter-revolutionaries.

"Calling on the Telephone" begins with the first voice (A) directing the players in the children's game of telephone; the second voice (B) then completes the line. In this type of musical call and response, the voices complete their musical lines before joining together for the final four phrases. The expression and tempo markings indicate "enthusiastically" and "a little fast." While the song's musical style is unremarkable, the final line accommodates a mouthful of political jargon.

The lyrics place the international socialist movement directly into the everyday activity of children playing. The call includes two clearly politicized markers: (1) the positive identification of Asia, Africa, and Latin America, and (2) the negative identification of three enemies that socialist children of the world should unite in solidarity to defeat: imperialists, revisionists, and counter-revolutionaries. Asia, Africa, and Latin America are included as broad stroke references to regions with socialist allies and therefore favorable diplomatic relations with China, whereas North America and Europe are thus noticeably absent from the list. Such lyrics are remarkably propagandistic and bring complex political slogans and socialist ideology into the everyday language of children. Communications scholar Xing Lu was raised in China during the Cultural Revolution and writes,

> I considered myself one of the "children of Mao's era." My formative years coincided with his reign of influence. I was indoctrinated into his system of morality and attracted to the communist cause. From kindergarten on we were taught that we were the inheritors of the communist legacy, which promised an egalitarian society and the best possible life. Through songs, textbooks, and school rituals we learned how Mao and the Communist Party saved China and that many people sacrificed their lives to bring us the new China. Because of my blind faith in Mao, I regarded his revolutionary theories as absolute truth even though I did not understand them completely. I saw reality

in black and white terms. People were either class enemies or revolutionary comrades. Things were either right or wrong. (2004, 26)

"LITTLE" (*XIAO* 小) SONGS

A handful of song titles begin with the diminutive "Little." For example, there are five songs that all begin with the character "little" in the first four volumes of the *New Songs of the Battlefield* anthology. While this may be considered a somewhat arbitrary grouping, its applicability becomes apparent when compared to other patterns of repeated characters at the beginning of titles. For example, among the sixty-five children's songs in the *New Songs of the Battlefield* anthology, repeated characters at the beginning of titles include these:

we	我们	*women*	6 song titles (9 percent)
red	红	*hong*	6 song titles (9 percent)
little	小	*xiao*	5 song titles (8 percent)

The propagandistic linguistic style and tone of the Cultural Revolution can be seen throughout its music, performing arts, and visual arts. In music, operas, posters, and political slogans, the vocabulary is overtly propagandistic, with repeated keywords that facilitate memorization. As Xing Lu writes, "Repetition is a powerful means of persuasion in totalitarian societies. . . . The more frequently a line was repeated, the more likely it was to be remembered and accepted as truth" (2004, 105). For example, the words "we," "red," "big/great" (*da* 大), "toward" (*xiang* 向), "battle," (*zhan* 战), and "forward" (*qian* 前) appear with great frequency. These terms invoke solidarity in the revolution as well as general encouragement and vigor.[8] In the *New Songs of the Battlefield* anthology, the three most frequent characters at the beginning of song titles are "we," with 50 titles (9 percent); "red," with 54 titles (10 percent); and "big/great," with 103 song titles (18.5 percent). While "big" is the most commonly used character in

Table 3.7. "Little" (*xiao*) songs in *New Songs of the Battlefield* (selected examples)

Year	Title	Composer/lyricist
1972	"Tiny Ball Shines Silver Rays"	Shen Yisu/Ma Kaiyuan
1972	"Tiny Little Screw Cap"	Chen Shaolin/Sun Yu
1973	"Little Driver"	Su Yong/Zhang Dongfang
1974	"Little Pine Tree"	Fu Jing and Li Weicai/Fu Gengchen
1975	"Little Carrying Pole"	Liu Dezheng/Beijing Primary School Chinese Language Textbook

the general anthology, "little" is one of the most common song title characters for children's songs, and though there are only 6 titles that begin with "little" (a small sampling size, no pun intended), I still view this, as with most other propaganda, to be intentional. The diminutive "little" is a marker for children and children's culture and therefore a suitable keyword for children's songs of the Cultural Revolution.

The final example in this section, "Tiny Little Screw Cap," is at the heart of my investigation into children's songs in content, style, and reception. Musically, the song is a simple children's melody, with call and response sections and a generic ABA form. The song begins with a leader (or solo voice) calling out a short musical line that is then repeated by the group (chorus); the third time, the chorus completes the line (both musically and in lyrics) as opposed to continued repetition. In the next (B) section (measure 24) the group sings a short one-measure phrase that is then repeated by the instruments instead of a voice (see measures 25 and 27). A final three lines serve as a closing to the song with two lyrical lines and a final line that brings back the original A theme.

小小螺丝帽
TINY LITTLE SCREW CAP

（领）路边有颗螺丝帽，
Leader: On the roadside there is a screw cap,
（齐）路边有颗螺丝帽，螺丝帽，
Group: On the roadside there is a screw cap, a screw cap,
（领）弟弟上学看见了，
Leader: Little Brother sees it on the way to school,
（齐）看见了，看见了，看见了。
Group: [he] sees it, [he] sees it, [he] sees it.
（领）螺丝帽，虽然小，
Leader: The screw cap, although small,
（齐）祖国建设不可少。
Group: [it] is essential in the construction of the motherland.

捡起来，瞧一瞧，擦擦干净多么好。
Pick it up, wipe it clean, once it is all clean it is so pretty.
送给工人叔叔，把它装在机器上，嘿！
Bring it to Worker Uncle, put it in the machine, hey!
机器唱歌我们拍手笑。
The machine sings [hums] while we clap our hands.

(S) Lu bian you— ke— luo si— mao, (C) luo bian you ke luo si mao, luo si mao,

(S) di di—shang xue kan— jian— le. (C) Kan jian le, kan jian le, kan— jian— le.

(S) Luo si— mao,— sui ran— xiao, (C) zu guo jian she bu ke— shao.

Jian qi lai, qiao yi qiao, ca ca gan jing duo mo hao.

Song gei gong ren shu———— shu, ba ta zhuang zai— ji qi

shang, hei! Ji qi chang ge wo men pai shou xiao.————

(S) Solo
(C) Chorus

Example 3.4. "Tiny Little Screw Cap"

The lyrics tell the story of a young child ("Little Brother") who discovers a screw cap on the side of the road on the way to school; the child dusts it off and hands it over to a worker ("Uncle") to be used in his machine. Though the screw cap is small in size, it is not insignificant in the essential large-scale work of building the nation. Here children are again connected to the larger work of the nation; specifically, though small in size (or age), children are identified as a valuable part of the larger "machine" (or nation). "Tiny Little Screw Cap" thus specifically identifies children within messages of nation building and underscores their contribution to society at large. Connecting children to the political activity of the day gave them a clearly defined path to their role in the contemporary (as youth) and future (as adults) socialist society. Moreover, the frequency with which individuals encountered and engaged with propaganda music is one of the defining aspects of music from the Cultural Revolution. For children, propaganda music was a daily back-drop to childhood, pulling them into the political storm that surrounded them. The songs gave them both something to do on a daily basis and an explicit role in the frenetic commotion of the Cultural Revolution.

Propaganda and Childhood

According to ethnomusicologist Patricia Shehan Campbell, "Children are a product of social organization, and they do not move through increasingly advanced stages of their biological and neurological growth without being shaped by a constellation of forces within their environments, not the least of which are the musical genres which their societies value and thus preserve" (2006, 434). Her research on music in childhood illuminates several important elements of children's songs from the Cultural Revolution. First, music is commonly considered an artistic expression of human emotion and experience. Second, as generations of anthropologists and ethnomusicologists have explored, music is a central site for processes of enculturation. Such sentiments are evident in discussions of Chinese children's songs. As Chen Chaoxia writes, "Beautiful children's songs will inspire children's thinking in all aspects, giving them a beautiful experience, but also cultivate their sentiments" (2009, 499). In a 2017 *Guangming ribao* (Enlightenment daily) newspaper article, Guo Chao describes children's songs as "the breast milk that guides children to learn the language" and as "crucial to children's growth" (2017, 9). So what happens when music is controlled for political purposes and filled with propagandistic ideology and language? What happens when the process of enculturation is politicized? Can music still serve as a so-called resting spot (Campbell and Scott-Kassner 2014, 13)? Children's songs from the Cultural Revolution may serve as one example for consideration.

Mao presented ideas for the radical transformation of music in his 1942 "Talks at the Yan'an Conference on Literature and Art." Zhou Enlai's Sanhua policy that followed Mao's 1942 talks specifically outlined how to transform both the function and the content of music and the arts. Applied to music of the Cultural Revolution such as the songs included in *New Songs of the Battlefield*, only the *content* of the music was fully altered. The *function* of music was never successfully transformed, but this failed attempt carries significant and lasting implications. The extreme politicization of music, in content and function, is seemingly at odds with what one may imagine for children's songs. In particular, the cross-cultural functions of music mostly prevailed over the attempted political transformation of its meaning. My fieldwork reveals that many individuals who grew up with the children's songs of the Cultural Revolution still benefited from music on individual, social, and emotional levels, despite extremely politicized and propagandistic efforts. As *erhu* musician Wang Guowei (who is discussed in detail in chapter 4) shared with me,

> The impact of this kind of music on me is too deep. I grew up during this era. Most of what I learned as a young person was connected to this type of music. Now it gives me a lot of memories of that time, those melodies, those voices are all engraved in my mind and in my heart. I still play it until today. Although it is revolutionary music, because it has been closely linked to me in that era, there is still a very deep feeling that I associate with this music. (2018, e-mail correspondence)

Campbell and Scott-Kassner open their text *Music in Childhood* with reference to anthropologist Alan P. Merriam's 1964 list of "Music's Many Functions":

1. emotional expression
2. aesthetic enjoyment
3. entertainment
4. communication
5. symbolic representation (symbols within the text, notation, and cultural meaning of the sounds)
6. physical response (dancing and other physical activity)
7. enforcement of conformity to social norms (instruction through song and rhymes)
8. validation of social institutions and religious rituals (use of music in religious services and state occasions)
9. contribution to the continuity and stability of culture (music as an expression of cultural values)
10. contribution to the integration of society (use of music to bring people together) (2014, 3–7)

The children's songs maintain these cross-cultural functions by integrating Mao and Zhou's cultural policies within the *New Songs of the Battlefield*. The propagandistic nature of children's songs from the Cultural Revolution makes the interplay of these functions rather disturbing. While I focus here on the cross-cultural functions of music, a distinction from "universals" bears repeating. Throughout history, many scholars have sought to identify so-called universals in music; however, the search for universals runs counter to the foundation of ethnomusicology. As Anne Rasmussen recently stated in response to a 2018 study, "While music is universal, its meaning is not" (qtd. in Marshall 2018).

In the case of the children's songs from the Cultural Revolution, the use and benefit of music were fully exploited to bring the message and ideology of a political movement to an entire generation of children in China. Political propaganda directed at children is certainly not exclusive to music of the Cultural Revolution, the Chinese Communist Party, or China alone. Patriotic songs for children have appeared across time and space. For example, Noriko Manabe writes about Japanese school songs during World War II that focused on instilling the national spirit, expanding empire, and glorifying the military (2013, 102–4): "Among the vast repertoire of Japanese school songs, perhaps the most thought provoking—and least well known—are those songs taught during World War II. Soaked with propagandistic messages, they assert the superiority of Japan over other nations, the glory of dying for one's country, the romantic imagery of conquered territories, and the joys of toiling in weapons factories, among other things" (96). Manabe considers the songs for schoolchildren to be an "important part of the wartime propaganda machine" and continues to explore the values reinforced, behaviors encouraged, and legacy of the songs in the schoolchildren after the war (96).

Donna Kwon's recent study of North Korean children's performances circulating online provides yet another, and here a contemporary, example of the role of children in propaganda culture. Kwon writes how, "in North Korean ideology, children are especially significant because they function in various forms of expressive North Korean media as aspirational subjects within the imagined patriarchal nation-state where Kim Il-Sung—and to a lesser extent, his male successors—are assumed as father figures" (2019, 7).

Juliane Brauer, in her study of music as a form of torture in Nazi concentration and extermination camps, examines how another totalitarian regime exploited the power of music. She identifies how "the power of music lies in its abilities to shape notions of identity, subjectivity, and belonging. For this reason, a focus on the body and emotions, both of which are targeted by torture, can go a considerable way toward offering an explanation of the potentially torturous nature of music" (2016, 7). Brauer's emphasis on the body and emotions provides a mechanism for unpacking the distinction between the transformation of function and content in children's songs of the Cultural Revolution. As Brauer explains,

> Music itself has no inherent meaning or emotional content. This is what makes the contact zone necessary and productive. Music's effect and the emotions attached to music are strongly linked to experiences, those at the time of listening as well as past experiences that have already been internalized

in the listener. The effect also depends on the circumstances surrounding perception, concrete practice, and performance. Furthermore, the impact of music is not entirely determined by the individual listener; it is dependent on broader, shared social factors and is subject to change over time. (2016, 9)

Guido Fackler, also writing on the role of music in concentration camps, quotes Christoph Daxelmüller's concept of "the prisoner as a cultural being" when noting that, "nevertheless, the fact that music was performed in the camps forces us to realize that the prisoners should not be regarded as an undifferentiated 'grey mass'" (Fackler 2007, 25). Thus, the emotions that are linked to individual experiences, and their broader social context, make clear the complexity of how members of a generation experience, and later remember, the music of their childhood. In other words, while political propaganda explicitly changed the content of children's songs by adding overt political messages, the *function* of music was much more difficult to transform. Ethnographic accounts of individuals who came of age during the Cultural Revolution offer insight into the lived experience of a childhood immersed in political propaganda.

The Past and the Present: Chen Jiebing

"Most people my age probably don't remember all [of the songs], but I remember them all. I don't know if you know my story? I went to the navy when I was nine years old" (Chen J. 2015, personal interview).[9] Each time I meet with Chen Jiebing, I am inspired by her energy and enthusiasm. She brings light into our conversations about dark and traumatic events with a resilience that is due in part to a lifetime of stage experience. Chen grew up in Shanghai as the youngest of five children. She watched as her father, a history professor, was sent off to a work camp after her family was labeled as one of the "Five Categories of Black Elements" or Hei wu lei (黑五类), a designation that identified her family as anti-revolutionary.[10] Because of her father's profession, her family was denounced and became a target of the Cultural Revolution. She herself was quite young at the time, but her older siblings had their careers cut short and were unable to continue their schooling. Several of them were sent out to the countryside to labor with the masses as a form of so-called reeducation. In attempts to respond to the new future awaiting his children, Chen's father thought the children should each learn a special skill that would create an opportunity for them in the new political and cultural environment. He met a famous musician,

Figure 3.1. Chen Jiebing, five years old (photo courtesy of Chen Jiebing)

He Bing, in his work camp and asked him to teach each of his children a different musical instrument. By then it was impossible to buy the instruments, so Chen's father himself made a *pipa* (plucked pear-shaped lute), a *yangqin* (hammered dulcimer), an *erhu*, and a *dizi*. Despite the low quality of the homemade instruments, the children were very serious and practiced for hours every day. Eventually He Bing said he could no longer teach the children as they had all surpassed his level, and he encouraged them to find new teachers to develop their craft.

"During that time, it's in the 1960s, so there are only eight [professional] model Beijing opera groups. All of a sudden army, air force, navy, [were] coming to all different big cities looking to audition young musicians. They are the only place [that would] hire professional musicians." Chen Jiebing explained how the musicians were part of a large group to entertain the soldiers. "If people grew up [during] that time they all know how important [it is] for you to get in, you can't believe how nice, especially for us because we are bad [Hei wu lei]. . . . Basically if you can get in, that means the government can accept you, you don't have a problem anymore." "And your family?" I asked. Chen Jiebing quickly responded, "Oh! My family can be turned around from 'black' to 'red'!" (referring to the Hei wu lei or "Five Categories of Black Elements" campaign).

Chen Jiebing and her sisters took every opportunity to audition. Yet they repeatedly failed to advance, largely due to their family being denounced, but sometimes because of their young ages. The musical groups were looking for musicians around the age of eighteen, and Chen's sisters were not yet of age. Chen herself was only nine but would claim that she was twelve because she thought "it sounds a little better." Finally, after one audition with the navy, the officials liked what they heard and told the family that they would have an answer in three days. On the third day they visited the family home to announce an invitation for Chen Jiebing to join the navy orchestra. Chen Jiebing recalled that "my sisters were very sad. Because they are older, they actually have to go to the countryside. . . . I was only nine years old and I wouldn't need to go [to labor in the countryside] right away. And my parents were very upset. Sad. Because they thought I was too young." The navy officials spoke with Chen Jiebing's parents and promised to take good care of their daughter. They said they needed to take her with them that day but would not leave immediately. The officials said they would tell her parents when they could come to the train station. But as Chen Jiebing explained, "Actually they didn't want my parents to change their mind. We left the next morning. My parents didn't see me again until one year later."

Chen Jiebing credits her father's foresight to teach her *erhu* and *jinghu* (京胡), a two-stringed bowed fiddle used in Beijing opera, for the opportunity to play in the orchestra. At the time, the eight model works (*yangbanxi*) were the only approved music; they prominently featured the *jinghu*, and Chen Jiebing's youth, memory, and stamina allowed her to easily recall the model works and play them repeatedly. "I think that's the only reason they want[ed] the youngest, because I play[ed] *jinghu*," she explained. Two years later, the army orchestra selected one of her sisters to also play *erhu*. Chen Jiebing stayed with the navy orchestra for thirteen years, and her sister played with the army orchestra for sixteen years. "I have to say, sounds like a strange story. But actually, very good ending for us. . . . [Often] people don't understand this kind of story. But for us, how important you change, you become a professional musician. We were so poor. We actually didn't have enough food. You don't even worry about that. We had uniforms. We don't really need to buy [anything]. I actually sent money back to my parents. And then my parents, their situation totally changed."

Chen Jiebing believes she would not "even be here" today if it was not for the Cultural Revolution. It is clear that her family was a direct target of the Cultural

Revolution after being labeled anti-revolutionary because of their class background. Though she did not state it explicitly, the physical threat to herself and her family was apparent, and the opportunity to join the navy orchestra and transform her family's class status in Cultural Revolution politics was a lifesaving moment. "I was very fortunate and benefited greatly growing up as a child with revolutionary music. Having joined the Naval military orchestral group at age 9, I not only developed my musical talents but received my education and learning about life's disciplines from the Military Service. Revolutionary music was very much the central core of life—practice, performance, entertain the troops, and to serve the country" (Chen J. 2018, e-mail correspondence).

Playing in the navy orchestra shaped Chen Jiebing both as an individual and as a musician. The musicians themselves were soldiers, wearing uniforms, completing physical training, and performing required drills. But at the same time, they were also practicing and rehearsing and performing nearly every day. Some of the teenage members of dance troupes were also very young, but

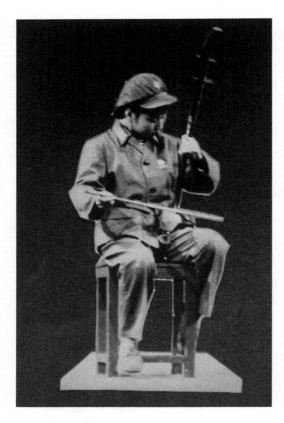

Figure 3.2. Chen Jiebing performing a solo onstage during her first year in the navy. She had to sit on a low stool because her feet could not touch the ground. (photo courtesy of Chen Jiebing)

Figure 3.3. Chen Jiebing performing with *yangqin* dulcimer accompaniment (music competition between the three military branches: air force, navy, and army) (photo courtesy of Chen Jiebing)

Chen Jiebing was by far the youngest of the musicians. She remembered how some orchestra members were bitter and unsupportive because of her age and her struggles to complete basic training drills. As a group, when the orchestra competed against other units, it would nearly always lose because of her young age and thus less developed physical strength and ability.

> Because of me our group was always the slowest. So, they don't treat me as a soldier because I am so spoiled and I'm younger. It's funny, the soldier[s], they don't really treat me that nice. They want to be equal. But the big boss is always nice to me because I am so young. Their daughter, sons [were] even older than me. They are much older. So, you can see the difference . . . so every night I have to think about [how] I am not nine years old any more. Because they tell me, don't think about yourself as nine years old anymore, you are a soldier. Which is true.

As a young performer and musician, Chen Jiebing developed her skills and gained direct access to opportunities that she believes were unique to the Cultural Revolution era. For example, instead of studying with one sole teacher, the orchestra would make arrangements for her to go directly to a composer to learn more about a specific piece, or to a region to learn more about folk music from that area. Chen Jiebing credits the thirteen years of regular and extensive performance for her development as a musician. And in addition to engaging with the music as a performer, she also had to sing the songs on a daily basis. Life during the Cultural Revolution was filled with daily meetings and gatherings for different groups, and each meeting or gathering would begin and end with a song (or two or three). Chen Jiebing explained, "Before Mao died people sing them all the time. Wherever you go they have a big speaker, a park, even on the street, they play the songs . . . and we would sing them too. Everybody had to sing them. For a big meeting, everyone had to stand up [and] sing some special song. It is ridiculous, you know, but it is part of history." At that time, Chen Jiebing said, there was only one picture and one message, neither of which was ever questioned. When China opened following Mao's death, people had access to more pictures, more messages, and more media and could start to think more critically about the messages of the Cultural Revolution era.

Conclusions

Children's songs from the Cultural Revolution are just one example of the "darker side of music," which Patricia Shehan Campbell and Trevor Wiggins reference in the introduction to *The Oxford Handbook of Children's Musical Cultures*: "Given the extent of hardship and conflict around the world, fascinating work lies ahead as to the role of music for children in challenging situations of work as child soldiers and of their struggles in families suffering the effects of failing economies. Such research would be difficult to arrange, and it should be no surprise that there is very little extant literature about the darker side of music by and for children" (2013, 19). The techniques of politicizing the content of music, directly placing children within socialist action (action songs), and repeatedly identifying children within the political campaigns of the day ("little" or *xiao* songs) brought the storm of the Cultural Revolution directly into the everyday lives of children. These techniques followed Zhou Enlai's scientific summary of characteristics for socialist artistic forms known as the "Three Processes of Transformation." Specifically, politicizing the content speaks to the first process, "revolutionize," and the identification of children within socialist action and political campaigns speaks to the second process, "national-ize." To be sure, the minds behind these children's songs and the cultural policies that informed them were clearly aware of the power of music:

for example, the upbeat and simple children's songs in *New Songs of the Battlefield* maintained the first six cross-cultural functions on Merriam's 1964 list. Since music is one of several processes of enculturation, the last four functions on Merriam's list maintained their power to teach children about cultural value with the political ideology and language of Cultural Revolution politics. Finally, disseminating the political ideology through children's songs was an important contribution to the charge to "popularize" within the processes of transformation, as children's songs would educate the next generation of socialist society.

The political language of these songs may initially surprise an outside observer. Stereotypically, children's songs talk about everyday life and play with simple and upbeat themes, yet the lyrics reek of political jargon, themes, and language that would otherwise seem out of place in an idealized (or romanticized?) ordinary child's life. For example, songs such as the classic "I Love Beijing's Tiananmen" appears to be a simple song, instilling patriotism and connecting children to the capital and the nation. But songs such as "Study Well and Make Progress Every Day" and "Calling on the Telephone" take things a step closer to Cultural Revolution ideology with lines such as "to fully defeat imperialists, revisionists, and counter-revolutionaries." And in songs such as "Lin Biao and Confucius Are Both Bad Things" and "Tiny Little Screw Cap," children are directed to actively participate in political criticism and nation building.

Chen Jiebing describes music from the Cultural Revolution as fighting songs because everyone should have been fighting for the revolution. "At that time you cannot be soft. . . . If you are soft in any way they will call you bourgeoisie" (2015, personal interview). These were not the ordinary days of childhood, but the Cultural Revolution era was far from ordinary. The political and cultural disruptions to everyday life were extraordinary and taken to historical extremes. When the lived experience of individuals who grew up with the children's songs is taken into consideration, the relevance, significance, and impact of the songs become increasingly apparent. While politicized lyrics may seem outdated or irrelevant, the emotional, social, and personal memories that individuals attach to these songs are essential for understanding the complexity of music in childhood.

Many individuals who grew up during the Cultural Revolution suggested to me that they engaged in a type of selective listening to or processing of the political language of the time. They could process only so much given their level of maturity, and much of the political language was above their comprehension or attention. As Wang Guowei shared,

Revolutionary music has a great influence on the children of the Cultural Revolution generation. Because at that time all people in mainland China could only listen to such music. These were broadcast on the radio every day, so many songs, as well as model operas . . . can be sung by almost everyone. Although the children at that time may not fully understand what they sang, the melody and lyrics left an indelible impression in their minds and hearts; influencing the generation's understanding and judgment of the world, society, things, and aesthetics. (2018, e-mail correspondence)

While the practice of actively choosing what to process and what to discard is commonplace throughout musical childhoods,[11] the extreme level of dissemination coupled with cultural isolation provides a unique context.

Communications scholar Xing Lu turns to Hannah Arendt's work on Nazi speech patterns to explain how "the purpose of totalitarian indoctrination is to ensure the absolute mind control of authoritarian leaders" (2004, 36–37). In her work on Japanese school songs during World War II, Noriko Manabe aptly writes, "An egg cannot be unscrambled; given how pervasive wartime propaganda was in the schools and media, and how impressionable most children would have been, it would seem likely that these childhood teachings somehow affected the way these children thought as adults" (2013, 111). During the Cultural Revolution, children could focus, either consciously or subconsciously, on the nonpolitical aspects of the music, yet it would have been difficult, if not impossible, to completely discard or divorce the political aspects of music, especially in one's subconscious mind, given the oppressive and all-encompassing context of the Cultural Revolution. Looking at the songs during our interview, Chen Jiebing laughed and said that though they are ridiculous, these songs are indeed part of history. As for her personal history, she was able to transform the class status of her family entirely as a result of her role as a musician of revolutionary music. When I asked Chen Jiebing and Wang Guowei if children's songs during the Cultural Revolution were still able to serve as an escape from the political turmoil of the adult world, Chen Jiebing responded, "No, quite the opposite. . . . Revolutionary music was used as propaganda and to engage children in joining the cultural revolution movement" (2018, e-mail correspondence). Wang Guowei responded, "To remove the lyrics from that kind of music, to appreciate and feel only the musical aspects . . . to a certain extent there could be the experience of escaping from the real world" (2018, e-mail correspondence).

As always, an individual's process of enculturation and social positioning, especially nationality and the type of government under which one comes of age, will both directly and indirectly inform one's response to music used as political propaganda. Writing about music and propaganda in 1983, Arnold Perris noted that "the control of art for official information goes against the grain of the creative spirit, we suppose"; and yet it is commonplace across time and place to employ music to disseminate ideas, information, and values (1983, 1). Yet when music is controlled for political and extramusical functions and that music is in fact children's music, alarm bells seem to go off for many observers. Based on my experience sharing these children's songs in the United States, I am certain that responses differ according to nationality, age, and other social identities and life experiences. As Perris writes, "The Westerner's presumptions arise in part because the term propaganda has acquired an odious meaning: it is a technique of distortion, often with evil intent" (1). While I am not certain if this alarm for propaganda in children's music is limited to so-called Western ways of thinking, I have observed two recurring and distinct viewpoints when presenting research in the United States on this topic. Some vehemently believe such music to be a violation of humanity and consider music to be the "resting spot" that Campbell and Scott-Kasner describe. But others, understanding propaganda as one of the many ways that music functions in society, tend to vary in their degrees of tolerance, intolerance, and acceptance. For example, what role do anti-communist sentiments play in one's response to children's songs of the Cultural Revolution? Where is the line between enculturation and indoctrination? When do patriotic songs turn to propaganda? And ultimately, how can we begin to understand the impact of propaganda in a child's world?

In her ongoing studies of Cultural Revolution culture, Barbara Mittler writes, "Propaganda is manipulated and manipulative. . . . A system creating propaganda is to be despised; everybody hopes for it to end" (2008, 466). And yet, Cultural Revolution propaganda art continues to experience popularity and revivals in certain circles. Mittler thus asks, "How does one explain why a people will not reject outright the propaganda art of a time that for many of them conjures up painful memories, memories of torture and violence, of slander and treason, of psychological strain and terror, of madness and even death?" (2012, 8). I believe that children's songs and the capacity that music has to play in one's process of enculturation may provide one piece to this puzzle. Future cross-cultural and multi-sited research projects may provide more nuanced accounts and perspectives.

Music has been used as political propaganda repeatedly in different times and places around the world. The exploitation of music for political propaganda clearly impacts the ability of music to remain as a "resting spot" or "calm from the storm," to which Campbell and Scott-Kassner refer (2014, 13). In the songs of *New Songs of the Battlefield*, the function of music was exploited but was never successfully transformed. And though music, at times, still had the ability to serve as a site for enjoyment and socialization, children's music of the Cultural Revolution politicized an art form often considered to be a safe space for our youngest and most innocent and vulnerable members of society who were only beginning to develop critical thinking skills. In these moments, we would do well to examine how and why we are drawing distinctions between enculturation and indoctrination, between patriotism and propaganda—and ultimately to give pause and consideration to the long-lasting impact both on individuals and on their eventual participation in society as adults.

Memories of the Battlefield

"Learning Music to Avoid Going 'Up to the Mountains and Down to the Countryside'"

Description: The interview subject was born in the 1960s and lived in an urban area of Beijing, as well as in a rural area of Hunan, from 1966 to 1976.[1] Her family background was classified as government officer and her occupation during the Cultural Revolution was student. The highest level of education she has achieved is graduate. The interview was conducted in person in Cranbury, New Jersey. Note: At the interviewee's request, the video of this interview has been replaced with a still photo obscuring the interviewee's identity.

INTERVIEWER: *Hello! Thank you for accepting my interview. First, could you tell me which decade you were born in? You don't need to say the exact year; just the decade will do, such as "1950s," "1960s," "1970s."*

I was born in the 1960s.

INTERVIEWER: *Where did you live in China from 1966 to 1976?*

Beijing.

INTERVIEWER: *Since you were born in the '60s, you must have some memories of those 10 years. If we only give you about 10 minutes, what would you most like to share? . . . Without arranging your speech too much, what would you most like to say?*

What memories I have, or what influence the things that happened during those years had on my later life?

INTERVIEWER: *The memories or impressions of those 10 years—you can talk about anything you like.*

I remember when I was small, probably when I was in elementary school, my mom [was working at] Beijing Institute of Architectural Engineering; her workplace was quite far away from our home. My mom would take me to school every morning. We would either take a long-distance bus or a local bus. I remember one time it was especially crowded, and we couldn't get on, so we gave up and decided to take the next bus. At that time, the violent struggle in schools was exceptionally fierce. My mom and I got on the next bus. We were riding along when we saw that the bus in front of us had tipped. There was a group of people there, fighting. Our bus just drove past.

INTERVIEWER: *What do you mean? It tipped over?*

I mean it had flipped into the ditch. That road was really narrow. It was a road leading to the outskirts; that university was in the outskirts. Although our home was outside the city as well, [the university] was even farther away. We saw that bus tipped over, with a bunch of people fighting. At that time, my mom's university had split into [two factions]: the "Old 81" and the "New 81"; I can't remember that clearly. Anyway, the students were fighting there. Sometimes we'd be at the movies, just watching the movie, and [students] would just start fighting.

INTERVIEWER: *You're talking about "violent struggle," right?*

Right. I didn't understand "violent struggle"; I was only in first grade at that time. I remember these incidents really well. Then, my mom's university started to send down [employees]. I don't know why, but they were sent to a university in Changde, Hunan [Province]. I went with her and attended elementary school there. Every day I walked from the university campus to the elementary school, and I had to cross a lot of farmland, as well as pass a lot of the houses in the village in Changde, Hunan. I remember so well, every day I went to school, I felt really scared. Why? There were snakes in the fields. On the way back there were dogs. Every day there'd be dogs barking and howling, and chasing me. Later I could run really fast, probably because I'd practiced while living there! Often I'd be running along, with dogs chasing at my heels. In the end, they never caught me. Sometimes I'd fall down and they'd run off. Later on I found out, if a dog is chasing you and you suddenly drop to its level, it'll back off. This left a deep impression on me; its influence on the rest of my life is that later on, I couldn't leave Beijing city limits. I was really afraid to leave urban Beijing because I could recognize the difference between the city and what was outside the city. Of course, later on, my mom left that university.

INTERVIEWER: *How long did you stay in Changde?*

We must've been there a year, and then we came back. The school still exists. My father was still in Beijing. [So, my mother] was sent back. Another thing I remember is that after I came back, the school I had been going to [before I left] would not accept me on the grounds that I was an outsider.

INTERVIEWER: *At that time there was discrimination against outsiders?*

I think there was. It seemed like [they thought], you are from Changde in Hunan Province, so you can't keep up with [our school's coursework]. Actually, my exam scores were excellent, but they still didn't let me go to first grade. However, we were separated into classes based on home address. Out of nowhere, a new school was established, so I went there, because my original school wouldn't let me in! So this memory is deep, and this had a big influence on my life. Later on, I passed the university entrance examination, and all the schools I applied to were in Beijing; I didn't dare go outside Beijing. There was another incident that affected my life later on. At that time there were "welcome groups," who received visitors.

INTERVIEWER: *This was called "welcoming outside guests."*

Right, "welcoming outside guests." Our school was near the Beijing Workers' Stadium. We'd dance the "welcoming guests dance." Those who danced a bit better than others or those who were prettier were put in the first row. Another thing is that the Workers' Stadium had a lot of activities, and they needed some people to lead the teams in. For example, the national soccer league tournament, or the youth soccer league tournament. They'd choose some people and train them to hold signs, for example "Youth Soccer Team," "China National Soccer Team," etc. I forget what all the names were. I was among the 12 people chosen by the school.

INTERVIEWER: *Because you were pretty?*

It wasn't that I was pretty; it was that [the 12 of us] were high-spirited. We were training . . . together all the time, and became good friends. We kept in touch even after I came to the United States. Up until today, my middle school classmates and I have kept in touch, and we often get together and go to one another's homes. So this was a lot of fun, and [what's more], at school other people would refer to us as "those 12 people," and my vanity at the time was really . . .

INTERVIEWER: *At that time, this would've been considered a political assignment, right?*

One thing was that it was a political position, but as Americans might say, you were popular. . . . It wasn't like how my son and daughter think of "popular" in America, which means that a person is good at sports. At that time, we were joining political activities, and we were the first group guests saw when they arrived. You welcomed visitors, you were up in front, [or] you were in the marching band; this was different from other people.

INTERVIEWER: *This must have satisfied your vanity.*

Oh, of course! Up until today I still think of it is as really . . . well, this is something I remember really well. Also, during the Cultural Revolution, I was supposed to go "down to the countryside." I was totally unwilling to leave Beijing. Some people said, "You can study the accordion," so I started studying at home.

INTERVIEWER: *At that time, in Beijing, studying musical instruments at home was called "having a specialized skill."*

Right, right: "having a specialized skill." Later on, one of the neighbors in our courtyard mentioned that Beijing Children's Palace was enrolling students. They had a training class. I studied on my own, and took my accordion with me to take the [admissions] test, and passed. After that class ended, they chose one student from each district, and I was the only one from Chaoyang District chosen. So, it was just four students studying with the teacher—one [student] from each district. Since I had been to Changde that time [when I was younger], I was unwilling to leave Beijing. I saw people older than me going "up to the mountains and down to the countryside." They had no choice; it seemed like they had nowhere to go after graduating high school, that they could only go "up to the mountains and down to the countryside." But if you got involved in the arts as a career path, you could avoid this. I recall this clearly; I studied and practiced with all my heart, so I was the only person chosen from Chaoyang District. After that, I'd go to the teacher's house to study. But the teacher said to me, "Why are you studying accordion?" I said I didn't want to go "up to the mountains and down to the countryside."

INTERVIEWER: *Ha! So honest!*

I was the oldest in my family, and my younger brother's health was not good. I'd certainly be the one going down, but I did not want to go at all. I thought maybe I could join an art troupe, or something like that. The teacher said, "You probably won't be able to get what you want just by playing the accordion. In an art troupe, the one who plays the accordion can usually also play the piano." She told me, "If you can only play the accordion, that's not enough. However, you're already too old to start learning piano." I said, "What can I do?" I didn't want to go "up to the mountains and down to the country-side," didn't want to go to the countryside, because my experience in Changde was such a . . .

INTERVIEWER: *A nightmare.*

Yeah, a *nightmare.* . . . Later, the teacher said, "Open your mouth, and let me look at your teeth." She said, "Not bad. You can study the flute. I promise that you can study with the best [flute teacher] at the Central Conservatory of Music"—because my teacher taught piano at the Central Conservatory of Music—"[If] you study flute, you'll definitely pass the test, since they lack people in flute, especially girls." So, I went back and told my parents I was going to study flute. Later, [after] the Tangshan Earthquake, the university entrance exam [was reinstated]. So, I was quite lucky.

INTERVIEWER: *So, the original motivation for you studying an instrument was that you didn't want to go "up to the mountains and down to the countryside."*

Right. That's what it was. But later it had a benefit to my whole life. Later, my [interest] in music . . . At the Children's Palace, the teacher didn't just teach me how to play the accordion, but also taught me some music theory. When I went to her house, she also taught me some other things. During these 10 years, I didn't really study. Still, carrying the signs [for the welcome reception] helped me make a group of friends, and that was really happy. [As for] study-ing musical instruments, if there hadn't been these 10 years [of the Cultural Revolution] . . . if there had been [the opportunity] to take the university entrance exam [all along], I don't know if I would have studied instruments. I really don't know. So, what I mean is that I benefited . . . from those 10 years for my whole life . . . , and I also gained friendship. . . . Also, my experience in Changde made me feel I had to depend on my own hard work. If you work hard on your own, you'll definitely achieve what you want.

INTERVIEWER: *You wanted to avoid going "up to the mountains and down to the countryside," so you worked hard at studying an instrument.*

Yes, I worked hard learning instruments. Later, for the university entrance exam, I drew on this experience of working hard at music. At that time, I hadn't been studying [academic subjects] much, so I had to study math, physics, and chemistry all on my own. After that, I tested well in math, and took part in a Beijing math competition. I remember that for the university entrance exam, my score in math was really high, but my other scores were not. I scored second place in math, which was not bad at all, though there were a lot of people who got that second-highest score. It was the same with chemistry: I studied incredibly hard, all by myself. So, I think that experience was a kind of training for life. That's how I'd put it. That's it.

INTERVIEWER: *Thank you for accepting my interview.*

4

MUSIC AND MEMORY

My mother and [one of] my undergraduate teachers happen to be around the same age, but their feelings about the Cultural Revolution are completely different; this has left me with a deep impression. My mom told me that although she went "down to the countryside," when she looks back on that time period now, she has good memories. These days, she and the classmates with whom she went "down to the countryside" often get on WeChat and sing songs from the Cultural Revolution era. During holidays, they take turns singing songs from those times. So, she really misses it.

—East Asian Library, University Library System (ULS), University of Pittsburgh, "Two People Born in the Same Year Have Completely Opposite Feelings about the Cultural Revolution" video, January 15, 2016

Many individuals who grew up during the Cultural Revolution consider its art and music, though dripping with political propaganda, to be the representative sights and sounds of their childhood and coming of age. Scholars have beautifully examined the arts in general (such as Mittler 2012 and Clark 2008), visual art (including Ho 2018 and King 2010), and various collections of music with attention to the model revolutionary works (such as McDougall 1984 and Clark, Pang, and Tsai 2016), yet the most focused English-language attention on revolutionary songs has been limited to Isabel Wong's chapter in Bonnie S. McDougall's 1984 anthology. Outside of the arts, humanities and social science scholars have focused on the trauma and devastation of the Cultural Revolution and the recent boom and expansion of the Chinese economy. In my fieldwork, I discovered that most individuals would not offer an unsolicited outpouring of personal stories or observations regarding the Cultural Revolution. Yet upon flipping through an old songbook or reading a few song titles, many respondents began to reminisce about their own experiences and offered personal commentaries on the period. The songs frequently served as a powerful trigger for an individual's emotions and memories, though they were often not generated by the music itself (that is, the aural element such as humming a melody or perhaps hearing a recording) but rather by a song title or a snippet of lyrics. Music can evoke the memories and emotions of the Cultural Revolution period that might otherwise be forgotten.

This chapter examines the unique and heightened level of nostalgia often felt by one generation amid overwhelmingly negative, traumatic, or unattached accounts reported by other generations. It explores how music serves as a vehicle through which individuals transcend time and space and access significant emotions from their youth and assesses music's capacity to trigger memory and nostalgia. It then considers how one's political outlook develops (Schumann and Scott 1989), the significance of one's individual and group experiences during this time period (Halbwachs 1992), and unique patterns in how older adults remember their coming of age (Jansari and Parkin 1996). Finally, it looks at how the contemporary context and rapid changes in modern China are instrumental to the way individuals remember the past through the lens of today.

Generations

The overwhelming nostalgia expressed by some of my interviewees initially took me by surprise. I had anticipated that some individuals would be bitter, others would be silent, and some would be embarrassed or unattached. The historic period is known for extreme chaos, upheaval, and destruction, so negative reactions were to be expected. But I had not predicted the positive memories that would be stirred through conversations about Cultural Revolution music. As I interviewed more people and conducted the 2003 survey, it was clear that one's age during the Cultural Revolution played an important role in how one recollected the time period. However, direct experience was not the only indicator of how much, or how well, people remembered the songs. I observed that individuals who were children or young adults during the Cultural Revolution recalled far more of the music than the older generations, despite the older generations' direct experiences. Those who were children or young adults during the Cultural Revolution remember the songs more fondly and with overwhelming feelings of nostalgia. When I shared these responses with political scientist Tang Wenfang, he quickly pointed out that broad characterizations could be made depending on one's age in relation to the emergence of the CCP and the start of the Cultural Revolution. Noting when individuals came of age (around the age of eighteen) and how

Table 4.1. Pre-socialist, socialist, Cultural Revolution, and reform generations

	Age in 1949	Age in 1966	Age in 1976
Reform generation (b. 1961 and later)	not yet born	ages 5 and under or not yet born	ages 15 and under or not yet born
Cultural Revolution generation (b. 1950–60)	not yet born	ages 6–16	ages 16–26
Socialist generation (b. 1933–49)	ages < 16	ages 17–33	ages 27–43
Pre-socialist generation (b. 1916–32)	ages 17–33	ages 34–50	ages 44–60

that timing corresponds to China's contemporary political history provide important generational cohorts for my research. Based on this organization of generations, Professor Tang and I were able to identify four distinct groups: the pre-socialist generation, the socialist generation, the Cultural Revolution generation, and the reform generation. These categories are defined in table 4.1. Though three of these four generations directly experienced the Cultural Revolution, only the socialist and pre-socialist generations report overwhelmingly negative or painful memories.

The older generations (pre-socialist and socialist generations) were socialized and politicized before the CCP took power in 1949; therefore they had little to no connection with the Cultural Revolution politics and, along with their advanced age, were not particularly motivated or energized by the music of the Cultural Revolution. In my fieldwork and interviews, people in these groups were quick to dismiss any mention of the Cultural Revolution and generally did not have any significant connection to the music. Typical responses to the music were negative or simply absent, particularly from those of the socialist generation, who may have experienced some of the most devastating disruptions to their adult lives as a result of the Cultural Revolution.

The members of the Cultural Revolution generation are the ones who consistently captured my attention. These are the individuals whose eyes lit up when flipping through a songbook. These are people who still remember every word of a Cultural Revolution song. These are the ones who can still find moments to smile when reflecting on their days during the Cultural Revolution—not because they were free from the devastation or because they were untouched by the political and cultural chaos but because that time encompassed their childhood. No matter how violent, traumatic, and devastating the time period may have been, the Cultural Revolution years were their formative years. And when put in contrast to the present of contemporary China, many remembered moments of goodness in the face of evil. When they had sung, they had done so in unison, and they had known what to expect. The predictability of that bygone environment, despite the atrocities, offers some comfort in the face of contemporary China's uncertainties and isolation.

For the reform and younger generations who lack a complete formal education on the Cultural Revolution, the era can feel like a bit of a myth. Some believe there is great value in studying, learning, and understanding, while others do not. Some laugh and some cry. Some have heard stories from their grandparents and parents, while others have heard nothing. The generational divides are distinct. As those who belong to the Cultural Revolution generation get older, the histories, memories, and emotions may continue to fade even deeper into the distance.

Music, Memory, and Nostalgia

The emotional power of music and its ability to bolster memory can be understood through multiple disciplinary lenses. In his research on music and nationalism, ethnomusicologist Thomas Turino examines music as an indicator of emotion and meaning and suggests that music is a compelling mode of indexing, or representing and signifying emotion (2000, 174). In *Music as Social Life: The Politics of Participation*, Turino explains why music matters and argues that "musical participation and experience are valuable for the processes of personal and social integration that make us whole" (2008, 1).

With regard to memory, psychologist Anthony Storr states, "The mnemonic power of music is still evident in modern culture. Many of us remember the words of songs and poems more accurately than we can remember prose" (1992, 21). Accordingly, music can aid in processes of memorization as well as in processes of recollecting past events and emotions. Turino's and Storr's research addresses two key issues in music and memory: music is an indicator that has the potential to manifest powerful emotions in individuals, which may be intensified in a group setting; and music is an effective means of enhancing memory, which is an important component of the process of stirring up recollections of one's past, albeit selectively constructed reproductions of that past.

These reproductions are often created similarly among groups that share common features or experiences. Sociologist Maurice Halbwachs identifies collective memory as a socially constructed notion and asserts that "while the collective memory endures and draws strength from its base in a coherent body of people, it is individuals as group members who remember" (qtd. in Coser 1992, 22). According to Halbwachs, collective memory is initially a personal memory, yet personal memory is directly influenced by an individual's relationship to a group. The songs of the Cultural Revolution may represent a means for eliciting the emotions and memories of the past. The meanings and emotions that an individual experienced during the Cultural Revolution resurface upon listening to a song, reading a songbook, or simply hearing a song title.

The majority of the 2003 survey respondent comments from the Cultural Revolution generation included favorable statements like "When I hear this music it takes me back" and "When I hear this music it makes me very excited." A woman academic in the city of Beijing mentioned the gravity of the Cultural Revolution period but continued into a nostalgic reflection that the music inspired: "For the country, the Cultural Revolution was a period of difficult memories and history. As a person, I really keep a strong memory of it and the music makes me think a lot about the past and brings my memories back."

An examination of the contemporary knowledge of and attitudes toward the *New Songs of the Battlefield* anthology reveals a number of themes, the most prevalent of which is nostalgia. Scholars continue to define and discuss the concept and construction of nostalgia in a variety of contexts.[1] Geremie Barmé defines nostalgia as "a longing for or painful yearning to return home" and "a condition of being lost to a familiar abode, an exile from home and, as such, [it] is said to be closely related to the homing instinct" (1999, 317). In her work on nostalgia and the Japanese popular songs known as *enka*, Christine Yano identifies nostalgia as a variable cultural practice. Her specific research demonstrates how music invokes a collective memory of the nation's painful past (2002, 14). In contrast to their contemporary context, Japanese audiences find great comfort in the longing for a constructed past of simple, raw, and powerful emotions (182).

Three key themes underline these definitions of nostalgia: they are understood as a means to create a site of memory, as a way to recover past emotions, and as a new way of imagining communities. Nostalgia as a means to create a site of memory represents an attempt to construct meaning for past experiences and emotions in light of one's current environment, surfacing as a means of clarifying and positioning oneself and one's identity during moments of confusion (Barmé 1999, 319). Or, as Storr writes, "making sense out of anything depends upon relating one thing with another, upon discovering or imposing order" (1992, 180). Nostalgia as a recovery of past emotions often stems from a sense of loss, perceived either in the past or in the present; these emotions are recovered to resurrect feelings of having endured great hardship or to recall lost feelings of joy and simplicity. Nostalgia as a new way of imagining communities expands on the issue of defining one's identity and place in the world by emphasizing the powerful and dynamic element of shared experience (Sant Cassia 2000, 299). The dramatic events of the Cultural Revolution serve as a way for individuals to identify with one another and discover a sense of solidarity through shared personal histories.

The nostalgia for the *New Songs of the Battlefield* anthology, and revolutionary music in general, manifests all three of these themes. Beginning in the 1990s and continuing into the twenty-first century, economic reforms in China have created a rapidly changing lifestyle for urban Chinese. Confronted with this changing environment, older generations have experienced a sense of loss or confusion and thus search into their past for the familiar. Past experiences, positive or negative, provide signposts for an individual's sense of self and as a result offer meaning to the present. Nostalgia as a site of memory is therefore fueled by the changes in contemporary society.

Following my initial fieldwork in China, I tried to make sense of patterns I observed in responses to the *New Songs of the Battlefield* anthology. Some individuals were deeply invested in my research and were highly motivated and energized to talk about the songs and their associated memories. Others were quick to dismiss the songs and responded with anger, sadness, and general bitterness. Many were silent and refused to speak about Cultural Revolution music or anything associated with that era. A fourth group knew very little and was surprised by Cultural Revolution–era lyrics. After developing four distinct cohort groups based on generation and China's political history, I began to focus on what I refer to as the Cultural Revolution generation. This generation came of age during the Cultural Revolution and consequently has a unique lived experience that distinguishes the types of memories and emotions that are evoked from Cultural Revolution music. Writing about Maurice Halbwachs's concepts of collective memory and the significance of groups, Lewis Coser explains how "of course individuals who remember, not groups or institutions, but these individuals, being located in a specific group context, draw on that context to remember or create the past" (1992, 22).

Sociologists Howard Schuman and Jacqueline Scott's study on generations and collective memory explains how the political events of one's youth are the "most" significant and "most" remembered (1989) and that one's unique character and personal political outlook are developed between the ages of seventeen and twenty-five. Building on Halbwachs's concepts of collective memory, Schuman and Scott identify three points to explain the maximum impact of youth: (1) individuals cannot recall events before their own lifetime; (2) a certain level of intellectual maturation is necessary to form a personal and political outlook; and (3) events are most strongly registered during adolescence and early adulthood given the impact of primacy, or the significance of experiencing something for the first time (1989, 360). As a result, patterns of memory coincide along age groups to create distinct generational imprinting; these memories are socially constructed (Coser 1992, 22) and therefore create collective memories that are unique to the historical, political, and social backdrop.

As Vivian Wagner points out in an examination of Red Guard songs from the Cultural Revolution, the impact of Cultural Revolution propaganda is immeasurable, particularly when it comes to music. Every individual campaign was accompanied by music (2001, 1–2), and all areas of China were inundated with the select few songs, operas, and movies over a short period of time. The isolation of material disseminated through government media accounts for this high level of saturation. In many ways, the *New Songs of the Battlefield* anthology continued along the same course as the Red Guard songs from the early years of the Cultural Revolution. The songs provided a means for individuals, young and old, to join in solidarity to express their commitment and dedication to the Communist Party, to fulfill the need to belong to a group, and to demonstrate one's allegiance to that group. The songs also provided a rare outlet for excitement and camaraderie for the nation's youth. As one survey respondent stated, "I personally really liked being there in the chorus." Despite the political turmoil, the youth were often caught up in the thrill of such a mass movement.

A woman who came of age during the Cultural Revolution, Zhang Haihui, remembered "everyone" singing numbers from the *New Songs of the Battlefield* during that time. Afterward, "everyone had their own personal/ individual tastes. . . . But then [during the Cultural Revolution] everyone was singing together and everyone could sing them in a group. But eventually everything became individual" (2018, personal interview).

Results from my 2003 public opinion survey confirm that the lyrics of revolutionary music became more inspirational as respondents' age increased, and the personal experience of chanting slogans, attending rallies, and other group events directly impacted one's emotional responses and memories. As Schuman and Scott suggest, "For most of us it is the intersection of personal and national history that provides the most vital and remembered connection to the times we had lived through" (1989, 380). The power of music does not lie in the melody alone; in this context, the revolutionary lyrics inspired unity, the singing in groups produced potent emotional responses, and the emotions and memories that were associated with the songs directly correlated to specific generations.

Remembering the Revolution

"During the Cultural Revolution, we were always in a group, surrounded by others, the group identity was so important and we did everything together. Nowadays, the city is filled with individuals who are self-absorbed and merely interested in earning more money. There is no longer any group identity. Hearing the *New Songs of the Battlefield* brings me back to a really exciting time of my life, that was full of energy" (Huang 2003, personal interview).[2] This Beijing-based businesswoman's reflection illustrates the clear effect that one's age has on memory construction and the impact of firsthand experience. The present, or the context in which the past is reconstructed, must be considered when examining someone's memory. In the late 1970s, just a few years after the end of the Cultural Revolution, reproductions of Cultural Revolution and pre–Cultural Revolution films, songs, and books were released in attempts to "recover" the past (Barmé 1999, 318). Individuals were already beginning their attempt to reclaim what they considered to be their "lost past."

As time passes, older generations frequently look back at the Cultural Revolution period (and life under Mao) as a time when life was much simpler and lacked the complexities of contemporary Chinese society. This perspective is common among the "educated youth" or "sent-down youth" (*zhishi qingnian* or *zhiqing* 知识青年),[3] members of the Cultural Revolution generation who spent some of their formative years away from their families, working throughout rural China. Beginning in the late 1970s and continuing throughout the 1980s, the sent-down youth began returning to the cities; soon after, they began sharing their experiences through what is often labeled the "literature of the wounded" (see Gold 1980; McLaren 1979). By the 1990s, the sent-down youth began shifting their perspective and focus of their experiences during the Cultural Revolution from tales of suffering to an overwhelming nostalgia. Barmé describes how levels of nostalgia increased during the 1990s as individuals viewed the earlier decades as a time of "simple emotions and plain living" (1999, 323–24).

Alternative interpretations or modes of reflection can be found in English-language publications of personal memoirs from individuals who survived the Cultural Revolution, which began appearing in North America and the United Kingdom in the 1980s and were published with greater frequency throughout the 1990s. Some of the more well-known accounts include *Life and Death in Shanghai* (Cheng 1986), *Wild Swans* (Chang 1991), *Red Azalea* (Min 1994), and *Red Scarf Girl* (J.-L. Jiang 1997). Much of the literature exposed tragic firsthand accounts of loss and suffering endured by individuals and their families during the Cultural Revolution.

By the late 1990s, scholars started to analyze the personal accounts in a new light, and their observations provide an alternative perspective and critique of both the Cultural Revolution experience and its representations. One example is the collection of essays *Some of Us*, edited by Xueping Zhong, Zheng Wang, and Bai Di (2001). These essays focus upon the "intersection between 'official ideology' and 'lived experience'" (xvii). The contributors, urban women who endured the Cultural Revolution and went on to establish themselves as academics throughout North America, attempt to provide an alternative perspective on life under Mao. The approach is a drastic departure from the earlier accounts that focus on loss and suffering. I observe a similar contradiction between the unquestionably negative portrayal of the Cultural Revolution and individuals' positive association of the *New Songs of the Battlefield* anthology. The high-spirited youths who enjoyed these songs are not necessarily naive or indifferent to the tragedies and hardships of the historic period; instead, the songs may trigger the spirit of one's childhood, adolescence, or young adulthood through the phenomena of memory and nostalgia.

During the 1990s, a resurgence in the popularity of revolutionary music emerged upon the release of contemporary arrangements. The most prominently featured releases included the remake of the classic "East Is Red." Scholars such as Xiaomei Chen (1999), Mercedes Dujunco (2002), Michael Dutton (1999), Gregory Lee (1995), Sheldon Lu (1996), and Sue Tuohy (1999, 2001) have examined this resurgence of allegiance to Mao. Generally, these scholars agree that the return to Mao in postmodern China may be interpreted as a reaction to Deng Xiaoping and the transformation into an open economy within a socialist society. Many who belong to the older generations have found it difficult to accept the drastic economic reforms and increase in materialism. Yunxiang Yan provides a thorough examination of the impact of these huge shifts in *The Individualization of Chinese Society* (2009). In my conversations, individuals in the older generations frequently noted being shocked by the shift to consumer culture in China and an increasingly individual-focused society (particularly in comparison with their youth and young adulthood). For example, Sheldon Lu proposes that the return of allegiance to Mao in the 1990s was driven by older generations' dissatisfaction with Deng Xiaoping (1996, 156). Lu explains further that the older generations' nostalgia for Mao and life under Mao is "directly related to the fact that their childhood and youth were spent, and 'lost,' in the heyday of Mao worship" (156).

Dutton describes how "the revolution returns as product" (1999, 269), and Dujunco provides further explanation for the sudden "Mao craze" by noting how the increase in earning and buying power in Chinese society led to individuals' ability to "indulge in nostalgia for the revolutionary years of their youth" (2002, 34). Through interviews with younger Chinese individuals, Xiaomei Chen observed, "When asked about the impression they had obtained of the Cultural Revolution from their parents, young people described it as an era when people were sincere, passionate, and enthusiastic about their ideals. The parents characterized the period as free, one in which drugs and prostitution were unknown, with low and stable grocery prices, a low crime rate, and more honest officials" (1999, 119).

Though my own research suggests that the "East Is Red" Mao craze has passed, the impact of the fad is still felt today. Cassettes of revolutionary music remixes were an attractive new commodity, particularly for individuals with disposable income for the first time in decades. And the 1990s remakes of Cultural Revolution songs and other revolutionary music made a lasting impression upon a large section of contemporary Chinese society.[4] Yet outside the reform generation, the majority of the public preferred the originals. The attachment to the songs in their original Cultural Revolution format remains strong for three of the four generations, though the preference for the songs in their original format may not be solely a question of aesthetics but rather one of the entire musical context, including their dissemination and production.

The 1990s Mao craze and contemporary attitudes in general have been deeply affected by significant changes in the consumption and production of music. Respondents commonly referred to the powerful force of group identity during the Cultural Revolution and contrasted it to the individualistic nature of contemporary Chinese society. This shift includes the mediums in which the songs have been played. During the Cultural Revolution, the *New Songs of the Battlefield* were broadcast and published repeatedly through the main channels of government media, including cable radio, wireless radio, and newspapers. The songs were then sung regularly, typically in formal group contexts such as work or school meetings and rallies. Today, the main channels of government media have largely been replaced by the internet, television, and recordings (audio and video). And while censorship still exists, the range of media available to individuals today is much more dynamic and wide than any earlier period in Chinese history. Moreover, songs are rarely sung in the same context as in the Cultural Revolution period; instead, individuals sing songs by themselves or at karaoke gatherings. These changes in modern China and in individuals' daily lives play a critical role in defining how individuals remember the past.

The Past and the Present: Wang Guowei

Wang Guowei is an accomplished *erhu* musician now based in New York City. He credits the Cultural Revolution as being not only influential but also responsible for his life as a professional musician: "To be honest, the Cultural Revolution affected me hugely. If it weren't for the revolution, I probably wouldn't have become a professional musician. I would more likely have become someone like my brother, just playing music at a certain level but not professionally. Because in our entire family no one does or did music [as a profession], and since we were very young our parents always told us that we needed to study hard and that studying was all about science" (2014, personal interview).[5]

At the onset of the Cultural Revolution, Wang Guowei was a young boy living with his family in Shanghai. His father had previously owned a small shop, and their family was considered bourgeoisie due to his background as a merchant. Wang Guowei shared, "Of course, when we look back today, we can think of the negative effects and pains that the revolution brought to China as a whole. But when I was little, I never thought about this. The only impression I had was that it was frightful [*kepa* 可怕]. . . . I was always scared because of my father's situation. Perhaps if my father was a common worker then it might have been less terrifying for our family."

During the Cultural Revolution, it was commonplace for Red Guards to unexpectedly raid a house to clear it of any displays or artifacts of the "Four Olds" (old culture, old customs, old habits, and old ideas) and to publicly criticize people's "errors." As a young child, Wang Guowei constantly feared for his father's well-being. "Whenever my father didn't come back from work at the regular time my mother would take me with her to my father's company to check to see if he was being criticized [*pidou* 批斗] or if he was suddenly locked up." Wang Guowei shared that during the Cultural Revolution he was "so young, really young, I didn't understand a thing. But I did have this impression in my memory."

During his childhood, Wang Guowei attended regular study groups where he was instructed to read, recite, and discuss the quotations of Mao Zedong. When school was in session, he learned all the writings of Mao Zedong but nothing about Tang or Song dynasty poetry—the classical literature that Chinese students before and after the Cultural Revolution were typically required to master as a sign of a so-called proper education. According to Wang Guowei, who was in middle school at the end of the Cultural Revolution, these changes from studying classical literature to Mao and back to classical literature again were not sudden; it was not until the mid-1980s and the leadership of Deng Xiaoping that differences became noticeable.

As Wang Guowei noted, "My background of learning music, 90 percent of what I played, was the Cultural Revolution music. Because at the time, all we heard was what was broadcast on the radio; and during the Cultural Revolution all that was on the radio was revolutionary music. There was no traditional Chinese music and there was no Western music, you wouldn't hear it." Later in our conversation, he said that occasionally one might hear of a traditional Chinese or Western musician or composition, but these mentions were always made in private. Wang Guowei would only occasionally catch bits of traditional Chinese or Western classical music behind closed doors, but this knowledge was rarely practical. For example, one teacher told Wang Guowei that in order to study the *erhu*, one must study the compositions of Liu Tianhua—whose compositions had been banned.

Wang Guowei started playing with different instruments around the age of five; his older brother informally served as his first music teacher, introducing him to a variety of instruments (first the harmonica, then the flute, and later the accordion) when he noticed Wang Guowei's interest and abilities. When Wang Guowei was eleven years old—which, he said, is "not very young for musicians who want to pursue a professional career"—his father located an *erhu* teacher who provided private lessons. This happy circumstance enabled him to progress much faster.

When Wang Guowei first started his *erhu* lessons, he played simple arrangements of revolutionary music like "East Is Red" and children's songs such as "I Love Beijing's Tiananmen"; most of these works were rearranged pieces from model revolutionary operas and ballets. Wang Guowei shared that everyone was playing the same music, just at different levels: "There

Figure 4.1. Wang Guowei with his *erhu*, 1972, in front of the family house in Shanghai (photo courtesy of Wang Guowei)

Figure 4.2. Wang Guowei, 1972 (photo courtesy of Wang Guowei)

was nothing else to practice, the entire musical world of China, including students in the conservatories and myself, we all played the same kind of music, except they'd play a harder version, but it was all the same revolutionary opera music and songs."

I asked Wang Guowei if he knew of the *New Songs of the Battlefield* anthology, and he immediately exclaimed, "Yes! I know all of them. I can sing them all." I then asked him about the memories that are sparked when he now looks at the songs, to which he sighed and replied, "Too much . . . you see, I can sing nearly all of them. [I've been singing them] ever since I was very young." He praised many of the songs, even though the lyrics were "all about Mao," noting that most of these so-called good songs were actually folk songs that predated the Cultural Revolution. Unlike other generations, his introduction to folk songs was given through the prism of revolutionary music:

> Before the revolution I didn't really know anything. I didn't really learn music either; I started learning music when the revolution started. And maybe my brother knew something about folk songs before the revolution. But these folk songs, if it weren't for the new lyrics, the influence might not be as big as it is now on the Chinese people. It was because of the lyrics during that time, singing about Mao Zedong and the Communist Party of China, and playing it every day, that the songs had such a powerful influence.

Wang Guowei explained that the revolutionary music always surrounded him and that most people learned, and usually memorized, most of this music effortlessly. Even those who were disinterested in music learned it; the repetition was unavoidable.

So how was this music received? If revolutionary music was all that one heard and all that one was able to sing, learn, and perform, what type of meaning does it hold for individuals today? Wang Guowei enthusiastically responded,

> Personally? Personally, I actually do quite like these things. I'm not talking about politics; I'm only talking in terms of music, or the melody. And this has a lot to do with a person's background. If it weren't for my generation, the younger generation would take no interest in these kinds of things. For example, I know a kid, his father was watching the model operas, and the kid said, "Why would you still watch something like that?" But for me, it's a kind of memory, my childhood and how I grew up, so I feel a sense of familiarity when I hear the melody, and that is something I can't cut off.

Wang Guowei talked about the musical value of revolutionary music while discussing the children's song "I Love Beijing's Tiananmen":

Is it a children's song with a lot of musical value? Not necessarily. Yet it made an impression on me, because it was part of my process growing up, personally. So, I would still go and watch the model revolutionary opera, even though it is different from how I felt when I was young. Now I would know how to analyze it and feel that some of the content is over the top . . . it is not natural. I would reflect on it, but I'd still feel a sense of familiarity. When I listen to the melody, I don't care about the lyrics; I feel close to it. It brought back a lot of memories, a lot.

Wang Guowei hesitated when I asked him about opportunities to hear revolutionary music and operas in China today. He told me that performances of popular revolutionary operas and ballets are given now and then as public performances. Many songs, operas, and ballets from the Cultural Revolution have been posted online at sites such as YouTube, but most "ordinary" people are no longer interested. He said, "But my generation and the generations before me will listen to them. I think I'm the last generation who really went through the revolution and still remember it; the generation after me didn't go through the revolution."

For Wang Guowei's generation, education and careers were on a much different path than for any other generation in China. For example, most families, especially ones with targeted class backgrounds, would need to send at least one child out to the countryside for manual labor. Wang came from a family of three children, and the fact that his father was a small business owner made them all targets of the Cultural Revolution; the family knew that at least one or more of the children would be sent out to the countryside. Wang's parents intentionally cultivated his musical talents in the hope that they would provide their son with opportunities; even if Wang Guowei was sent out to the countryside, he would not be asked to farm and would be allowed to play in a musical group. Wang Guowei explained, "So for my parents, this was the most important reason for me to learn music; for me of course [it] is the same, but at the same time, I also really liked music. I just didn't really understand when I was young."[6]

Working as a musician provided Wang Guowei with increased opportunities during the Cultural Revolution and in the years following. He played in a "youth palace" Chinese orchestra (*shaonian gongmin yuetuan* 少年宫民乐团) from a young age and later rose to prominence via the Shanghai People's Broadcasting Station Youth Orchestra (Shanghai guangbo renmin diantai shao'er yuedui 上海广播人民电台少儿乐队). Still attending high school in 1978, an opportunity arose to audition for the Shanghai National Orchestra. Wang Guowei was accepted under unusual conditions; he was only seventeen, much younger than most of the applicants:

At the time if you got into a professional group or orchestra, it was really the best career, especially for those who played in the opera during the Cultural Revolution. The treatments they received were so different. They got to have new clothes and eat chocolate; I mean, chocolate at the time was so rare! But those who are in the opera got to have chocolate, and everyone wanted to have that life. So when I got in the professional orchestra, I didn't even hesitate. I dropped out of high school, since getting in was extremely difficult.

Wang Guowei credits the Cultural Revolution as perhaps the key influence on his path toward becoming a professional musician. He shared that "if it wasn't for the Cultural Revolution, I think I wouldn't have done this. It'd just be my free-time hobby to play an instrument or something. I might be doing research instead, because I can work in a lab all day without a problem. I'm actually not a performer type of person; I'm more of a research person." Wang Guowei moved to the United States in 1996, quickly established himself in New York as an accomplished *erhu* musician, and has played and taught professionally ever since. During one of our meetings in New York he thanked me for talking with him about the music in particular, and the time period in general, as it allowed him the rare opportunity to reflect and reminisce. The Cultural Revolution is a huge part of who he is, and why he is who he is, but there seems to be no one for him to discuss it with: "The Cultural Revolution influenced and affected my life greatly; it set my life path, really. It was the revolution that made me who I am today. My family wouldn't have thought to let me become a professional musician; even until now I'm still the only one in the family who is a professional musician, so I am completely the product of the Cultural Revolution."

The Past and the Present: Chen Xiaojie

I met Chen Xiaojie,[7] who resides in Flushing, New York, through a family friend. Chen Xiaojie and her husband are part of a group of Chinese friends who gather once a week to sing karaoke together. The night I visited their gathering, nearly twenty people were in attendance when the evening began, though I learned later that people would come and go throughout the evening. The group was primarily made up of seniors in their sixties or seventies, roughly a third of the group was in their forties, and a few were in their twenties or thirties. The leader of the group hosted the evening in his basement, where a makeshift karaoke bar had been set up for this single purpose. The basement had a large-screen television, a book for selecting songs, and a bar and benches and was filled with posters of famous singers from across East Asia. Everyone brought a dish or two to serve anyone who arrived hungry.

Chen Xiaojie was full of energy, easy to talk to, and comfortable with herself and others. With her white hair, big smile, and jewelry, it is hard to imagine the years she spent suffering in the countryside outside Shanghai. Chen was eager to help and enjoyed conversation, and I often had to remind her that I was there to listen and to learn about her life. She laughed and had an uplifting air and expressed pain only when she recalled the suffering of her faraway past.

Chen Xiaojie and I found a quiet spot upstairs in the living room. She was enthusiastic and eager to hear what I had to say. She told me that her family was originally from Shanghai and that she came to the United States in 1983. When I asked her how she explained the Cultural Revolution period to non-Chinese Americans, she quickly responded, "No, no, no, no, no. Americans? I don't talk about this with Americans. I work with all *laowai* [老外], and everyone is too busy. We wouldn't talk about such things. Americans, they're not interested. Like you, you're interested, so you want to know. But most people, they're not interested. There's no time to talk about such things. They go to work to work. Nobody asks me about before [how it was]." Chen Xiaojie used a few terms that were common to overseas Chinese but may be misleading to someone unfamiliar with the diasporic community. For example, the common usage of the term "American" is a masked reference to race/ethnicity as well as to nationality; it assumes a white American and overlooks entire communities of Chinese Americans and other people of color. She also referred to Americans as *laowai*, the Chinese term for "foreigner," revealing her China-based orientation even though she has lived in the United States for three decades. And despite this China-based orientation in her own identity and relation to others in the United States, her response disclosed how in other ways she is removed from her early adulthood in rural China. It is not a part of her present public or shared identity; rather, it is a distant past both in time and space.

Chen Xiaojie's family was originally from a wealthy family in urban Shanghai. Because of their class status, her family was targeted as soon as the Communist Party of China took power in 1949. Chen Xiaojie's mother initially fled to Hong Kong and later to the United States, leaving her five children behind. As Chen said, her mother never suffered like her children, or as the Chinese expression goes, "She never tasted the bitter" (*ta meiyou chi guo ku*

她沒有吃過苦). Chen and her four siblings were spread all across China and had no contact with each other throughout the 1950s, 1960s, and 1970s, until their mother applied for visas for them to join her in the United States in the 1980s.

When the CCP came into power, Chen Xiaojie had just graduated from a specialty school; because of her class background, she ended up living in the rural countryside outside of Shanghai for more than twenty years to "'reform' [*gaizao* 改造] your way of thinking," as Chen laughingly put it. The transition to the countryside was a tremendous shock: "We were so poor. We had nothing to eat; maybe some sweet potatoes but no rice. It was so miserable, but at that time I was so young and had no choice. If it was miserable, then you just had to be miserable." As she told me about her struggles in the countryside, she repeatedly used the phrase *chengfen bu hao* (成分不好), a loaded phrase that indicates "class background is not good" and literally refers to "bad ingredients," "bad composition," or "bad birth." Her frequent employment of this phrase underlined the enduring power of class status in 1950s and 1960s China.

Chen Xiaojie was the first person I interviewed or spoke to who experienced the Cultural Revolution in the countryside. I had previously heard and read about the distinctions between the urban and rural areas, but Chen's descriptions paint a vivid personal picture. As she spoke about music during the Cultural Revolution, it became evident that her life had been dominated by manual labor, scarcity of resources, and her targeted social status. She suffered alongside the local peasants, labored with them, and endured the same scarcity of resources. Yet she was always considered to be different and was cast as an outsider. Chen Xiaojie said that while she eventually made friends, she was extremely isolated and lonely.

When I asked Chen Xiaojie about music during the Cultural Revolution, she said that the sights and sounds of political propaganda in the cities constantly overwhelmed her. However, she lived at the foot of a mountain in an extremely rural area, where residents had to take a two-hour tractor ride to a tiny village to buy anything. Chen said, "So you just wake up, work, eat, and go to sleep. Not much opportunity to hear or sing these songs." With a little more conversation, she admitted that those who enjoyed singing would seek out any music that was available to them. Since Chen liked to sing, especially songs from the model operas, she learned much of the revolutionary music. As we flipped through the *New Songs of the Battlefield* anthology, she enthusiastically pointed to her favorites and said she learned to sing them because they were "nice sounding" (*haoting* 好听), but songs that were extremely political or revolutionary were "not good, so I wouldn't learn to sing them because I didn't like them."

Like many upper-class Shanghai residents in the decades leading up to CCP rule, Chen Xiaojie's family had listened to a lot of foreign and foreign-influenced music. Eventually, Chen found the political propaganda music of the Cultural Revolution displeasing. When I asked if she had ever listened to any of this "foreign" music in the countryside, Chen emphatically shouted, "NO! Oh no! . . . In the countryside it was even stricter than other places; it was forbidden." Since she was originally from Shanghai, all of Chen's clothes were of much higher quality than those of the local peasants. While she considered them to be quite meager, the local peasants would comment on how beautiful her clothes were. "So, you wouldn't go listen to that foreign music [if you were already so different]."

As she paged through the songbooks, Chen Xiaojie did not recognize the vast majority of the songs. She said that they "have such a strong odor of politics," and she was disinterested in the music. Periodically, she had been interested in model operas and learned to sing some songs. But when we took a close look at them, she expressed few specific memories or personal attachments and noted that most people in her generation are equally apathetic. Still, Chen Xiaojie believes that the music, and the time period, serve as history and that this history is very deep (*hen shen* 很深). She closed by sharing that "a lot of people suffered a lot of bitterness"—or pain or hardship (*shou le hen duo ku* 受了很多苦)—"so we can't forget all of this; and it is important to research this music."

Conclusions

In the search for one's past and the familiar, the shared past—the collective memory—proves to be a formidable asset. In the case of the Cultural Revolution, the intense shared experience can unite individuals and allow them to identify with a group. Comparing an average person's life during the Cultural Revolution to their life today reveals an overwhelming shift in focus from the group to the individual. The shift can serve as a key impetus for nostalgia and a yearning for the imagined community of the past.

As a recovery of past emotions, nostalgia for the Cultural Revolution seeks to remove the pain. While individuals like Chen Xiaojie still mourn the loss and tragedy of their past, many others, like Wang Guowei, look back to recover a sense of solidarity, camaraderie, and simplicity, and music commonly triggers this sense of nostalgia. The emotional power of music and the meanings that it constructs allow basic emotions to be carried through the complex web of politics and history. Nostalgia becomes an attempt to recover the positive emotions of the past, though not necessarily an attempt to recreate or rebuild them. Wang Guowei shared, "See, talking to you about these songs [to help you better understand] also gives me the opportunity to reminisce [*huiyi* 回忆]. Because there aren't many who research this, and especially because I'm here [in the United States] . . . there's no one to talk about this with" (2015, personal interview).

A company employee from the suburbs of Beijing was one of many respondents who suggested that revolutionary songs should continue to be promoted, stating that "in contrast to today's music, the revolutionary music of the past was very encouraging and got people excited, the media should play some more." A retired resident of Shanghai responded, "When you listen to this music it gets you very excited, I hope to hear it all the time."

Both Wang Guowei and Chen Xiaojie repeatedly expressed the importance of studying music from the Cultural Revolution, which was the defining time period in their lives. In both positive and negative ways, the politics directly impacted their life paths and the trajectories for their future. Chen Xiaojie's hardship through her time in the countryside parallels most pictures that are painted about life during the Cultural Revolution, particularly those that are drawn outside China. And while Chen Xiaojie did not want to disclose her exact age, her family history suggests that she is most likely of the "socialist generation" or at the older end of the "Cultural Revolution generation." Her age, coupled with the hardship of decades of labor in the countryside, was reflected in her overwhelmingly negative reflections and lack of connection to the *New Songs of the Battlefield* anthology.

Wang Guowei's experiences complicate this narrative of trauma, as his career as a professional musician may not have ever come to be without the particulars of the Cultural Revolution. The safety of a career in music protected him and his family during and after the Cultural Revolution, and his current-day nostalgia, and the excitement and enthusiasm with which he reminisced about music from his childhood, is completely understandable. The excitement, the energy, and the nostalgia would otherwise be untapped or difficult to access without music. Wang Guowei's story is representative of the unique particulars of the Cultural Revolution generation, especially given the primary role of music in his personal and professional lives, both past and present.

Music is a powerful vehicle for emotions and memory; perhaps this is why the use of music in disseminating revolutionary content has such an emotional and long-lasting impact. In a general sense, the emotive power of music helps explain how and why these songs can trigger such a strong sense of nostalgia. The semiotic function of music allows individuals to attach their own individual meanings to music or sound. This often facilitates memory, thereby creating a powerful signifier, and hearing a few notes or reading a few lines of a song may spark a powerful emotional response. Music has also been identified as a means of arousing individuals, and the heightened emotional response to music can enhance and strengthen one's memory. An individual's age and his or her related association to a particular generation play a leading role in the construction of collective memories. Schuman and Scott have identified the effects of generational imprinting and conclude that an individual's experiences as a youth remain prominent in one's memory for the remainder of one's life. Firsthand experience deeply affects an individual's memory, and the full context of an event, including one's emotional response to it, is difficult to convey once the moment has passed. During the Cultural Revolution, the repetitive propaganda and energetic fervor deeply influenced people's emotional responses to music. The revolutionary language, such as the lyrics of the songs in the *New Songs of the Battlefield* anthology, had a striking impact, particularly on the youth. Through the medium of music, their lyrics inspired individuals and provided a means for group identification.

The impact of firsthand experience and context in general may begin to explain why those of the Cultural Revolution generation find these lyrics so encouraging. As age increases, music triggers nostalgia and lyrics inspire encouragement, and members of the Cultural Revolution generation naturally have more emotional meanings attached to music and lyrics than younger generations. Those of the Cultural Revolution generation experienced these meanings while simultaneously negotiating their present context in contemporary China or outside of China, which has resulted in a marked personal contrast between their past and present lives. This phenomenon is described by psychologists Ashok Jansari and Alan J. Parkin as the "reminiscence bump," a concept that explains the "disproportionally higher recall of early-life memories by older adults" (1996, 85). In other words, older adults have an increased number of memories from adolescence and young adulthood because it is a period of life when one experiences so many firsts along with a lot of repetition in one's twenties. Later on, "life review starts to happen" in the mid-thirties, and then after age forty-five there are fewer recent or new events (85). Steve Janssen, Antonio Chessa, and Jaap Murre (2005) extend the discussion of the "reminiscence bump" in their work:

130 · CHAPTER 4

"The presence of the reminiscence bump in young adults and the stronger reminiscence effect in older adults suggest that two processes affect the reminiscence bump phenomenon. *First, events in adolescence are encoded more strongly than events that occur in other life periods (differential encoding). Second, because these events are initially stored more intensely, they will be retrieved more frequently.* Therefore, these events will become even stronger at a later age (differential sampling)" (666, emphasis added). Those of the generation I call the Cultural Revolution generation (born between 1950 and 1960) reached midlife in the 1990s and 2000s. The reminiscence bump helps begin to explain why and how they may have stronger memories from their youth than from other time periods in their life.[8]

For members of the Cultural Revolution generation, their maturation into adulthood occurred during a period of extremely heightened emotions, and the events of this era are remembered most significantly and often most fondly. The camaraderie, group participation, and energy of the Cultural Revolution are difficult to find in contemporary Chinese society; thus, in an attempt to negotiate one's identity in contemporary China, the constructed memory of an energetic youth provides an individual with comfort and thereby triggers waves of nostalgia. Contemporary Chinese society and individuals' personal and political outlook also affect how they construct memories of the past. A reviewer of an earlier publication insightfully articulated that the "encouraging" element that the songs inspire today may account for a comparative or relative relationship.[9]

The *New Songs of the Battlefield* anthology was an attempt to mobilize the masses, educating them about political campaigns and official ideologies through forms and styles already familiar and accessible to them. However, the signs and symbols themselves (that is, the music and melodies) are remembered beyond the political content. How the songs are remembered today and who remembers them demonstrate that members of the Cultural Revolution generation have attached deeply emotional meanings to the music; in their contemporary lives, the music provokes otherwise untapped memories of childhood and youth.

Memories of the Battlefield

"You Hear These Songs and You Are Inspired"

When I walked up the stairs to Jin Laoshi's office in early 2018, I immediately flashed back to visiting her office years before when I was a young graduate student.[1] She greeted me with the same warm smile, and we picked up our conversation as if no time had passed. The mutual respect and connection were still there, as was the shared interest in telling the story of a seemingly distant time and place. Jin Laoshi studied English and graduated from a college in Shanghai in 1964, two years before the official beginning of the Cultural Revolution. After graduating, she began what was originally scheduled as a two-year teachers' training class; however, the training was cut short because the cohort was required to go out to the countryside as their participation in the nationwide "Socialist Education Movement" (Shehuizhuyi jiaoyu yundong 社会主义教育运动) and "Four Cleanups" (Si qing yundong 四清运动).[2] "We were supposed to stay in the countryside for a year but had to return to school earlier because [of] the Cultural Revolution" (Jin Laoshi 2018, e-mail correspondence).

August 12, 1966: "This day I remember too clearly," Jin Laoshi explained when I asked her about the early days of the Cultural Revolution (2018, personal interview).[3] Everyone was writing "big character posters" (*dazibao* 大字报) that criticized individuals who were known to have worked with the Guomindang (the Nationalist Party 国民党; also known as Kuomintang or KMT) or associated with foreigners or other types of so-called reactionary affiliations. Without much guidance or verification, older professors were labeled as reactionary and anti-revolutionary, as well as with "really ugly names." Then the posters led to struggle meetings known as "Douguihui" (斗鬼会), literally "Meeting to Battle the Ghosts [or Demons]," a reference to a 1966 slogan, "Sweeping Away All the Monsters and Demons" (Niu gui she shen 牛鬼蛇神), or "Monsters and Demons" for short.[4] The slogan was popularized after a 1966 editorial had mobilized the masses to demon-ize class enemies (X. Lu 2004, 59; K.-S. Li 1995, 292, quoting *The Great Socialist Cultural Revolution*, 1–6). At the onset of the Cultural Revo-lution, this slogan was employed to label anyone with an unfavorable class background. Once labeled, the enemy was typically subjected to public humiliation and often physical violence.

On August 12 Jin Laoshi went to work to find the Red Guards already on campus, leading a meeting from up on a stage in the campus playground. "The Red Guards were on the stage and we all sat below. They wrote these big poster boards, gave them [the accused] the tall pointy hat, [and] hung a label around their neck. They brought them to the stage and criticized them." But then the tone shifted. People in the audience started to write notes and pass them up to the Red Guards. Jin explained that colleagues were turning each other in. Suddenly the Red Guards would read a note and then take someone from the audience and put that person on the stage for criticism. "So, everyone was extremely tense, because you didn't know who would get called up on stage." Eventually the accused were all pulled down and forced to crawl on the ground. The Red Guards covered them with paste and then doused them with black ink, turning their heads and skin gray to make them look like a devil (referring to the "Monsters and Demons" campaign). "They were crawling on the ground. I remember that day so clearly. To me I can never forget that . . . that picture is still in my mind today. Because I never could have imagined treating other people like this. And these were all our teachers." It was after this experience that the intensity and uncertainty of the Cultural Revolution sunk in, "because you just never knew what was going to happen."

The Cultural Revolution was marked by these types of dynamics: the political climate was intense, struggle and criticism manifested themselves physically, and political campaigns were constantly shifting. As a new graduate and new teacher, Jin Laoshi witnessed the suffering of her senior teachers, and physical violence also became part of the everyday sounds and sights: "There were quite a few people in the end who could not take it and commit[ted] suicide. We knew this because we were all at school. We had a big building and they locked up some teachers in there. And at night we would hear people shouting, prob-ably being beaten, and we could hear this. People locked up, unable to go home."

But Jin Laoshi believes that the violence was perhaps more subdued in Shanghai when compared with Beijing, as it was common to describe *wendou* (文斗), or battle of words, in Shanghai, whereas in Beijing there was much more *wudou* (武斗), or battle of weapons. When I asked Jin what it was like for her to witness such acts and be in such an environment, she responded, "I was so young, so I did not suffer in the same way. I was not exactly [from] a *gongren* [工人, or laboring class] family, but I was still considered simple. . . . Of course some things I cannot forget. I will never forget." She later said, "At that time, someone like me, I did not really suffer much criticism. But the big thing is that we did not have anything else to do at that point. Just meetings, meetings, meetings."

One phrase that Jin Laoshi used stuck with me: *wanquan meiyou shiqing* (完全没有事情). "Absolutely nothing to do" is one way to translate this, and we talked at length about how this experience of being idle (and without purpose or direction) was clearly a challenge for her. Following the intense and chaotic opening of the Cultural Revolution, things started to settle. By 1968–69, Jin Laoshi stated, "There was just no business left. Not even meetings. How would you have anything else to meet about? Also, no classes to attend." Everyone was still receiving their salary, so some colleagues just stopped coming in to work. Jin Laoshi and many of her colleagues maintained a sense of obligation, especially since they were still collecting a salary, and they dutifully came in to work every day. "So, we would just chat, the men would play poker, the women would knit sweaters, etc. If we did have to hold a meeting, we would go to the meeting. If we did not have a meeting, we would just sit around. At that time there just was not anything to do."

According to Jin Laoshi, the college began to offer classes for the workers, peasants, and soldiers in a program that was known as *gongnongbing xueyuan* (工农兵学员), or "worker-peasant-soldier students," around 1971. Jin spoke fondly of her time teaching these students as they were dedicated, committed, respectful, and not afraid to *chiku* (吃苦), a Chinese expression that literally means "eat bitterness," in this instance referring to her students' ability to endure hardships. The phrase *chiku* evokes an important political movement of the 1950s and 1960s known as *yiku sitian* ("recalling bitterness and reflecting on sweetness" 忆苦思甜):[5]

I still remember at the beginning of every class. There was a leader of Gongxuandui [Workers Propaganda Team 工宣队]. That person (a woman) would always start the class. *Yiku sitian*, do you know that? You have to recall the bitter days in the past, in the old society. And then think of the happy days now. You have to make a comparison to love life now and you need to be grateful. This was required. Then she talked about how everything was so hard in the past and how well she was doing now. At the end she would teach one English phrase, "Long live Chairman Mao." Every semester was her teaching this class at the beginning. Only after that, could we start to teach.

Once the *gongnongbing xueyuan* classes began, Jin Laoshi's daily life was transformed. No longer idly passing time, she and her colleagues were busy with long days of teaching. "We worked with them from morning to night. All the way to 9 or 10 p.m., then we would go back to the classroom and start preparing class for the next day. We wouldn't have a voice left and we would use our own money to buy medicine. . . . We were all very *renzhen* [serious or earnest 认真]." Jin Laoshi and the other junior teachers lived at the school. "We had a classroom where junior faculty slept. No beds. Mattresses on the floor. During the day we were with students. And then we slept in the classroom at night." Jin taught the students English and courses that included intensive reading, speaking, and listening. Because some students were from the villages, they came to her classes without much of an educational foundation. Many had not completed middle school, and some came in with only a very basic elementary school background. Jin Laoshi often had to cover basic content first in Chinese before moving into their English lessons so the students could comprehend the material itself. Most of these students would not have had the opportunity to study at the college level were it not for the Cultural Revolution and as a result were incredibly dedicated to the curriculum.

As a scholar and educator of language, Jin Laoshi shared many insights that helped me understand the particularities of Cultural Revolution propaganda from a linguistic perspective. We had met when I was a student, beginning to analyze the *New Songs of the Battlefield* anthology. We would discuss many aspects of the Cultural Revolution beyond language, including her own personal experiences in China during the time. When we met again in 2018, she graciously agreed to speak with me about what it meant for the CCP to revolutionize music during the Cultural Revolution. Jin Laoshi described the language of the Cultural Revolution as "very special. An interesting topic," and she raised a point that I frequently heard in my interviews: "Looking now and listening to the song lyrics, sometimes I think, 'This sounds . . . funny or ridiculous,' you know. But now, I would not say or sing these things. I think about how we could have been so naive then." Jin Laoshi told me how she heard the songs every day, all day, and everywhere. Revolutionary songs such as those appearing in *New Songs of the Battlefield* were broadcast publicly on TV, radio, and in public spaces. They were sung before, during, and after all meetings at school. "*Feichang shuxi* [extremely familiar 非常熟习] because we sang all of them. And if we were not singing them, we would constantly hear them . . . back then we were singing them all the time, all day long. I could sing them from start to finish."

Jin Laoshi explained how at the time she and her friends would not question the lyrics or the revolutionary propaganda. "At that time, we did not have an ounce of this way of thinking. We thought it was all so good. That it is what we should be singing. And that it had a good benefit [*haochu* 好处]. Younger people like us, we were into the up-beat songs. Revolutionary songs were incredibly inspiring." Jin Laoshi credits both the melodies and the lyrics for the rousing nature of the songs. "The songs give you inspiration. You hear these songs and you are inspired. You will not feel down. Sometimes you come across some difficulties, some troubles; you sing these songs and you would forget about it. You would put it aside. You would, along with everyone, sing together."

How and why were ordinary individuals inspired by the revolutionary songs? Jin Laoshi attributes the phenomenon to a sense of purpose, a goal, and a future that the inspirational lyrics provided, particularly to the younger generations in China during the Cultural Revolution. "Lyrics at that time were very spiritual," she said, at a time when the only approved organized religion or spirituality was the cult of personality surrounding Mao Zedong. She also observed the sense of unity in the revolutionary lyrics: "not about you as an individual, or your small family, but it is all bigger; the country, the world." Jin identifies these attributes as part of the nuance of the Cultural Revolution. It cannot be simply characterized as exclusively positive or negative; there were some moments of humanity within this storm of evil and trauma. She later expressed, "The Cultural Revolution was not all about the songs. And the songs are not all about the Cultural Revolution. . . . Some aspects are still relevant." She then mentioned a particular song as we wrapped up our interview, "Sewing Kit Is an Heirloom" ("Zhenxianbao shi chuanjiabao" 针线包是传家宝) (music example 4.1).

针线包是传家宝
SEWING KIT IS AN HEIRLOOM

小小针线包，革命传家宝，
Tiny little sewing kit, [is a] revolutionary heirloom,
当年红军爬雪山，用它补棉袄；
When the Red Army climbed the snow-capped mountains,
    [they] used it to patch up quilted jackets;

小小针线包，革命是传家宝，
Tiny little sewing kit, [is a] revolutionary heirloom,
解放军叔叔随身带，缝补鞋和帽。
Uncle PLA [People's Liberation Army] keeps it on hand, sewing
    shoes and caps.

我们红小兵，接过传家宝，
We the Little Red Guards, will take over the heirloom,
艰苦奋斗好传统，永远要记牢。
To work arduously is a good tradition, we must always remember.
艰苦奋斗好传统，永远要记牢。
To work arduously is a good tradition, we must always remember.

The politicization of music is multilayered in this example. The lyrics reference the resilience and resourcefulness of the Red Army (Hongjun 红军) and members of the People's Liberation Army (Jiefangjun 解放军) in times past who carried a little sewing kit as they climbed up snow-capped mountains to mend shoes and caps. As a children's song, the lyrics also speak to the next generation of soldiers, connecting the "Little Red Guards" (Hongxiaobing 红小兵) to their "uncle" (*shushu* 叔叔) soldiers and identifying them as next in line within a glorious and revolutionary tradition. Translated as a "family heirloom" or "cherished tradition," *chuanjiabao* (传家宝) includes the character *bao* (宝), which invokes the sentiment of something precious and darling (it is also part of the term for baby: *baobei* [宝贝]). The lyrics connect children to the history and future of the nation and inspire them to be resourceful and work hard. As Jin Laoshi looked over the

affectionately, moderato

Xiao xiao zhen xian bao, ge ming chuan jia bao, dang nian hong jun

pa xue shan, yong ta bu mian ao; xiao xiao zhen xian bao,

ge ming chuan jia bao, jie fang jun shu shu sui shen dai, feng bu xie he

mao. Wo men hong xiao bing, jie guo chuang jia bao,

jian ku fen dou hao chuan tong, yong yuan yao ji lao. Jian ku fen dou

hao chuan tong, yong yuan yao ji lao._____

Example 4.1. "Sewing Kit Is an Heirloom"

score she remarked, "You could change some of the lyrics a little bit. But the melody you can keep. Like 'Sewing Kit Is an Heirloom,' they wanted everyone to take good care of everything and reuse everything. This basic meaning is not evil [*huai* 坏]; you do not have to criticize it all."

5

CONCLUSIONS

Just how and why did Mao and the CCP specifically utilize music as a weapon during the Cultural Revolution? And how might we understand the impact of the music as remembered today? In this chapter I begin with an overview of the weaponization of music through the framework of the cultural policy known as "Three Processes of Transformation." I then move on to explore twenty-first-century China to better understand the present from which individuals currently remember the past. Finally, I thread together conversations of the senses, memory, violence, and trauma to ultimately explore three questions: Why music? Why does this matter today? What can we learn?

Transformation

Learning how and why music was weaponized as part of CCP propaganda during the Cultural Revolution helps one understand the short-term and long-term impact of the music. In *Rhetoric of the Cultural Revolution*, Xing Lu addresses the CCP's use of music when she writes, "Songs became instruments of socialization, political control, and ideological persuasion in Communist China during the Cultural Revolution. They were part of a mechanism intended to remold the thought processes of almost one quarter of the human race. They were utilized in a campaign to mobilize the population to achieve specific goals such as disseminating radical ideas, eradicating class enemies, and maximizing cultlike devotion to Mao and the Communist Party" (2004, 120).

In a later text (*The Rhetoric of Mao Zedong*), Xing Lu states, "Mao Zedong's legacy, both good and bad, is still alive, glorified by some Chinese people even as it continues to haunt others" (2017, 14). Lu's careful and meticulous analysis of Mao's rhetoric offers important insight into understanding the music of the Cultural Revolution through its design, implementation, and reception. She summarizes the five major rhetorical themes of the Cultural Revolution—moral appeals, mythmaking, conspiracy theory, dehumanization, and radicalization—and writes that "some of these themes can be traced to classical Chinese rhetoric, and some bear close resemblance to the rhetoric of Stalin's Russia and Nazi Germany" (2004, 184). Lu joins other scholars such as Barbara Mittler (2008) and Isabel Wong (1984) in drawing careful connections from cultural and historical practices that predate the Cultural Revolution. While there is a continuation of practices, there are also distinctions to be noted within the Cultural Revolution.

Zhou Enlai's cultural policy of "Three Processes of Transformation" (San-hua 三化), an extension of Mao's 1942 "Talks at the Yan'an Conference on Literature and Art," provides a framework for understanding the *how* and *why* behind the politicization (or, in the language of the Chinese Cultural Revolution, the revolutionization) of music. The policy provided a clear road map for how Mao Zedong and the CCP attempted to transform both the content and the function of music.

REVOLUTIONIZE

Once the content was revolutionized, the CCP turned to the revolutionization of the function of music. As Xing Lu writes, "The singing of quotation songs helped with the memorization of Mao's instructions and sayings. Memorizing classics by heart has been a Chinese tradition" (2004, 121). In this way, Mao and the CCP capitalized on certain Chinese traditions such as memorization and recitation and coupled this with totalitarian control, including an environment of fear and violence, to transform the function of music. During the Cultural Revolution the CCP maintained tight control over the arts, and its music, though ubiquitous, was uniform and unchanging. The extreme and totalitarian level of dissemination resulted in a revolutionization of the senses. Individuals encountered the revolution at every corner and with nearly every sense: propaganda posters were visible everywhere one looked; sounds of propaganda music filled the air both inside and outside of the home; and the revolution was physically embodied through such activities as group singing and loyalty dances. Propaganda arts educated the masses on how to participate in society (DeMare 2015, 4–5) and motivated individuals to participate (Ho 2018, 3).

NATIONALIZE

In retrospect, the success of the CCP in "nationalizing" music was due to its ability to capture the youth. Today, the children's songs have the strongest long-term impact, despite making up only a small percentage of the political propaganda at the time. The children's songs gave the youth a path toward becoming members of a socialist society; they provided a moral compass and educated children on how to join in the revolution. Yet, in the long run, the political message faded as the children became adults and developed their own consciousness and political outlook. As a result of more lived experience, perhaps more education, and, as always, distance and time, these children developed critical thinking skills. While the music most directly and strongly impacted this generation, the political message is not at the heart of the contemporary memory of the songs. Many people still maintain a strong connection to the music, which continues to take folks back to their childhood. Yet the politics is nearly always secondary to the human and lived experience. I have yet to meet an individual who upholds the political campaigns of the Cultural Revolution without question. Some components and threads are still held dear by some, but the overwhelming majority see the politics as outdated and out of touch. Yet the music still serves as the soundtrack of their youth.

POPULARIZE

To "popularize" music involved efforts to get the revolutionary music out to the masses and to make revolutionary music an everyday component of people's lives. Utilizing forms that were familiar to the masses made the message accessible and engaging and helped disseminate the music far and wide. Political propaganda surrounded individuals at every step throughout their day. Daily life in the urban centers versus rural countryside certainly varied, as exemplified in the story of Chen Xiaojie versus the others who are featured in this book.

Similar to the efforts of nationalizing music and making it truly *of* the people, efforts to popularize required not only that the revolutionary art be disseminated but that the masses accept it and see themselves in it in order to popularize it and make it truly *of*, *by*, and *for* the people. These efforts were not limited to the Cultural Revolution period alone. As Sue Tuohy writes of song movements throughout modern China, "Song movements embraced two missions: to learn from and to teach the people. These missions reflect a tension found throughout the century in the dual goals of representing and transforming the people" (2001, 115). Nationalizing music required a knowledge of popular and historical traditions, styles, and aesthetics.

The CCP could not have predicted its decades-long success of popularizing music, now tied to the post-socialist society of twenty-first-century China, where nostalgic memories are embedded in the music. Sheldon Lu explains how "human beings are haunted by history and memory. The engagement with the socialist and communist past comes in a variety of positions, ranging from nostalgia and longing to revulsion and rejection" (2007, 131). The capacity for music to carry one back to another time, place, moment, and emotion, coupled with the remarkable changes in society between the Cultural Revolution and twenty-first-century China, has contributed to the long-term "success" of this popularization of revolutionary music.

Of course, this nostalgia and longing for the past is not merely a simplistic yearning for one's youth. Sheldon Lu describes how the contemporary "post-socialist" moment of reflecting back nostalgically on the predictable socialist days of one's youth during the Cultural Revolution offers a way, or a space, or a moment, to simultaneously process the past and the present in hopes of better understanding what comes next. He writes, "Longing for the socialist past does not imply a simplistic, naive return to the negative aspects of Stalinism or Maoism. Post-socialist nostalgia for the future is a reflective and self-reflexive reaction to both the truths and the tragedies of the past in anticipation of a better future" (2007, 132). An example here comes to mind from a story a Chinese student in the United States recently shared with me. She was curious to speak with me about my research on the Cultural Revolution period, just as I was interested to hear about her impressions of the period as someone born in China in the late 1990s and raised in Shanghai in the early years of the twenty-first century. When I asked how she knew of the music at all (since most students I speak with are typically not familiar with the period, its history, or its music), she responded that her father had sung Cultural Revolution (and other revolutionary) songs to her ever since she was a child. She continued on to say that her father loves to sing and would replace "Mao Zedong" with her own three-character name as a way to praise and adore her; simultaneously, and she only came to realize this as she was a bit older, he sang the songs as a way to express his frustration and resentment for what he lost as someone who grew up in China during the Cultural Revolution. An individual critical of Mao Zedong and the Cultural Revolution period, he used the songs, ever so familiar to him, to teach his daughter about the country's history and his history. And he also sang the songs to shower his daughter with love and attention, a far cry from the original intention of the revolutionary songs (Yang 2018, personal interview).[1]

Impacts of the Cultural Revolution on Chinese Society

The "Great Proletarian Cultural Revolution" was Mao's attempt to mobilize the masses in a large-scale social revolution that would aid in developing a solid socialist economic base while transforming the ideology of the people. The revolution stressed economic and political reform, but its very name explicitly stated a goal to transform the nation through arts, literature, and education—in other words, culture. Many scholars today emphasize the devastating effects of the Cultural Revolution on writers, artists, and intellectuals (see Harding 1993; Hsu 1995; and Meisner 1999). As Immanuel C. Y. Hsu states, "Poignantly, the Cultural Revolution turned out to be anticultural, anti-intellectual, and anti-scientific; for knowledge was considered the source of reactionary and bourgeois thought and action" (1995, 703). In addition to the loss of creative and artistic production during the Cultural Revolution, many historical cultural artifacts were destroyed.

The Cultural Revolution also had a powerful effect on education. Though some reforms benefited the education system, the cessation of classes during the Cultural Revolution resulted in what many refer to today as the "educated youth" (*zhishi qingnian* 知识青年). Also labeled the "lost generation" or "sent-down youth," this generation was taken to the countryside to serve the revolution through manual labor and in turn to "learn" from the peasants. The loss in creative, artistic, and scientific production of the older generations, the lack of education in the "sent-down youth," and the subsequent lack of trained teachers for the following generations damaged the educational growth of three generations (Hsu 1995, 703).

Alternatively, some of the reorganization of the curriculum and methods during and after the Cultural Revolution provided increased opportunities for rural, non-elite populations (J. Wang 1998). However, standards within the educational system declined: students were selected for their class background as opposed to academic merit, the curriculum was highly politicized, the length of schooling was reduced, and a greater emphasis on manual labor was instituted (Harding 1997, 241).

The Cultural Revolution also increased rural communities' access to education, medicine, and health care. In the early 1960s, health care was concentrated in the urban areas. Mao criticized this imbalance and called for more emphasis on common health care and a decrease in advanced research within cities (Meisner 1986, 378–79). As a result, trained health professionals gave rudimentary instruction to young people, including many peasants, and sent them out to the rural areas to care for the masses. Many of the young peasants—labeled "barefoot doctors" (*qijiao yisheng* 赤脚医生) as a designation of their peasant-class background—received minimal training and administered only basic health care.

Arts, education, health care, and rural community life are only four examples here of many areas impacted by the Cultural Revolution. It is imperative that differing historical interpretations are considered when analyzing the Cultural Revolution. Scholars such as Harry Harding and Maurice Meisner outline some of these gains and losses but state that, since the Cultural Revolution policies were largely reversed in subsequent years, they had little long-term impact. Other scholars, such as Hsu, stress the importance of the disruption and losses in labor, industry, and agriculture during the era. Scholars will certainly be unraveling the impact of the Cultural Revolution on modern China for decades to come as access to documents increase and different social, political, and cultural tides shift, allowing for different types of inquiry.

China in the Twenty-First Century

The ways in which the music of the Cultural Revolution is remembered and the ties of these memories to the Cultural Revolution are both infused with the realities of the present. As Sheldon Lu writes, "To fully comprehend the past is to come to terms with the present—the present historical circumstances, socioeconomic conditions, and mode of production" (2007, 138). The changes in people's lives from the Cultural Revolution to twenty-first-century China are multifaceted. For most, especially in urban areas, precious little remains constant: people experience different political landscapes, different societal landscapes, different cultural landscapes, and different daily lives. Such stark differences, coupled with an aging population, create an environment that is ripe for nostalgia. Sheldon Lu writes of this nostalgia for the "socialist past" in contemporary Chinese cinema as a direct reaction against "the present capitalist consumer society" (131). He continues on to explain how "socialism during the 1950s to 1970s has conveniently come to signify values and ideals that are putatively absent today—idealism, egalitarianism, self-sacrifice, and innocence" (131).

I observed the same reactions in my interviews with individuals while they reminisced about their Cultural Revolution days through music. The music of the Cultural Revolution is full of propagandistic rhetoric with stark images of good and bad, right and wrong, and specific ideological messages; there is no confusing whom to support, what to promote, and how to spend one's day. Such clear messages, though troubling and no longer politically, culturally, or personally relevant, still provide a clarity that is often absent in twenty-first-century China. Writing in 2007, Sheldon Lu described a "postsocialist China" as a moment of negotiating the aftermath of a socialist revolution bleeding into economic reforms and rapid development. He went on to explain how "postsocialism is everyday life, in which ordinary citizens struggle to make a transition from the guarantees and rigidity of socialist welfare to the fluctuations and freedom of a mass consumer society. . . . Postsocialism is a battlefield of intellectual and ideological contention between different persuasions" (2007, 209). His use of the term "battlefield" gives me pause; the ideological battlefield of the Cultural Revolution appears to maintain its relevance even in the drastically shifting landscape of twenty-first-century China.

Working with memory requires an understanding of the present from which the journey begins. When I first started my research on *New Songs of the Battlefield* anthology in 2001, China was in a different moment than when Sheldon Lu was writing in 2007, just as we are in a different moment as I write these words in 2019. Each of these moments deserves its own focus, but my primary concern here is the tension between the past and the present. The efforts of the CCP to transform China into a socialist society, and the political propaganda music that supported these efforts, still resonate today. In 2007 Lu wrote how "postsocialism is not the end of socialism. It is an expectant present moment of unprecedented social experimentation that looks in two directions—back to the past and forward to the future. It feels nostalgia for the revolutionary past even as it enters the doors of the supermarket of capitalism" (210). In other words, the postsocialist moment Lu describes involves a complex web of looking back to the past as a means to understand and cope with one's present. For socialist efforts, the first decade of the twenty-first century in China was a time of growth that was accompanied by confusion and, in the eyes of many observers, contradictions. Rapid increases in economic development provided a new wealth of choices in consumption, and the results bore more of a resemblance to capitalism than to socialism. Navigating these choices created a perplexing reality for many individuals in their daily lives, particularly when contrasted to the predictability of life during the Cultural Revolution.

Today the present has once again shifted. Xi Jinping, president of the PRC and general secretary of the CCP, continues Deng Xiaoping's description of "socialism with Chinese characteristics" (Xi 2014) to describe the political and economic condition in twenty-first-century China. What does this mean for the relationship between music and politics? In what way does the CCP still seek to maintain control of the arts? And ultimately, is the CCP still interested in utilizing the arts as part of a cultural army and continuing a totalitarian control of the arts? Three recent moments come to mind that respond to these questions: Xi Jinping's 2014 speech at the Conference on Literature and Art, the 2018 ban on hip-hop culture and tattoos on television, and Xi Jinping's comments at the 2018 commemoration of Marx's birthday.

First, in 2014 Xi Jinping presented a speech at the Conference on Literature and Art,[2] after which journalists commented on the direct connections to Mao Zedong's cultural policies and the 1942 talks at Yan'an.[3] President Xi emphasized the importance of culture and the arts for the "rejuvenation" (*fuxing* 复兴)—pointedly replacing "revolution"—of China.[4] Quoting Mao, Marx, and Lenin, Xi recentered the socialist discourse with such statements as, "The Chinese spirit is the soul of socialist literature and art" (see Boehler and Piao 2015). The remarks connect socialism with Xi's ideological and political vision for the arts and stand as a sharp and direct criticism of some of the so-called downfalls in arts and culture since the opening of China's economic markets. Resonating directly with Mao's earlier talks outlining literature and the arts as part of a cultural army, Xi states that

> our society is at a moment of great intellectual activity. It is an era of big collisions of ideas and blending of cultures, which has generated quite a few problems. One of the most prominent is that some people lack values. There is no good and evil in their views, there is no bottom line to their actions, they dare to do everything that violates party discipline and the nation's laws. They dare to do everything that is unethical. There is no sense of nation, sense of community, sense of family. There is no right or wrong, there is nothing that isn't questioned, no knowledge of beauty and ugliness, no distinction between fragrant and odorous, there is ignorance and extravagance. This is the root cause for all kinds of problems in society. If these are not effectively solved, it will be difficult to move forward in the Reform and Opening and the socialist modernization drive. (qtd. in Boehler and Piao 2015)

This notion of a lack of values as a direct result of the Cultural Revolution comes up repeatedly in my fieldwork. Individuals mention how the political chaos, violence, and disruption to traditional Chinese societal values broke down one's moral compass and corroded interpersonal relationships. I have heard firsthand and read secondhand about the absolute shock of those who witnessed the degradation and violence that marked the Cultural Revolution. The traumas of enacting, witnessing, and experiencing violence continue to manifest in society long after the acts of violence themselves have ceased.

During President Xi's speech, he discussed the absence of a sense of community and drew a distinction between the "fragrant" and the "odorous"—ideas that the CCP clearly and relentlessly disseminated through multiple channels throughout the Cultural Revolution. The preface of the *New Songs of the Battlefield* anthology includes the declaration that "yellow flowers on the battlefield are especially fragrant," and President Xi's current rhetoric had direct connections to the ideology and rhetoric of the anthology. Although efforts to "rejuvenate" China have replaced the former revolutionary emphasis, the sentiment remains the same—as do the criticisms. Literature and arts are central to China's path to socialism.

We can see the direct application and consequence of Xi's statements four years after he made them. In early 2018, the State Administration of Press, Publication, Radio, Film and Television banned from television any actors with tattoos or depictions of "hip hop culture, sub-culture (non-mainstream culture) and dispirited culture (decadent culture)" (Quackenbush and Chen 2018). Once again, the government banned any art that was not aligned with the party's image of socialist values.

The year 2018 also marked the two-hundred-year celebration of Marx's birthday. President Xi's comments at the celebration included, "Hold high the banner of socialism with Chinese characteristics" and "Work tirelessly to realize the Chinese dream of national rejuvenation," two points that were directly taken from his speech to the Nineteenth National Congress held in 2017 (Xi 2017). President Xi's connecting of Marx, Mao, and socialism with today's China demonstrates the relevance of studying Cultural Revolution arts; the period was neither a historical "other" nor a passing phase. These extreme policies and their enforcement are significant and point to a need for further interdisciplinary critical scholarship of the Cultural Revolution era. The economic development, expansion of cultural landscape, and new choices in consumption present a different environment, but music and politics are still central to the party and to understanding Chinese culture and society. In the 2014 talks, the 2017 speech to Congress, and the 2018 censorship movement, Xi was reinforcing the CCP's control in general, and specifically indicating that the party should control what arts should and could be following the periods of liberalization. These statements and actions demonstrate the continued efforts by the CCP to utilize arts as a political tool nearly eighty years after Mao's Yan'an talks.

Music, Senses, Violence, Trauma

Writing about modern China, Sue Tuohy explains how, "in musical performance, citizens do not merely 'read' the nation; they see, hear, and participate in it" (2001, 124). Furthermore, she describes the "broad processes of musical nationalism accompanying the transformation of China" that were at peak intensity during the Cultural Revolution as being "repeated, reproduced, reorganized, and interrelated day by day in diverse settings, working together to portray the temporal and spatial dimensions of the nation. They give concrete form to the abstract concepts of the unity, historical longevity, national destiny, and order of the nation through a soundtrack that permeates the daily life of citizens throughout the PRC. These musical activities function as performances of the social imaginary" (124).

The CCP's attempts to develop a musical nationalism reflect a practice that spans much of the twentieth and twenty-first centuries, with a heightened intensity during the Cultural Revolution. Tuohy's work examines the "mutually transformative process of making music national and of realizing the nation musically" (2001, 108) and similarly encourages a push beyond sound itself to understand how music can serve as "an active means by which to experience the nation, by which to feel and act national" (109). Thus, musical activities play an important role in realizing the abstract concepts of socialism and provide a regular and repeated vehicle for people to engage and embody the political ideology. Put another way, the revolution required the mobilization of the masses where individuals and groups actively embodied the political ideology.

Along these lines, in his study of listening, music, and wartime, Martin Daughtry argues that "sound territorializes space, both at the macro level of the neighborhood and at the micro level, within the fluid-filled spaces of the body" (2015, 20). Furthermore, he contends that "if the soundscape concept is to be brought into alignment with the most incisive new work on sound and listening, we will need to reattach its abstract ear to a historically and culturally inflected body; conceive of that body as one that sounds while listening, listens while sounding, and learns while doing both; and emplace that body within an ever-changing series of overlapping vibrational environments" (122–23). In the context of the Cultural Revolution, Daughtry's call for an attention to the ear and ultimately to the body provides a depth of understanding for how music during the Cultural Revolution impacted individuals in the short term and continues to do so in the long term. Andrew Jones's work helps to illustrate how CCP strategies engaged similar techniques with that of mass media and popular songs from other places such as the United States and Europe. In his discussion of quotation songs (the songs that predated the Cultural Revolution in which Mao Zedong quotes were set to music), Jones explains that the songs were designed for portability and with a hook.

> This portability, as envisioned by those who originally promoted these songs at the very height of the Red Guard movement of September 1966 in the pages of the *People's Daily*, would not only annihilate spatial and temporal limitations, but also penetrate psychological barriers as well. . . . Interestingly enough, this description, in its emphasis *on the ability of these songs to record, broadcast, and enable Mao Zedong thought to saturate social, somatic, and psychological space*, reads almost uncannily like an account of the ethereal yet ubiquitous powers of mass media itself. This is not merely a rhetorical accident. (2014, 45, emphasis added)

In his discussion on pop music form, Jones continues on to emphasize how with repetition comes mastery and with mastery comes mobilization (2014, 47). And this mobilization during the Cultural Revolution was embodied through song: "Here, not only does the song effect the Chairman's teleportation, but the body of the singer itself becomes a resonant medium upon which the quotation is printed" (54). The pervasive, repetitive, and relentless dissemination of Cultural Revolution propaganda created an environment of constant stimulation, of seeing, hearing, and feeling the political propaganda, an engagement of nearly all of the senses. This leads to the important work of Tomie Hahn on listening, transmission, and the body. She describes the senses and how they "reside in a unique position as the interface between body, self, and the world. They are beautiful transmission devices, through which we take in information, comprehend the experience, assign meaning, and often react to the stimuli" (2007, 3). Yet the transmission devices which Hahn refers to as "beautiful" were exploited in Cultural Revolution propaganda. Thus, the music of the Cultural Revolution provides a site to critically examine the vibrations of sound, not only as musical or even physical vibrations but as the embodiment of the sensory environment.

In his discussions of theater during the Cultural Revolution, Brian DeMare explains how "the dramatic quality of Maoist revolution . . . had a powerful legacy for the PRC era, ensuring that political life in Mao's China was profoundly theatrical" (2015, 6–7). DeMare cites Barbara Mittler's work, in which she underscores how the audience "formed and enacted" propaganda art (qtd. in DeMare 2015, 7), and thus to understand Cultural Revolution culture requires an acknowledgment of moments of agency under extreme restriction and censorship. With such agency comes embodiment. If we push beyond sound itself, either in its physical vibrations or musical characteristics, and view sound and listening as an embodied experience, then the intensity of the Cultural Revolution environment takes on a new level of agitation. The Cultural Revolution is frequently cited as a unique period for its history, politics, and cultural environment. To consider the body in discussions of political propaganda (and music in particular) is to give attention to a sensory environment of historic extremes. Mittler aptly describes the "sensual experience that the Cultural Revolution was—its images, its sounds, its smells, and its touch" (2012, 32). And I return to Ban Wang's work on the aesthetic:

> The cultural character of the Revolution points to the eminently aesthetic dimension of political life during those tumultuous years. The aethestic . . . does not pertain simply to the arts or literature or even aesthetic theories, but embraces human pleasure and pain, enthusiasm and despair. . . . The aesthetic here is whatever impinges on the intimately sensory and sensual strata of our existence; it is our psychic and bodily conditions and the symbolic forms expressing them. In this broad sense, the aesthetic is an existential category, part of life, something lived and experienced at the ends of one's nerves and tasted on the tip of one's tongue. In this light, a cultural event becomes a vast stage for aestheticized politics. (1997, 195)

Inspired by both Mittler's and Ban Wang's rich contributions to understanding the Cultural Revolution, my work here considers how we may underscore the extreme nature of this sensory experience: the weaponization of music, the dissemination of propaganda arts, and the revolutionization of the senses. Moreover, this all occurred along with intense acts of violence and moments of trauma and, for some, concurrently with their influential period of development as children and youth.

In "When Music Is Violence," music critic Alex Ross writes, "When music is applied to warlike ends, we tend to believe that it has been turned against its innocent nature. . . . We resist evidence suggesting that music can cloud reason, stir rage, cause pain, even kill. . . . Despite the cultural catastrophe of Nazi Germany, the Romantic idealization of music persists" (2016). I have observed this romantic idealization of music and, though I did not directly experience the Cultural Revolution, at times embodied it myself. Yet for individuals who lived through this period, or for individuals with some connection to violence and trauma, music can equal violence. As Ross mentions, there is a long history around the world connecting music and war, and yet the supposed "innocent nature" of music is upheld by many. We can look back to early rulers and philosophers and their attention to the power of music and its ability to govern and influence the masses. Citing an example from ancient China, Ross writes, "The Chinese 'Book of Rites' differentiated between the joyous sound of a well-ruled state and the resentful sound of a confused one." Likewise, many scholars examine the long history of music and governance in China, such as Tuohy, who notes how "over two thousand years ago, Marquis Yi displayed the character and power of the state of Zheng through a magnificent set of bronze bells" (2001, 107). Mao and the CCP built upon this tradition in a new way to serve the revolution and transform China into a socialist society.

One of the defining characteristics of the Cultural Revolution is the violent means by which political campaigns and directives were carried out. The extreme measures of ideological transformation were realized both physically and psychologically. The devastation to individuals, groups, and the nation, though glossed over in CCP historical accounts, are of tragic proportions. In *The Turbulent Decade* (1996), Jiaqi Yan and Gao Gao conclude,

> For China, the Cultural Revolution remains a colossal catastrophe in which human rights, democracy, the rule of law, and civilization itself were unprecedentedly trampled. Not only was the president persecuted to death, tens of millions of innocent people were also attacked and maltreated. According to a Xinhua News Agency report on the trial of Jiang Qing and others in November 1980, some 34,800 people were persecuted to death. This figure is probably an extremely conservative estimate. Culture was devastated and the economy almost collapsed. . . . In these irrational years, the whole of China tumbled into insanity. (1996, 529)

With insanity and violence comes trauma. In the CR/10 collection (in the East Asian Library at the University of Pittsburgh) alone, physical violence and suicide are commonplace reflections. I have yet to meet someone, whether a perpetrator, target, witness, or bystander, who does not cite some personal story of violence from the Cultural Revolution. The environment of violence (often deeply personal, at times chaotic, and, for many, sustained over long periods of time) has a lasting impact on both individuals and society at large. Martin Daughtry captures the suspension of time when he describes trauma as an "'impossible event,' one that cannot be incorporated into one's ongoing self-narrative and so creates a circular temporality of flashbacks in which 'the past is always present'" (2015, 7). At the end of

Daughtry's *Listening to War* he asks, "How insidiously powerful is music as a carrier of traumatic memory?" (109), and this question is acutely relevant to the remembering of the Cultural Revolution through music. Jin Laoshi's and Zhang Haihui's stories demonstrate how, through processes of remembering, the music of the Cultural Revolution can play an important role in accessing the memories, emotions, and lived experience of the Cultural Revolution. And through the stories of Wang Guowei and Chen Jiebing, we learn how the Cultural Revolution was a defining time period in these two artists' lives. The meanings, emotions, and memories associated with the music far exceed the political design and at times contradict or supersede it. Propaganda arts and propaganda culture deserve our full and critical attention because of the humanity embedded within them.

The Battlefield

My mother, together with five members of her family, left China in 1949 to escape communism. As such, I grew up hearing stories of the Cultural Revolution as tales of what could have happened to our family. As a teenager I voraciously read memoirs of individuals who lived through the Cultural Revolution, taking in story after story of tragedy and hardship. As a college student I was introduced to scholarship on the Cultural Revolution period and began learning about it in a classroom with my professors and peers. Through this experience, I started to place the time period within a larger analytical framework of political history. As a graduate student I conducted ethnographic fieldwork to document the *New Songs of the Battlefield* anthology from the Cultural Revolution. Now, as an ethnographer, scholar, and educator, I write these words more than forty years after the end of the Cultural Revolution in an attempt to give voice to an important chapter in music, memory, violence, and trauma.

So, as we consider how Mao and the CCP utilized music as a weapon during the Cultural Revolution, we must ask, Why music? As Martin Daughtry writes, "The psychological wounds inflicted at the nexus of sound and violence are profound, albeit poorly understood" (2015, 98). Daughtry shares that an earlier title for his book was "Sound Wounds" (271). The totalitarian control and sensory environment of the extreme was an exploitation of music and humanity. Though *New Songs of the Battlefield* opens with the quotation "Yellow flowers on the battlefield are especially fragrant," understanding the design, implementation, and impact of propaganda music reveals that the trauma of so-called fragrance lingers on for generations.

Why does this matter today? Sue Tuohy mentions ancient bells as one of the earliest examples of Chinese rulers utilizing music to govern and how this practice continues centuries later: "Although I have come across no mention of retuning bells at recent Chinese Communist Party (CCP) conferences, the government of the PRC continues to display its power musically" (2001, 112). While I was originally developing this conclusion, a former student sent me a link to a CCP propaganda video of a children's song, "Belt and Road Is How" (New China TV 2018), promoting the Belt and Road Initiative, a twenty-first-century CCP economic development project launched by Xi Jinping in 2013. When I asked her where she had seen this, she then forwarded a link to a recent clip from John Oliver's late-night TV show (Oliver 2018). We know that the impact of the music continues on, and yet such contemporary examples demonstrate a continued practice of utilizing music and the arts to govern.

Finally, what can we learn? Xing Lu captures the essence of Mao's rhetoric by explaining how Mao united Chinese people, moved China to a different social structure and institutional practice, reshaped Chinese cultural habits and ideological beliefs, and instilled a new consciousness and new hope for the future (2017, 185). The impact of Mao's rhetoric was, and continues to be, great. Lu writes, "By the end of the Cultural Revolution many who grew up with the revolutionary slogans, songs, model operas, wall posters, and loyalty dances of the ten years of chaos became disillusioned with politics and began to pursue material well-being. The horror of revolution was over, but its impact on Chinese thought, culture, and communication lingers to this day" (192).

The emotions, the memories, and the lived experience of those who endured the traumatic decade are bound within the lyrics and melodies of revolutionary songs. Though some of the reflections are linked to the Chinese Communist Party's original efforts for an ideological transformation, other reflections are deeply personal, individual, and connected to a memory of something larger than a political campaign. In this totalitarian environment of extremes, music assaulted the senses, often in pursuit of violent ends. But today, this music can also provide solace for a generation as its members recall a radically different era. In these moments, this music is no longer a weapon but can offer something else: perhaps a sense of something familiar or a memory of one's childhood. To be sure, there are as many memories and emotions as there are individuals remembering, and I share my observations here on individual stories as well as trends and patterns that emerged in my research while absolutely respecting and recognizing the individuality and exceptions.

In the end, did music as Mao's weapon "work"? I have argued here at times yes and at times no. Writing these words more than four decades after the end of the Cultural Revolution, the question that remains for me is this: What are the long-term impacts of the politicization and weaponization of music, especially during one's childhood and youth? And once again, how can we explain the distinctions between enculturation and indoctrination, between patriotism and propaganda? While the songs of the *New Songs of the Battlefield* anthology are seemingly locked into a time, place, and politics of a closed chapter in China's history, their reverberations continue to be felt today.

Brief Historical Context
of the Cultural Revolution

Many leading scholars cite a handful of specific incidents and trends in the first two decades of the Chinese Communist Party rule that appear to have instigated the Cultural Revolution (see Clark 2008; Esherick, Pickowicz, and Walder 2006; Fairbank 1987; M. Gao 2008; Harding 1993; Hsu 1995; MacFarquhar and Schoenhals 2006; Meisner 1986; Spence 1990; and Yan and Gao 1996). These incidents and trends can be categorized into four major waves that follow a loose chronological order leading up to the formal launch of the Cultural Revolution in 1966.

The first wave developed in the 1950s, when China's relations with the Soviet Union began to crumble. The deterioration of relations was largely due to the ideological conflicts between Josef Stalin's successor, Nikita Khrushchev, and China's leader, Mao Zedong. In 1956, three years after Stalin's death, Khrushchev gave a landmark speech denouncing Stalin as a tyrant and criticizing his cult of personality. Mao questioned Khrushchev's ideology and theory as the two leaders drifted apart. From 1957 to 1959, Mao visited the Soviet Union once and Khrushchev made two visits to China; the meetings did not go well. Khrushchev was irritated with Mao's policies and actions leading up to the Taiwan Straits crisis of 1958 and refused to support China during the conflict. By the mid-1960s, Khrushchev pulled all Soviet technicians out of China and broke an agreement to provide China with an atomic weapon.

The second wave developed from the fallout after a series of CCP campaigns failed during the late 1950s and into the 1960s. The most often-cited campaign was the General Line of Socialist Construction (Shehuizhuyi jianshe zongluxian 社会主义建设总路), which included the Three Red Banners (Sanmian hongqi 三面红旗): the General Line (Zhongluxian 总路线), the Great Leap Forward (Da yue jin 大跃进), and the People's Commune Movement (Renmin gongshe yundong 人民公社运动). At the second session of the Eighth Party Congress in May 1958, Mao's General Line "Go all out, aim high, and achieve greater, faster, better and more economical results in building socialism" was adopted and the Great Leap Forward was launched. The movement was an attempt to boost industrial production to surpass Britain in fifteen years or less. Related to the Great Leap Forward, the People's Commune Movement reorganized peasant life in an attempt to utilize and control all rural labor power to increase production (K.-S. Li 1995, 372–75).

The movements brought about great economic decline and devastation, resulting in growing criticism of Mao and his ideologies. The Eighth Plenum of the Eighth Party Congress met in Lushan during the summer of 1959 to discuss, among other things, how to "correct the mistakes of the Three Red Banners" (Yan and Gao 1996, 3). Several leading officials commented on the failures of the Three Red Banners and suggested a shift away from its political and ideological emphasis. Mao circulated a letter written by Defense Minister Peng Dehuai that addressed issues of socialist transformation and the failures of certain campaigns. Many leaders began to agree with Peng's statements, and Mao began criticizing Peng as a revisionist. The criticisms escalated and led to the eventual dismissal of Peng, who was replaced by Lin Biao, a proven military leader and close supporter of Mao (Leiberthal 1997, 101).

In the following years, the country continued to suffer from declines in agricultural and industrial production, poor weather, and the removal of the Soviet scientists. The Ninth Plenum of the Eighth Party Congress was called in early 1961 to address the country's concerns. Mao proposed further investigation and stated, "To protect the Three Red Banners, China must war with the rest of the world, including large numbers of the opposition group and the skeptical group within the Party" (Yan and Gao 1996, 5). Mao began to raise concerns about the return of capitalism and leaders who supported Soviet revisionism. Liu Shaoqi was soon perceived as one of the leaders of the revisionists, which led to growing tension between Mao and Liu. These power struggles represent the third major wave that led to the Cultural Revolution.

The fourth major wave surfaced amid growing tensions and division within Chinese leadership. In 1962, Mao introduced the Socialist Education Movement (Shehuizhuyi jiaoyu yundong), an attempt to transform the economy, political organization, and ideology through socialist education (Meisner 1986, 288). The movement soon became known by one of its resolutions, the "Four Cleanups" (Si qing yundong), an attempt to "clean politics, clean economics, clean organization, and clean ideology" (292). It became a focal point for the battles between Mao and Liu; the two leaders debated for the next few years as Mao continued to question Liu and his "revisionist" followers.

Mao believed that "revisionists" and their "counter-revolutionary" plots were already permeating not only the Chinese leadership but the arts, literature, and the educational system as well. Mao began dismissing and demoting those labeled as "revisionists" to strengthen his position and weaken Liu's. At the end of 1965, major criticism surrounding the play *Hai rui* (Dismissed from office) sparked a string of debates regarding arts and politics. On November 10, 1965, Yao Wenyuan (editor in chief of the *Liberation Army Daily*) wrote a scathing editorial of the play written by Wu Han, an academic who also served as the deputy mayor of Beijing.

Historian Immanuel C. Y. Hsu identifies the editorial as the firing of "the first salvo of the Cultural Revolution" (1995, 697). The editorial criticized Wu for the play's allusions to Mao as a greedy and unfair emperor who dismissed an honest official (Defense Minister Peng). In the following months, Wu Han, along with many others, was denounced for criticizing Mao and his policies. Targeting Wu Han was a powerful move for Mao since Wu was both a public official and a leading intellectual, and because Wu was affiliated with other so-called Black Gang members Deng Tuo and Liao Mosha, the criticisms also implicated their patron, Liu Shaoqi. Through these circles of connections, the accusations could also be traced back to Liu Shaoqi. The tension continued to rise and culminated in the formal launching of the Cultural Revolution on August 8, 1966.

Sixty-Five Children's Songs
in *New Songs of the Battlefield*

Chinese title and English transliteration	English translation	Volume and page no.
Zhufu Maozhuxi wanshouwujiang 祝福毛主席万寿无疆	Wish Chairman Mao a Long Life	I-58
Haohao xuexi tiantian xiangshang 好好学习天天向上	Study Well and Make Progress Every Day	I-149
Wo ai Beijing Tiananmen 我爱北京天安门	I Love Beijing's Tiananmen	I-150
Huoche xiangzhe Shaoshan pao 火车向着韶山跑	The Train Runs toward Shaoshan	I-151
Women shi Hongxiaobing 我们是红小兵	We Are Little Red Soldiers	I-153
Daqing hua kai biandi hong 大庆花开遍地红	The Flowers of Daqing Bloom in Red	I-154
Xiaoxiao luosimao 小小螺丝帽	Tiny Little Screw Cap	I-155
Wo shi gongshe xiao sheyuan 我是公社小社员	I Am a Little Member of the Commune	I-156
Zhenxianbao shi chuanjiabao 针线包是传家宝	Sewing Kit Is an Heirloom	I-157
Xiaoxiao qiu'er shan yinguang 小小球儿闪银光	Tiny Ball Shines Silver Rays	I-158
Ge ming gushihui 革命故事会	Revolution Story Telling	I-158
Dajia laizuo guangbocao 大家来做广播操	Everybody Come Do Radio Broadcast Exercises	I-159
Gesheng feichu xin wowo 歌声飞出新窝窝	Songs Fly Out of Our New Village Homes	II-36
Gesheng women de xin Xizhang 歌唱我们的新西藏	Sing in Praise of Our New Tibet	II-39

Chinese title and English transliteration	English translation	Volume and page no.
Zheng xiang yidui qin xiongdi 真象一对亲兄弟	They Are Really Like Two Blood Brothers	II-136
Women shi Maozhuxi de Hongxiaobing 我们是毛主席的红小兵	We Are Chairman Mao's Little Red Soldiers	II-191
Hongxiaobing chengzhang quan kao dang 红小兵成长全靠党	The Little Red Soldiers Growing Up Rely Completely upon the Party	II-192
Xiao siji 小司机	Little Driver	II-194
Zhangda dangge hao sheyuan 长大当个好社员	Grow Up to Be a Good Member of the Commune	II-196
Woshi gongshe xiao mumin 我是公社小牧民	I Am the Little Herdsman of the Commune	II-197
Congxiao zhagen zai caoyuan 从小扎根在草原	Rooted in the Grasslands from Childhood	II-198
Fengshou geer fei man shan 丰收歌儿飞满山	Song of Bumper Harvest Flies to All the Mountain	II-200
Zhong kuihua 种葵花	Plant Sunflowers	II-201
Zhi shumiao 植树苗	Plant Tree Seedlings	II-202
Song siliao 送饲料	Delivering Feed	II-203
Wei ji 喂鸡	Feeding the Chickens	II-205
Da dianhua 打电话	Calling on the Telephone	II-206
Qishang xiao muma 骑上小木马	Ride the Little Rocking Horse	II-206
Women shi Maozhuxi de Hongxiaobing 我们是毛主席的红小兵	We Are Chairman Mao's Little Red Soldiers	III-206
Hongxiaobing zhi ge 红小兵之歌	Song of the Little Red Soldiers	III-207
Women shi zhaoqipengbo de Hongxiaobing 我们是朝气蓬勃的红小兵	We Are Little Red Soldiers Full of Vigor and Vitality	III-208
Linbiao, Konglaoer dou shi huai dongxi 林彪，孔老二都是坏东西	Lin Biao, and Confucius Are Both Bad Things	III-209
Leifeng shushu wangzhe women xiao 雷锋叔叔望着我们笑	Uncle Lei Feng Smiles at Us	III-210
Women zhang zai Yanhe pang 我们长在延河旁	We Grow by the Side of the Yan River	III-212
Xiner shao gei Taiwan xiaopengyou 信儿捎给台湾小朋友	Letters Sent to the Children of Taiwan	III-214
Hongxiaobing xue gong ge 红小兵学工歌	Song of the Little Red Soldiers Learning Industrial Production	III-215
Jinggangshan xia zhong nangua 井冈山下种南瓜	Growing Pumpkins at the Foot of Jinggang Mountain	III-217

Chinese title and English transliteration	English translation	Volume and page no.
Hongxiaobing zhi yuwang 红小兵织渔网	The Little Red Soldiers Weave Fishnets	III-220
Qinjian jieyue ji xinjian 勤俭节约记心间	Remember in Your Heart to Work Hard and Economize	III-221
Xiao songshu 小松树	Little Pine Tree	III-222
Dakai zande shouyinji 打开咱的收音机	Turn on Our Radio	III-223
Hongxing ge 红星歌	Red Star Song	IV-193
Dangde guanghui zhaoliangle women xintian 党的光辉照亮了我们心田	The Brilliance of the Party Shines and Brightens our Heart	IV-195
Zai canlande wuxing hongqi xia 在灿烂的五星红旗下	Under the Magnificent Five-Starred Red Flag	IV-198
Gongren shifu jin xiao lai 工人师傅进校来	Master Workers Come into the Schools	IV-200
"Wu.Qi" lushang xiang qian pao "五。七" 路上向前跑	On the "5.7" [May 7 Directive] Road We Quickly Run Forward	IV-202
Pichou fandong de "San zi jing" 批臭反动的"三字经"	The "Three Character Classic" of Criticize Chou and Oppose Movement	IV-203
Xiu hongxing 绣红星	Embroider a Red Star	IV-204
Xiangjiao lin li gesheng xiang 橡胶林里歌声响	Sounds of Singing Ring through the Rubber Forests	IV-204
Shaonian yundongyuan jinxingqu 少年运动员进行曲	Marching Song of Junior Athletes	IV-206
Haidao Hongxiaobing 海岛红小兵	Island's Little Red Guards	IV-207
Women huainian Taiwan xiaopengyou 我们怀念台湾小朋友	We Cherish the Memory of the Children of Taiwan	IV-209
Hongxiaobing sao gu mang 红小兵扫谷忙	The Little Red Soldiers Are Busy Sweeping the Valleys	IV-210
Xiao biandan 小扁担	Little Carrying Pole	IV-211
Zuguo, wo ai ni 祖国，我爱你	Our Motherland, I Love You	V-228
Nanhai ertong ai Beijing 南海儿童爱北京	The Children of the South China Sea Love Beijing	V-229
Wei xinsheng shiwu qi guzhang 为新生事物齐鼓掌	All Applaud for the New Things	V-230
Xiangyangyuan li yangguang zhao 向阳院里阳光照	The Sun Shines in Xiangyang Courtyard	V-231
Tielu pu xiang Yanhe pang 铁路铺向延河旁	Pave the Iron Path toward the Side of Yan River	V-232
Chuchu shengkai Dazhai hua 处处盛开大寨花	The Flowers of Dazhai Blossom Everywhere	V-234

Chinese title and English transliteration	English translation	Volume and page no.
Zhangda dangge xin nongmin 长大当个新农民	Grow Up to Be a New Peasant	V-237
Caoyuan xiao xunluobing 草原小巡逻兵	Little Patrol Soldiers on the Grasslands	V-238
Donghai xiao minbing 東海小民兵	Minuteman of the East China Sea	V-239
Liangge da pingguo 两个大苹果	Two Big Apples	V-241
Women shi qin'aide haopengyou 我们是亲爱的好朋友	We Are Dear Friends	V-242

Chinese Character Glossary

Terms

bao	宝	treasure and/or precious
baobei	宝贝	baby
biaoyanchang/biaoyan ge	表演唱/表演歌	performance song
bu yiyang	不一样	different (lit. "not the same")
chengfen bu hao	成分不好	Chinese expression meaning "class background is not good"; lit. "bad ingredients" or "bad composition" or "bad birth"
chiku	吃苦	eat bitterness
chuanjiabao	传家宝	heirloom or treasure
da	大	big/great
Daqing	大庆	city in west of Heilongjiang province, Mao's model in industry
Da yuejin	大跃进	Great Leap Forward (campaign)
Dazhai	大寨	village in eastern Shanxi province, Mao's model in agriculture
dazibao	大字报	big character posters
difang xing	地方性	local quality
Douguihui	斗鬼会	"Meeting to Battle the Ghosts [or Demons]" (campaign)
duchang	独唱	solo
duichang	对唱	duet
erhu	二胡	two-stringed bowed fiddle
ertong biaoyanchang	儿童表演唱	children's performance song
ertong chang	儿童唱	children's song (lit. "children sing")
ertong duichang	儿童对唱	children's duet
ertong gequ	儿童歌曲	children's song(s)
ertong shenghuo	儿童生活	(songs of) children's activities
feichang shuxi	非常熟习	extremely familiar
fenfa	奋发	rousing/energetic
fuxing	复兴	rejuvenation
gaizao	改造	reform
geming	革命	revolution

geming gequ	革命歌曲	revolutionary songs (type of mass song)
geminghua	革命化	revolutionize
geming jiaoxiang yinyue	革命交响音乐	revolutionary symphony
geming lishi gequ	革命历史歌曲	revolutionary history songs
geming lishi minge	革命历史民歌	revolutionary history folk songs
geming minge	革命民歌	revolutionary folk songs
geming wenhua	革命文化	revolutionary culture
geyao	歌谣	type of folk song (see Wagner 2001); also ballad
ge zu ertong xinsheng	各族儿童心声	voices of children of all ethnic groups
gongnongbing xueyuan	工农兵学员	worker-peasant-soldier students
gongren	工人	laboring class; workers
guanxianyue	管弦乐	orchestra
guoji waijiao guanxi	国际外交关系	international diplomatic relations
haochu	好处	good benefit; good traits or characteristics
haoting	好听	"sounds nice" or "pleasing to the ear"
Hei wu lei	黑五类	Five Categories of Black Elements (campaign)
hen pi	狠批	ruthless criticism
hen shen	很深	very deep
hong	红	red
Hongbaoshu	红宝书	lit. *Red Treasure Book* (commonly known as the *Little Red Book*)
Hongjun	红军	Red Army (predecessor to People's Liberation Army)
Hongjun gequ	红军歌曲	Red Army song(s)
Hongweibing	红卫兵	Red Guard(s)
Hongxiaobing	红小兵	Little Red Guard(s)
huai	坏	evil or bad
huankuai di	欢快地	lively or happily
huiyi	回忆	reminisce
huiyi duibi	回忆对比	comparing past and present
huopo di	活泼地	vivaciously or lively
jianding youli	坚定有力	staunchly or firm and strong
Jiefangjun	解放军	People's Liberation Army (PLA)
jinghu	京胡	two-stringed bowed lute used in Beijing opera
jinxingqu	进行曲	march
jinxing sudu	进行速度	march speed (tempo)
jiu fengsu	旧风俗	old customs
jiu sixiang	旧思想	old thinking
jiu wenhua	旧文化	old culture
jiu xiguan	旧习惯	old habits
kepa	可怕	frightful
kexuede, minzude, dazhongde	科学的，民族的，大众的	scientific, national, popular (policy)
laowai	老外	informal term for foreigner
liang	辆	measure word (a word used together with a numeral to describe the size/amount of a noun) used for a vehicle/group of vehicles
liang'an guanxi	两岸关系	cross-strait relations
man su	慢速	slow speed (tempo)
minglang	明朗	bright and clear
minzu	民族	encompasses both ethnicity and nationality; no direct translation

minzuhua	民族化	nationalize
nannü ertong chang	男女儿童唱	song for boy(s) and girl(s)
nannüsheng duichang	男女声对唱	duet (man and woman)
nannü xiaohechang	男女小合唱	mixed small chorus
nansheng biaoyanchang	男声表演唱	men's performance song
nansheng duchang	男声独唱	man's solo
nansheng ertong chang	男声儿童唱	boy's song
nansheng hechang	男声合唱	men's chorus
nansheng xiaohechang	男声小合唱	men's small chorus
nan zhongyin duchang	男中音独唱	men's baritone solo
Niu gui she shen	牛鬼蛇神	"Sweeping Away All the Monsters and Demons" (slogan)
nü gaoyin duchang	女高音独唱	soprano solo
nüsheng biaoyanchang	女声表演唱	women's performance song
nüsheng duchang	女声独唱	woman's solo
nüsheng ertong chang	女声儿童唱	girl's song
nüsheng hechang	女声合唱	women's chorus
nüsheng qichang	女声齐唱	women's chorus in unison
nüsheng tanchang	女声弹唱	woman/women play (an instrument) and sing
nüsheng xiaohechang	女声小合唱	women's small chorus
pidou	批斗	to criticize
Pi Lin pi Kong yundong	批林批孔运动	Campaign to Criticize Lin Biao and Confucius
Po si jiu	破四旧	Smash the Four Olds (campaign) (sometimes referred to as "Four Olds")
qian	前	forward
qijiao yisheng	赤脚医生	barefoot doctors
qinqie di	亲切地	affectionately
qun	群	measure word (a word used together with a numeral to describe the size/amount of a noun) commonly used for a crowd or large group of people
qunzhonghua	群众化	popularize
relie	热烈	warm(ly) or enthusiastic(ally)
Renmin gongshe yundong	人民公社运动	People's Commune Movement (campaign)
Renmin ribao	人民日报	*People's Daily* (newspaper)
renzhen	认真	serious or earnest
reqing/reqingde	热情/地	enthusiastically or passionately
Sanhua	三化	Three Processes of Transformation (policy)
Sanjiehe	三结合	Three-in-One Alliance (policy)
Sanmian hongqi	三面红旗	Three Red Banners (campaign)
shange duichang	山歌对唱	mountain song duet
Shangshan xiaxiang	上山下乡	Up to the Mountains and Down to the Countryside (campaign)
shao kuai	稍快	a little fast (upbeat tempo)
Shehuizhuyi jianshe zongluxian	社会主义建设总路线	General Line of Socialist Construction (campaign)
Shehuizhuyi jiaoyu yundong	社会主义教育运动	Socialist Education Movement (campaign)
shijian xing	时间性	time quality
"shou le hen duo ku"	受了很多苦	"suffered a lot of bitterness [pain/hardship]"
shushu	叔叔	uncle
Si jiu	四旧	Four Olds (campaign) (see Po si jiu)

Si qing yundong	四清运动	Four Cleanups (campaign)
Siren bang	四人帮	Gang of Four
songge	颂歌	songs of praise
taikepa	太可怕	so horrible
"ta meiyou chi guo ku"	她没有吃過苦	"she never tasted the bitter"
Tiantian du	天天读	Read Every Day (campaign)
tongsheng ertong chang	童声儿童唱	children's song
wanquan meiyou shiqing	完全没有事情	absolutely nothing to do
wei Maozhuxici puqu	为毛主席词谱曲	Mao poetry songs (the poetry of Chairman Mao set to music)
wendou	文斗	battle of words
women	我们	we
Wuchan jieji wenhua dageming	无产阶级文化大革命	Great Proletarian Cultural Revolution
wudou	武斗	battle of weapons
wuqi	武器	weapon
xiang	向	toward
xiao	小	small or little
xiaohechang	小合唱	small chorus
Xin minzhuzhuyilun	新民主主义论	*On New Democracy*
xiyue di	喜悦地	delightfully or joyfully
yangbanxi	样板戏	model revolutionary works
yiku sitian	忆苦思甜	recalling bitterness and reflecting on sweetness
youpai	右派	rightist
yulu ge	语录歌	quotation songs
"Zai Yan'an wenyi zuotanhui shang de jianghua"	在延安文艺座谈会上的讲话	"Talks at the Yan'an Conference on Literature and Art"
zhan	战	battle
zhandi huanghua fenwai xiang	战地黄花分外香	yellow flowers on the battlefield are especially fragrant
Zhandi xinge	战地新歌	*New Songs of the Battlefield*
zhaoqi pengbo di	朝气蓬勃地	vibrantly
zhengzhi huodong	政治活动	(songs of) political activities
Zhiqu Weihushan	智取威虎山	*Taking Tiger Mountain by Strategy*
zhishi qingnian	知识青年	"educated youth" or "sent-down youth"; generation sent out to the countryside throughout the Cultural Revolution period
Zhongluxian	总路线	General Line (campaign)
zhong su	中速	medium speed/tempo
zhuangyan di	庄严地	stately, solemnly
ziyou di	自由地	freely
zichanjieji	资产阶级	bourgeoisie

Song Titles

"Aerbaniya, wo qinmi de tongzhi he dixiong"	阿尔巴尼亚，我亲密的同志和弟兄	"Albania, My Dear Comrade and Brother"
"Beijing songge"	北京颂歌	"Song in Praise of Beijing"
"Caoyuan shang de hongweibing jian daole Mao zhuxi"	草原上的红卫兵见到了毛主席	"Red Guards on the Grasslands Have Met Chairman Mao"

"Dahai hangxing kao duoshou"　大海航行靠舵手　　"Sailing the Seas Depends on the Helmsman"

"Da tanke"　打坦克　　"Strike the Tanks"

"Dazhai renxin xiang hongtaiyang"　大寨人心向红太阳　　"The Heart of the Dazhai People Is toward the Red Sun"

"Dongfang hong"　东方红　　"East Is Red"

"Fanshen daoqing"　翻身道情　　"The Song of Emancipation"

"Geming qingnian jinxingqu"　革命青年进行曲　　"Marching Song of the Revolutionary Youth"

"Gongnong yijia ren"　工农一家人　　"Workers and Peasants Are All One Family"

"Lingdao women shiye de hexin liliang shi Zhongguo Gongchandang"　领导我们事业的核心力量是中国共产党　　"The Force at the Core Leading Our Cause Forward Is the Communist Party of China"

"San da jilu ba xiang zhuyi"　三大纪律八项注意　　"Three Main Rules of Discipline and Eight Points for Attention"

"Tielu xiudao Miaojiazhai"　铁路修到苗家寨　　"The Railways Are Built Up to the Miao Village"

"Tuolajishou zhi ge"　拖拉机手之歌　　"Song of the Tractor Drivers"

"Wo ai Beijing Tiananmen"　我爱北京天安门　　"I Love Beijing's Tiananmen"

"Wuchanjieji wenhua dageming jiu shi hao"　无产阶级文化大革命就是好　　"The Great Proletarian Cultural Revolution Is Indeed Good"

"Zhenxianbao shi chuanjiabao"　针线包是传家宝　　"Sewing Kit Is an Heirloom"

Names

Cheng Tan　程坦

Chiang Kai-shek　蒋介石　　also romanized as Chiang Chieh-shih or Jiang Jieshi; also known as Chiang Chung-cheng (蒋中正)

Fu Jing　傅晶

Gao Shiheng　高士衡

He Zhaohua　何兆华

Hong Yuan　洪源

Jiang Qing　江青

Jin Guolin　金果临

Jin Yueling　金月苓

Li Dequan　李德全

Mao Zedong　毛泽东

Shen Yawei　沈亚威

Tian Guang　田光

Zhou Enlai　周恩来

Committees, Groups, Organizations, and Political Parties

Chuangzuo zu　创作组　　Composition Committee

Gongxuandui　工宣队　　Workers Propaganda Team

Guomindang (see also Kuomintang)　国民党　　Nationalist Party (commonly Kuomintang or KMT)

Guowuyuan wenhuazu geming gequ zhengji xiaozu　国务院文化组革命歌曲征集小组　　Revolutionary Song Collection Task Force, Cultural Affairs Office under the State Council

Guowuyuan wenhuazu wenyi chuangzuo lingdao xiaozu	国务院文化组文艺创作领导小组	Literary and Artistic Creation Leadership Task Force, Cultural Affairs Office under the State Council
Kuomintang (see also Guomindang)	国民党	Nationalist Party (commonly Kuomintang or KMT)
Shanghai guangbo renmin diantai shao'er yuedui	上海廣播人民電台少兒樂隊	Shanghai People's Broadcasting Station Youth Orchestra
Shanghaishi gongren wenhuagong wenyi xuexiban	上海市工人文化宫文艺学习班	Literature and Art Study Class, City of Shanghai Workers' Cultural Palace
shaonian gongmin yuetuan	少年宫民乐团	"youth palace" Chinese orchestra
Zhandi xinge bianxuan xiaozu	战地新歌编选小组	*New Songs of the Battlefield* Editorial Committee
Zhongguo Gongchandang	中国共产党	Chinese Communist Party (CCP); also translated as Communist Party of China (CPC)
Zhongguo yishu yanjiuyuan yinyue yanjiusuo	中国艺术研究院音乐研究所	Music Research Institute of the Chinese Academy of Arts
Zhonghua Renmin Gongheguo	中华人民共和国	People's Republic of China (PRC)
Zhongyang guangbo wengongtuan guanxianyuetuan	中央广播文工团管弦乐团	Central Broadcasting Cultural Workers' Troupe Orchestra
Zongzheng xuanchuan dui	总政宣传队	Central Political Propaganda Team

Notes

Chapter 1. Researching the Battlefield

1. With much appreciation to Tomie Hahn (2006) for thoughtfully and intricately theorizing a process that unfolded for me throughout this fieldwork project.

2. Portions of this manuscript appeared in my dissertation (Bryant 2004) and earlier publications (Bryant 2005, 2007, 2018a, and 2018b). An earlier version of portions of chapters 1 and 3 first appeared as "Music, Memory, and Nostalgia: Collective Memories of Cultural Revolution Songs in Contemporary China" in *The China Review* 5, no. 2: 151–75 © 2005. Reprinted with permission of the Editorial Board of *The China Review*.

3. CCP (Chinese Communist Party) and CPC (Communist Party of China) are two acronyms commonly used as English translations of the Chinese Zhongguo Gongchandang (中国共产党); I use the former throughout this text.

4. Jiang Z. writes, "Collecting a complete set of 'New Songs from the Battlefield' is really a great event in my collecting career" (2008, 18). For more on flexi-discs, see Laurence Coderre's entry in *The Mao Era in Objects*.

5. The survey was conducted by the Shanghai branch of Horizon during January and February 2003. For further description of the anthology, see Bryant 2004.

6. See the several entries in the bibliography under East Asian Library, University Library System (ULS), University of Pittsburgh.

7. A reviewer commented on the 1994 summary and asked how this is similar or different in 2020, an excellent question. CCP descriptions of the Cultural Revolution have changed throughout different times in response to the current political climate. References to the Cultural Revolution can also change in nuanced ways depending on the context of a speech or publication. The scrutiny of such changes is worthy of critical attention but not the focus of the current study.

8. Notable English-language memoirs include Liang and Shapiro (1983), Cheng (1986), Y. Gao (1987), Luo (1990), Chang (1991), Min (1994), J.-L. Jiang (1997), Pomfret (2007), and L. Zhang (2008). This is by no means an exhaustive list but rather an example of continued publications of memoirs over several decades. See also discussion in chapter 4.

9. Much has been written on music in concentration camps, including Karas (1985) and Rovit and Goldfarb (1999).

Chapter 2. Music and Politics

Portions of this chapter originally appeared as "Flowers on the Battlefield Are More Fragrant" by Lei Ouyang Bryant from *Asian Music*, Volume 38, Number 1, pp. 88–121. Copyright © 2007. Courtesy of the University of Texas Press. All rights reserved. Special thanks to the guest editors for that issue and the reviewers for their constructive and detailed comments during the review process.

1. See Bryant (2004) for an extended discussion of format, organization, compilation, and editing as well as personal accounts from composers.

2. The "Great Proletarian Cultural Revolution" is the official name of the movement; however, I refer to the movement throughout this text using the abbreviated English translation "Cultural Revolution."

3. The original group included Peng Zhen, Lu Dingyi, Kang Sheng, Zou Yang, and Wu Lengxi.

4. Jiang Qing, Wang Hongwen, Zhang Chunqiao, and Yao Wenyuan were all brought to trial in 1981 for their actions during the Cultural Revolution; they served their sentences and were eventually released. Jiang passed away in 1991, Wang in 1992, and Zhang and Yao both died in 2005.

5. My use of the term *revolutionary* here is specifically as a political tool in the social revolution and does not suggest broader definitions of "vanguard" or "groundbreaking fashion."

6. Mao presented his talks in May 1942 and a text was published later in 1943. See Mao 1967 as one original Chinese-language publication of the Yan'an talks from the Cultural Revolution period. See McDougall 1980 for an English translation of Mao's 1942 talks (based upon the 1943 Chinese-language publication).

7. The Chinese term *minzu* has no direct English translation; the term encompasses English-language concepts of ethnicity and nationality. Though I have translated *minzuhua* as "nationalize," I conceptualize the term in its Chinese meaning, incorporating elements of both ethnicity and the nation. The concept of *minzu* has been problematized by many scholars, most notably Crossley (1990), Duara (1995), Gladney (1994), Harrell (1990), and Khan (1996); see also Rees (2000) and Baranovitch (2003) for case studies of music and ethnic minorities.

8. See Baranovitch (2003), Harris (2004), Rees (2000), and C.-F. Wong (2010) for case studies of music and ethnic minorities in China.

9. Similarly, Clark mentions the policy in regard to model revolutionary ballets but does not expand (2008, 163).

10. See Ju (1993) and Liang (1993) from the 1990s, and post-2000 see Du (2019), Ren (2020), Zhou Y. (2012), Chen F. (2006), Gao H. (2010), Jiang Z. (2008), Fu (2012), Wei Jun (2007), Wang G. (2008), Wei Jianbin (2011), and Zhang J. (2018).

11. Clark's examination of cultural production is not limited to music but also uses three periods to discuss the Cultural Revolution: 1966–68, 1968–71, and 1971–76 (see 2008, 250).

12. The *East Is Red* production offers a wealth of discussion and analysis; on dance see Wilcox (2018), on song see Gibbs (2018), and on theater see X. Chen (2002).

13. See http://www.morningsun.org/east/index.html.

14. The civil war was disrupted by the War of Resistance against Japan. The PRC considers 1949 as the end of the civil war, when the Communist Party took power of China; however, the Republic of China (the Nationalist government that fled to the island of Taiwan) did not declare the war over until 1991.

15. The instrumental designation of "Chinese" or "Western European" orchestra appears simply to identify instrument type; further analysis may demonstrate a diversity of musical styles detached from the traditionally prescribed style of the particular instrument.

16. Can also be translated as "Liu Shaoqi, who do you think you are?"

17. See S. Jones (1999) and Kouwenhoven and Schimmelpenninck (1997) as examples for further reading.

18. See Bryant (2004) for details (including comprehensive catalog of songs); Bryant (2007) for select examples; and Feng (2004) for a Chinese-language overview of the anthology.

19. Performance songs (*biaoyan ge* 表演歌) are simple songs (usually for two or more voices) that tell a simple story and are often accompanied by movements or dance; this type of song was commonly used during the May Fourth Movement (1919) and the War of Resistance against Japan (1937–45) (Zhongguo yishu yanjiuyuan 1984, 27; Wagner 2001).

20. Translations provided by a member of the Chinese Foreign Ministry in Beijing.

21. Chen Feng (2006) and Jiang Zhiwei (2008) both expand the categories beyond the four stated in the 1972 preface. Chen expands the list of four categories to six, whereas Jiang lists eight. Neither includes a stand-alone category for ethnic minorities. Chen lists one category as "new things," including the new socialist society, but also many references to the younger generations and another stand-alone category for Red Guards and Little Red Guards (73). Jiang's expansion to eight categories includes a separate category for "Cultural Revolution" songs as well as a separation of workers, peasants, and soldiers into three distinct categories of "industry," "agriculture," and "military" (18).

22. See Bryant (2004) for a complete catalog of the anthology including original Chinese title, English transliteration, and English translation.

23. Musical examples are all transcribed by me (with support from student research assistants) based on the printed cipher notation score, unless otherwise noted. We have attempted to maintain all original articulations and musical markings, aside from transferring cipher notation into staff notation.

24. It is difficult to obtain original recordings of the *New Songs of the Battlefield* anthology; therefore, it is impossible at this point to state conclusively that a cappella recordings do not exist. However, all of the recordings that I have collected include some type of instrumental accompaniment. Furthermore, I have never heard of an a cappella recording in my discussions with individuals familiar with the Cultural Revolution period.

25. Zhong, Wang, and Di (2001) and Min (1994) are merely two examples of many contemporary memoirs and narratives that address the defeminization of women during the Cultural Revolution. See also X. Chen (2002) and Yue (1993).

26. General trends in the instrumental arrangements may be observed, yet a complete set of original recordings is necessary to provide any substantial validation.

27. A large number of the songs included in the anthology are credited to work or military units or collective composition and editing teams rather than to individual composers (see Bryant 2004).

28. Gao H. (2010) specifically cites "The Great Proletarian Cultural Revolution Is Indeed Good" as an example of the stiff and rigid musical styling of the period. Gao also writes of the widespread dissemination of the song, resulting in long-lasting familiarity.

29. The Chinese lyrics use measure words (a word used together with a numeral to describe the size/amount of a noun) of *liang* (辆) and *qun* (群) that may be used for a variety of objects; the greatest distinction here is that *liang* usually refers to some sort of vehicle or group of vehicles, and *qun* is commonly used for a crowd or large group of people.

30. An original recording (China Record BM-267) obtained from the Cultural Revolution period includes an arrangement of the song lasting 1 minute 32 seconds wherein the song is sung three times (resulting in nine repetitions of the two-line chorus).

31. I do not know the ethnicity (Han, Mongolian, or other) of Gao Shiheng and Li Dequan. Based on conversations with editors and composers, it appears that it was common practice for Han Chinese composers to develop songs representing non-Han peoples, often employing stereotypical representations. Yet at times exceptions did occur where a composer from an ethnic minority group was able to more accurately represent the musical traditions of that ethnic group. See Gao H. (2010) for a discussion of three individuals (a composer, a lyricist, and a tenor) connected to one of the most well-known songs about Hainan Island who never actually visited the island before composing and performing the piece.

32. Enver Hoxha (1908–85) was a founder and leader of the Albanian Communist Party beginning in 1941; he served in Albania as president (from post–World War II

to 1985), prime minister (1944–54), and minister of foreign affairs (1946–53). Under Enver Hoxha, Albania supported China after the Sino-Soviet split in 1960.

33. With thanks to an anonymous reader for pointing me to Schoenhals's *Doing Things with Words in Chinese Politics: Five Studies* (1992) as a classic text on the topic of the CCP use of language in propaganda.

34. Once again, it is important to emphasize the agency of individuals and dispel any notion of a monolithic response; yet trends and patterns do emerge through qualitative ethnographic accounts and quantitative market research survey; see Bryant (2004) for a detailed discussion of accounts of inspiring effects.

Memories of the Battlefield: "It's in Your Bones, It's in Your Blood"

1. All quotes are from my personal interview with Zhang Haihui in 2018 unless otherwise noted.

2. See full details of the project at http://culturalrevolution.pitt.edu.

Chapter 3. Music and Childhood

An earlier version of chapter 3 first appeared as "'Tiny Little Screw Cap' ('*Xiao Xiao Luosimao*'): Children's Songs from the Chinese Cultural Revolution" in *Music and Politics*, 12(1) ©2018. Reprinted with permission of the Editors of *Music and Politics*. Special thanks to the two anonymous reviewers for their constructive and detailed comments during the review process of the article.

1. In fact, Chen Chaoxia notes a contemporary decline in quality, number, and impact of children's songs, both political and apolitical, and links it to a falloff in the dissemination of all types of music in general (2009, 499).

2. See Kouwenhoven and Schimmelpenninck (1997) and S. Jones (1999) for ethnographic accounts of music during the Cultural Revolution.

3. A complete chart of all sixty-five song titles (Chinese, English transliteration, and English translation) appears as appendix B.

4. See Li Cheng (2010) for additional discussion of musical modes in children's songs. For an introduction to five Chinese systems of pitch names/notation and Western counterparts, see Lam (n.d.); Y. Chen (2001); and Zhongguo yishu yanjiuyuan (1984).

5. See Liu J. (2014).

6. I interviewed roughly a dozen undergraduate students originally from China between 2006 and 2014; the interviews were a combination of casual, semiformal, and formal interviews.

7. See Chiu and Zheng (2008); and Liu and Lu (2014a, 2014b).

8. For a discussion of keywords in *New Songs of the Battlefield*, see Bryant (2004, 99–104). See also Clark (2008); X. Lu (2004); Mittler (2012); and A. Jones (2014).

9. All quotes in this section are from my personal interview with Chen Jiebing in 2015 unless otherwise noted.

10. From K.-S. Li: "During the Cultural Revolution the theory of 'family lineage' dominated people's lives. If a person had his 'class status' listed as landlord, rich peasant, counter-revolutionary, bad element, or rightist, then he himself, his family members, and his descendants would be labeled under the 'five categories of black elements'" (1995, 150).

11. See Campbell and Wiggins (2013).

Memories of the Battlefield: "Learning Music to Avoid Going 'Up to the Mountains and Down to the Countryside'"

1. East Asian Library, University Library System (ULS), University of Pittsburgh, "Learning Music to Avoid Going 'Up to the Mountains and Down to the Countryside'" [CR10-0057-BEJ] *China's Cultural Revolution in Memories: The CR/10 Project*, video, 11m:28s. August 10, 2016. https://digital.library.pitt.edu/islandora/object/pitt%3A7198656/viewer. ©2016. Reprinted with permission of Zhang Haihui, Head, East Asian Library, University Library System, University of Pittsburgh. See also East Asian Library, University Library System (ULS), University of Pittsburgh (2017).

Chapter 4. Music and Memory

Earlier versions of this analysis appear in Bryant (2004) and as "Music, Memory, and Nostalgia: Collective Memories of Cultural Revolution Songs in Contemporary China," in *The China Review* 5(2): 151–175 ©2005. Reprinted with permission of the Editorial Board of *The China Review*. Special thanks go to Guobin Yang and the team of reviewers and editors involved in the special issue.

1. See Barmé (1999); Boym (2001); and Yano (2002).

2. Pseudonym by request.

3. With the majority of schools and universities closed down during the Cultural Revolution, the cities were overwhelmed with students. In order to ease the burden on the urban scene, the government employed a campaign to send the youth out to the countryside to learn from the peasants. The "Up to the Mountains and Down to the Countryside" (Shangshan xiaxiang 上山下乡) campaign resulted in tens of thousands of students moving out to rural areas throughout China for manual labor in rural farming communities, state farms, or state factories. Great distances separated many families, and the majority of students did not return to the cities until the end of the Cultural Revolution. See K.-S. Li (1995); and G. Yang (2003, 2000).

4. For example, see Dujunco (2002).

5. All of the quotes from Wang Guowei in this section are from his 2014 personal interview.

6. A reader shared that music and sports were two commonly pursued areas of training that parents sought out in hopes of providing future opportunities for their children.

7. "Chen Xiaojie" is a pseudonym the interviewee requested. "Chen Xiaojie" is Chinese for "Ms. Chen"; a common surname, it has the similar effect as "Jane Doe" in English. All of the quotes from her in this section are from her 2015 personal interview.

8. With thanks to former colleague Dominique Vuvan for introducing me to the concept of the "reminiscence bump" and literature in the field of psychology.

9. See Bryant (2005).

Memories of the Battlefield: "You Hear These Songs and You Are Inspired"

1. Pseudonym by request; Jin is a common Chinese surname, and "Jin Laoshi" translates in English to "Professor" or "Teacher Jin."

2. See "She jiao yundong" (社教运动) and "Si Qing" (四清) in K.-S. Li (1995, 401 and 429).

3. All of the quotes from Jin Laoshi in this section are from her 2018 personal interview unless otherwise noted.

4. See X. Lu (2004, 58–61) for additional background on this slogan.

5. See Ho (2018) for one discussion of *yiku sitian*.

Chapter 5. Conclusions

1. Pseudonym by request.

2. Available in Chinese at http://cpc.people.com.cn/n/2015/1015/c64094–27699249. html.

3. See Canaves (2015); Chin (2015); J. Hu (2015); and C. Huang (2014a, 2015b).

4. "Rejuvenation" is a recurring theme in Xi's contemporary statements. In fact, in 2018 China launched the world's longest high-speed (bullet) train connecting Beijing and Shanghai, known as the "Fuxing bullet train." See http://www.xinhuanet.com/english/2018–06/30/c_137291690.htm.

Bibliography

Abu-Lughod, Lila. 1991. "Writing against Culture." In *Recapturing Anthropology: Working in the Present*, edited by Richard G. Fox, 137–62. Santa Fe, NM: School of American Research Press.

———. 2000. "Locating Ethnography." *Ethnography* 1, no. 2: 261–67.

Baranovitch, Nimrod. 2003. *China's New Voices: Popular Music, Ethnicity, Gender, and Politics, 1978–1997*. Berkeley: University of California Press.

Barmé, Geremie. 1999. *In the Red: On Contemporary Chinese Culture*. New York: Columbia University Press.

———. 2016. "Red Allure and the Crimson Blindfold." In *Red Legacies in China: Cultural Afterlives of the Communist Revolution*, edited by Jie Li and Enhua Zhang, 355–86. Cambridge, MA: Harvard University Asia Center.

Boehler, Patrick, and Vanessa Piao. 2015. "Xi Jinping's Speech on the Arts Is Released, One Year Later." *New York Times: Sinospheres*. 15 October 2015.

Boym, Svetlana. 2001. *The Future of Nostalgia*. New York: Basic Books.

Brauer, Juliane. 2016. "How Can Music Be Torturous? Music in Nazi Concentration and Extermination Camps." *Music and Politics* 10, no. 1: 1–34.

Bryant, Lei Ouyang. 2004. "'New Songs of the Battlefield': Songs and Memories of the Chinese Cultural Revolution." PhD diss., University of Pittsburgh. http://etd.library.pitt.edu/ETD/available/etd-05052004-205332/.

———. 2005. "Music, Memory, and Nostalgia: Collective Memories of Cultural Revolution Songs in Contemporary China." *China Review* 5, no. 2: 151–75.

———. 2007. "Flowers on the Battlefield Are More Fragrant." *Asian Music* 38, no. 1: 88–121.

———. 2009. "Performing Race and Place in Asian America." *Asian Music* 40, no. 1: 4–30.

———. 2018a. "Teaching Mao through Music: Pedagogy and Practice in the Liberal Arts Classroom." *Journal of Music History Pedagogy* 8, no. 2: 30–61.

———. 2018b. "'Tiny Little Screw Cap' ('Xiao Xiao Luosimao'): Children's Songs from the Chinese Cultural Revolution." *Music and Politics* 12, no. 1.

Campbell, Patricia Shehan. 2006. "Global Perspectives." In *The Child as Musician: A Handbook of Musical Development*, edited by G. E. McPherson, 415–38. Oxford: Oxford University Press.

Campbell, Patricia Shehan, and Carol Scott-Kassner. 2014. *Music in Childhood: From Preschool through the Elementary Grades*. 4th ed. Boston: Schirmer Cengage.

Campbell, Patricia Shehan, and Trevor Wiggins, eds. 2013. *The Oxford Handbook of Children's Musical Cultures*. New York: Oxford University Press.

Canaves, Sky. 2015. "Chinese President's Speech on the Arts: The Hollywood Connection." *ChinaFilmInsider*, 20 October 2015. http://chinafilminsider.com/chinese-presidents-speech-on-the-arts-the-hollywood-connection/.

Chang, Jung. 1991. *Wild Swans: Three Daughters of China*. New York: Simon and Schuster.

Chen Chaoxia 陈朝霞. 2009. "Qianyi dangdai Zhongguo ertong gequ fazhan tedian" 浅议当代中国儿童歌曲发展特点 [On the characteristics of the development of contemporary Chinese children's songs]. *Keji xinxi* 科技信息 [Science and technology information] 19:499–500.

Chen Feng 晨枫. 2006. "Wenhua dageming shi nian zhong de gequ (1966–1976): *Zhandi xinge* de bianji chuban ji qi yingxiang cong" "文化大革命"十年中的歌曲 (1966–1976)《战地新歌》的编辑出版及其影响 [Songs in the ten years of the Cultural Revolution (1966–1976): Editing, publishing, and influences of *New Songs of the Battlefield*]. *Gequ* 歌曲 [Song] 9:72–73.

Chen, Xiaomei. 1999. "Growing Up with Posters in the Maoist Era." In *Picturing Power in the People's Republic of China: Posters of the Cultural Revolution*, edited by Harriet Evans and Stephanie Donald, 101–22. Maryland: Rowman and Littlefield.

———. 2002. *Acting the Right Part: Political Theater and Popular Drama in Contemporary China*. Honolulu: University of Hawai'i Press.

———. 2017. *Staging Chinese Revolution: Theater, Film, and the Afterlives of Propaganda*. New York: Columbia University Press.

Chen, Yingshi. 2001. "Theory and Notation in China." In *Garland Encyclopedia of World Music Volume 7, East Asia: China, Japan, and Korea*, edited by Robert C. Provine, Yosihiko Tokumaru, and Lawrence J. Witzleben, 153–64. New York: Routledge.

Cheng, Nien. 1986. *Life and Death in Shanghai*. New York: Grove Press.

Chin, Josh. 2015. "A Year after Xi's Landmark Speech on the Arts, Some Things Get Left Out." *Wall Street Journal*, 15 October 2015. https://blogs.wsj.com/chinarealtime/2015/10/15/ayearafterxislandmarkspeechonthearts somethingsgetleftout/?reflink=desktopwebshare_permalink.

Chiu, Melissa, and Shengtian Zheng. 2008. *Art and China's Revolution*. New York: Asia Society; New Haven: in association with Yale University Press.

Clark, Paul. 2008. *The Chinese Cultural Revolution: A History*. New York: Cambridge University Press.

Clark, Paul, Laikwan Pang, and Tsan-huang Tsai, eds. 2016. *Listening to China's Cultural Revolution: Music, Politics, and Cultural Continuities*. New York: Palgrave Macmillan.

Coderre, Laurence. n.d. "Flexi-Disc." The Mao Era in Objects. Accessed 30 September 2021. https://maoeraobjects.ac.uk/object-biographies/flexi-disc/.

Cook, Alexander C., ed. 2014. *Mao's Little Red Book: A Global History*. New York: Cambridge University Press.

Coser, Lewis, ed. and trans. 1992. *Maurice Halbwachs: On Collective Memory*. The Heritage of Sociology. Chicago: University of Chicago Press.

Crossley, Pamela Kyle. 1990. "Thinking about Ethnicity in Early Modern China." *Late Imperial China* 11, no. 1: 1–34.

Dai Jiafang 戴嘉枋. 2004. "Fusu yu zai chenlun—lun 'Wenge' qijian *Zhandi xinge* zhong de gequ chuangzuo" 复苏与再沉沦—论"文革"期间《战地新歌》中的歌曲创作 [Resuscitation and re-degradation—on "Cultural Revolution" period *New Songs of the Battlefield* composition]. *Zhongyang yinyue xueyuan xuebao* 中央音乐学院学报 [Journal of the Central Conservatory of Music] 4:71–84.

Daughtry, Martin. 2015. *Listening to War: Sound, Music, Trauma, and Survival in Wartime Iraq*. New York: Oxford University Press.

Daxelmüller, Christoph. 1998. "Kulturell Formen und Aktivitäten als Teil der Überlebens- und Vernichtungsstrategie in den Konzentrationslagern." In *Die nationalsozialistischen Konzentrationslager. Entwicklung und Struktur*, edited by Christoph Dieckmann, Ulrich Herbert, and Karin Orth, 2 vols. (Göttingen: Wallstein Verlag) 2: 983–1005.

DeMare, Brian James. 2015. *Mao's Cultural Army: Drama Troupes in China's Rural Revolution*. Cambridge: Cambridge University Press.

Deng Liqun 邓力群, Ma Hong 马洪, and Wu Heng 武衡, eds. 1997. *Dangdai Zhongguo yinyue* 当代中国音乐 [Contemporary Chinese music]. Beijing: Zhongguo yishu yanjiuyuan yinyue yanjiu suo 中国艺术研究院音乐研究所 [Chinese National Academy of Arts, Music Research Institute].

Dolby, A. W. E. 1976. *A History of Chinese Drama*. London: P. Elek.

Du Yang 杜洋. 2019. "*Zhandi xinge* qu ji de yishu jiazhi" 《战地新歌》曲集的艺术价值 [The artistic value of the collection of *New Songs of the Battlefield*]. *Xiju zhi jia* 戏剧之家 [Home drama] 33:58.

Duara, Prasenjit. 1995. *Rescuing History from the Nation: Questioning Narratives of Modern China*. Chicago: University of Chicago Press.

Dujunco, Mercedes. 2002. "Hybridity and Disjuncture in Mainland Chinese Popular Music." In *Global Goes Local: Popular Culture in Asia*, edited by Timothy Craig and Richard King, 25–39. Vancouver: University of British Columbia Press.

Dutton, Michael. 1999. *Streetlife China*. Cambridge: Cambridge University Press.

East Asian Library, University Library System (ULS), University of Pittsburgh. 2016a. "Two People Born in the Same Year Have Completely Opposite Feelings about the Cultural Revolution" [CR10-0028-JIL]. *China's Cultural Revolution in Memories: The CR/10 Project*, video, 3m:35s. January 15, 2016. https://digital.library.pitt.edu/islandora/object/pitt%3A7198598/viewer.

———. 2016b. "After a few years in the Countryside, We Found out that China was not as simple as we had imagined" [CR10-0034-BEJ]. *China's Cultural Revolution in Memories: The CR/10 Project*, video, 16m:08s. July 15, 2016. https://digital.library .pitt.edu/islandora/object/pitt%3A7198622/viewer.

———. 2016c. "Learning Music to Avoid Going 'Up to the Mountains and Down to the Countryside'" [CR10-0057-BEJ]. *China's Cultural Revolution in Memories: The CR/10 Project*, video, 11m:28s. August 10, 2016. https://digital.library.pitt.edu/ islandora/object/pitt%3A7198656/viewer.

———. 2017. "'Long live Chairman Mao; good health to Vice Chairman Lin!': Vivid Memories from the Countryside" [CR10-0008-HEB]. *China's Cultural Revolution in Memories: The CR/10 Project*, video, 17m:43s. March 27, 2017. https://digital .library.pitt.edu/islandora/object/pitt%3A7198579/viewer.

———. 2018. *China's Cultural Revolution in Memories: The CR/10 Project*. July 10, 2018.http://culturalrevolution.pitt.edu

Esherick, Joseph W., Paul G. Pickowicz, and Andrew G. Walder. 2006. *The Chinese Cultural Revolution as History*. Stanford: Stanford University Press.

Fackler, Guido. 2007. "Music in Concentration Camps 1933–1945." Translated from the German by Peter Logan (Wurzburg). *Music and Politics* 1, no. 1: 1–25.

Fairbank, John King. 1987. *The Great Chinese Revolution, 1800–1985*. New York: Harper Perennial.

Feng Zhiping 冯志平. 2004. "*Zhandi xinge* chubu yanjiu" 《战地新歌》初步研究 [Initial research on *New Songs of the Battlefield*]. *Yinyue yanjiu* 音乐研究 [Music research] 1: 79–87.

Fu Xiaoyu 符晓钰. 2012. "Yinyue yu shidai—yi 'wenge' shiqi gequ tedian wei li" 音乐 与时代—以 "文革" 时期歌曲特点为例 [Music and the times—taking the characteristics of songs during the "Cultural Revolution" as an example]. *Huanghe zhi sheng* [Song of the Yellow River] 18:38–39.

Gao Hong 高虹. 2010. "*Wo ai Wuzhishan, wo ai Wanquanhe* dansheng shimo" 《我 爱五指山, 我爱万泉河 》诞生始末 [*I love Wuzhishan, I love Wanquan River* the whole story]. *Chuancheng*传承 [Inheritance and innovation] 1:26–27.

Gao, Mobo C. F. 2008. *The Battle for China's Past: Mao and the Cultural Revolution*. London: Pluto Press.

Gao, Yuan. 1987. *Born Red: A Chronicle of the Cultural Revolution*. Stanford: Stanford University Press.

Gibbs, Levi S. 2018. *Song King: Connecting People, Places, and Past in Contemporary China*. Honolulu: University of Hawai'i Press.

Gilman, Lisa. 2016. *My Music, My War: The Listening Habits of U.S. Troops in Iraq and Afghanistan*. Middletown, CT: Wesleyan University Press.

Gladney, Dru. 1994. "Representing Nationality in China: Refiguring Majority/ Minority Identities." *Journal of Asian Studies* 53, no. 1: 92–123.

Glück, Judith, and Susan Bluck. 2007. "Looking Back across the Life Span: A Life Story Account of the Reminiscence Bump." *Memory and Cognition* 35, no. 8: 1928–39.

Gold, Thomas B. 1980. "Back to the City: The Return of Shanghai's Educated Youth." *China Quarterly* 84:55–70.

Günel, Gökçe, Saiba Varma, and Chika Watanabe. 2020. "A Manifesto for Patchwork Ethnography." Member Voices, *Fieldsights*, 9 June 2020. https://culanth.org/fieldsights/a-manifesto-for-patchwork-ethnography.

Guo Chao 郭超. 2017. "Zenyang rang jintian de haizi yongyou ziji de erge" 怎样让今天的孩子拥有自己的儿歌 [How to let today's children have their own children's songs]. *Guangming ribao* 光明日报 [Enlightenment daily], 14 June 2017: 9.

Hahn, Tomie. 2006. "Emerging Voices: Encounters with Reflexivity." *Atlantis* 30, no. 2: 88–99.

———. 2007. *Sensational Knowledge: Embodying Culture through Japanese Dance.* Middletown, CT: Wesleyan University Press.

Halbwachs, Maurice. (1950) 1980. *The Collective Memory.* New York: Harper.

———. 1992. *On Collective Memory.* Edited, translated, and with an introduction by Lewis A. Coser. The Heritage of Sociology. Chicago: University of Chicago Press.

Harding, Harry. 1993. "The Succession to Mao and the End of Maoism, 1969–1982." In *The Politics of China, 1949–1989,* edited by Roderick MacFarquhar, 248–339. Cambridge: Cambridge University Press.

———. 1997. "The Chinese State in Crisis, 1966–9." In *The Politics of China: The Eras of Mao and Deng,* edited by Roderick MacFarquhar, 148–247. New York: Cambridge University Press.

Harrell, Stevan. 1990. "Ethnicity, Local Interest, and the State: Yi Communities in Southwest China." *Comparative Studies in Society and History* 32, no. 2: 515–48.

Harris, Rachel. 2004. *Singing the Village: Music, Memory, and Ritual among the Sibe of Xinjiang.* Oxford: Oxford University Press.

Hinton, Harold C., ed. 1980. *The People's Republic of China, 1949–1979.* Wilmington, DE: Scholarly Resources.

Ho, Denise Y. 2018. *Curating Revolution: Politics on Display in Mao's China.* Cambridge: Cambridge University Press.

Holm, David. 1984. "Folk Art as Propaganda: The *Yangge* Movement in Yan'an." In *Popular Chinese Literature and Performing Arts in the People's Republic of China, 1949–1979,* edited by Bonnie S. McDougall, 3–35. Berkeley: University of California Press.

Hsu, Immanuel C. Y. 1995. *The Rise of Modern China.* Oxford: Oxford University Press and University of California Press.

Hu, Jack. 2015. "The Dark Historical Context Surrounding Chinese President Xi's Arts Speech." *Global Voices,* 24 October 2015. https://globalvoices.org/2015/10/24/%E2%80%8Bthe-dark-historical-context-surrounding-chinese-president-xis-arts-speech/.

Hu, Sheng, ed. 1994. *A Concise History of the Communist Party of China: Seventy Years of the CPC.* Beijing: Foreign Languages Press.

Huang, Cary. 2014a. "Xi, Mao and the Dark Art of Ideology." *South China Morning Post,* 21 October 2014. http://www.scmp.com/news/china/article/1620884/xi-mao-and-dark-art-ideology.

———. 2014b. "Xi Jinping's Call for Political Art Evokes Bad Memories of Cultural Revolution." *South China Morning Post*, 26 October 2014. http://www.scmp.com/comment/insight-opinion/article/1624554/xi-jinpings-call-political-art-evokes-bad-memories-cultural.

Huang, Zheping. 2018. "China's Huge Celebrations of Karl Marx Are Not Really about Marxism." *Quartz*, 4 May 2018. https://qz.com/1270109/chinas-communist-party-and-xi-jinping-are-celebrating-the-200th-birthday-of-karl-marx-with-a-vengeance/.

Jansari, Ashok, and Alan J. Parkin. 1996. "Things That Go Bump in Your Life: Explaining the Reminiscence Bump in Autopbiographical Memory." *Psychology and Aging* 11, no. 1: 85–91.

Janssen, Steve, Antonio Chessa, and Jaap Murre. 2005. "The Reminiscence Bump in Autobiographical Memory: Effects of Age, Gender, Education, and Culture." *Memory* 13, no. 6: 658–68.

Jiang, Ji-Li. 1997. *Red Scarf Girl: A Memoir of the Cultural Revolution*. New York: Harper Collins.

Jiang Zhiwei 江志伟. 2008. "'Wenge' zhencang pin *Zhandi xinge*" "文革" 珍藏品 《战地新歌》 ["Cultural Revolution" collection *New Songs of the Battlefield*]. *Beifang yinyue* 北方音乐 [Northern music] 10:18.

Jones, Andrew. 2014. "Quotation Songs: Portable Media and the Maoist Pop Song." In *Mao's Little Red Book: A Global History*, edited by Alexander C. Cook, 43–60. New York: Cambridge University Press.

Jones, Stephen. 1999. "Chinese Ritual Music under Mao and Deng." *British Journal of Ethnomusicology* 8:27–66.

Ju Qihong 居其宏. 1993. *20 shiji Zhongguo yinyue* 20世纪中国音乐 [20th century Chinese music]. Qingdao: Qingdao chubanshe 青岛出版社 [Qingdao Publishing House].

Karas, Joža. 1985. *Music in Terezín, 1941–1945*. Stuyvesant, NY: Pendragon Press.

Khan, Almaz. 1996. "Who Are the Mongols? State, Ethnicity, and the Politics of Representation in the PRC." In *Negotiating Ethnicities in China and Taiwan*, edited by M. J. Brown, 125–29. Berkeley: Institute of East Asian Studies, University of California, Berkeley, Center for Chinese Studies.

King, Richard, ed. 2010. *Art in Turmoil: The Chinese Cultural Revolution, 1966–1976*. Vancouver: University of British Columbia Press.

King, Richard, and Jan Walls. 2010. "Introduction: Vibrant Images of a Turbulent Decade." In *Art in Turmoil: The Chinese Cultural Revolution, 1966–1976*, edited by Richard King, 3–24. Vancouver: University of British Columbia Press.

Kouwenhoven, Frank, and Antoinet Schimmelpenninck. 1997. "Guo Wenjing—a Composer's Portrait: 'The Strings Going *Hong Hong Hong* and the Percussion *Bong Keeh*—That's My Voice!'" *CHIME* 10–11: 8–49.

Kwon, Donna. 2019. "Discrepant Kisses: The Reception and Remediation of North Korean Children's Performances Circulated on Social Media." *Music and Politics* 13, no. 1: 1–20.

Lam, Joseph. n.d. "China." *Oxford Music Online*. Accessed 1 December 2017. http://www.oxfordmusiconline.com:80/subscriber/article/grove/music/43141pg2.

Lee, Gregory. 1995. "The 'East Is Red' Goes Pop: Commodification, Hybridity and Nationalism in Chinese Popular Song and Its Televisual Performance." *Popular Music* 14, no. 1: 95–110.

Leiberthal, Kenneth. 1997. "The Great Leap Forward and the Split in the Yan'an Leadership, 1958–65." In *The Politics of China: The Eras of Mao and Deng*, edited by Roderick MacFarquhar, 87–147. New York: Cambridge University Press.

Li Cheng 李成. 2010. "Shilun 'wenge' shiqi de ertong gequ jiqi chuangzuo tezheng" 试论 "文革" 时期的儿童歌曲及其创作特征 [On children's songs and their creative features in the "Cultural Revolution" period]. *Yinyue tansuo* 音樂探索 [Explorations in music] 3:35–37.

Li Chunyan 李春雁. 2004. "'Wenge' shiqi de yuyan bianyi—yi *Zhandi xinge* geci wei li" "文革"时期的语言变异—以《战地新歌》歌词为例 [Language variation during the "Cultural Revolution" period—in *New Songs of the Battlefield* lyric examples]. *Liaoning gongxueyuan xuebao* 辽宁工学院学报 [Journal of the Liaoning Institute of Technology] 6, no. 5: 52–54.

Li, Jie. 2016. "Introduction: Discerning Red Legacies in China." In *Red Legacies in China: Cultural Afterlives of the Communist Revolution*, edited by Jie Li and Enhua Zhang, 1–22. Cambridge, MA: Harvard University Asia Center.

Li, Jie, and Enhua Zhang, eds. 2016. *Red Legacies in China: Cultural Afterlives of the Communist Revolution*. Cambridge, MA: Harvard University Asia Center.

Li, Kwok-Sing. 1995. *A Glossary of Political Terms of the People's Republic of China*. Translated by Marky Lok. Hong Kong: Chinese University Press.

Liang, Heng, and Judith Shapiro. 1983. *Son of the Revolution*. New York: Knopf.

Liang Maochun 梁茂春. 1993. *Zhongguo dangdai yinyue 1949–1989* 中国当代音乐 1949–1989 [Contemporary music of China 1949–1989]. Beijing: Beijing guangbo xueyuan chubanshe 北京广播学院出版社 [Beijing Broadcasting Institute Publishing House].

———. 2003. "Lun 'yuluge' xianxiang" 论"语录歌"现象 [On the phenomena of songs of Chairman Mao's quotations]. *Wuhan yinyue xueyuan xuebao* 武汉音乐学院学报 [Journal of Wuhan Conservatory of Music] 1:43–52.

———. 2008. "Lun 'wenge' shiqi de yishu gequ" 论"文革"时期的艺术歌曲 [On art songs of the "Cultural Revolution" period]. *Zhongyang yinyue xueyuan xuebao* 中央音乐学院学报 [Journal of the Central Conservatory of Music] 1:31–43.

Liu, Ding, and Carol Yinghua Lu. 2014a. "From the Issue of Art to the Issue of Position: The Echoes of Socialist Realism, Part I." *e-flux* 55. http://www.e-flux.com/journal/55/60315/from-the-issue-of-art-to-the-issue-of-position-the-echoes-of-socialist-realism-part-i/.

———. 2014b. "From the Issue of Art to the Issue of Position: The Echoes of Socialist Realism, Part II." *e-flux* 56. http://www.e-flux.com/journal/56/60367/from-the-issue-of-art-to-the-issue-of-position-the-echoes-of-socialist-realism-part-ii/.

Liu Jing 刘靖. 2014. "'Wenge' shiqi Zhongguo ertong gequ tanjiu—yi *Zhandi xinge weili*" "文革"时期中国儿童歌曲探究—以《战地新歌》为例 [A study of Chinese children's songs in the "Cultural Revolution" period—taking the *New Songs of the Battlefield* as an example]. *Bianjiang jingji yu wenhua* 边疆经济与文化 [The border economy and culture] 11, no. 131: 125–26.

Liu, Terence M. 2001. "Instruments: Erhu." In *Garland Encyclopedia of World Music Volume 7, East Asia: China, Japan, and Korea,* edited by Robert C. Provine, Yosihiko Tokumaru, and Lawrence J. Witzleben, 213–16. New York: Routledge.

Lu Lin 吕麟, Wang Anguo 王安国, Qiao Jianzhong 乔建中, Liang Maochun 梁茂春, Ju Qihong 居其宏, Cai Huoxing 曹火星, and Dai Penghai 戴鹏海. 1987. "Dangdai yinyue yantao hui shang de fa yan" 当代音乐研讨会上的发言 [Speech at the Contemporary Music Symposium]. *Renmin yinyue* 人民音乐 [People's music] 12:4–8.

Lu, Sheldon Hsiao-peng. 1996. "Postmodernity, Popular Culture, and the Intellectual: A Report on Post-Tiananmen China." *Boundary2* 23, no. 2: 139–69.

———. 2007. *Chinese Modernity and Global Biopolitics: Studies in Literature and Visual Culture.* Honolulu: University of Hawai'i Press.

Lu, Xing. 2004. *Rhetoric of the Chinese Cultural Revolution: The Impact on Chinese Thought, Culture, and Communication.* Columbia: University of South Carolina Press.

———. 2017. *The Rhetoric of Mao Zedong: Transforming China and Its People.* Columbia: University of South Carolina Press.

Luo, Zi-Ping. 1990. *A Generation Lost: China under the Cultural Revolution.* New York: H. Holt.

MacFarquhar, Roderick, ed. 1993. *The Politics of China, 1949–1989.* Cambridge: Cambridge University Press.

MacFarquhar, Roderick, and Michael Schoenhals. 2006. *Mao's Last Revolution.* Cambridge, MA: Belknap Press of Harvard University Press.

Manabe, Noriko. 2013. "Songs of Japanese Schoolchildren during World War II." In *The Oxford Handbook of Children's Musical Cultures,* edited by Patricia Shehan Campbell and Trevor Wiggins, 96–113. New York: Oxford University Press.

Mao Zedong 毛泽东. 1954. *On New Democracy.* Peking: Foreign Languages Press.

———. 1967. *Zai Yan'an wenyi zuotanhui shang de jianghua* 在延安文艺座谈会 [Talks at the Yan'an Conference on Literature and Art]. Beijing: Renmin chubanshe 北京：人民出版社 [Beijing: People's Publishing House].

Marshall, Alex. 2018. "Can You Tell a Lullaby from a Love Song? Find Out Now." *New York Times,* 25 January 2018.

McDougall, Bonnie S. 1980. *Mao Zedong's "Talks at the Yan'an Conference on Literature and Art": A Translation of the 1943 Text with Commentary.* Ann Arbor: Center for Chinese Studies, University of Michigan.

———, ed. 1984. *Popular Chinese Literature and Performing Arts in the People's Republic of China, 1949–1979.* Berkeley: University of California Press.

McLaren, Anne. 1979. "The Educated Youth Return: The Poster Campaign in Shanghai from November 1978 to March 1979." *Australian Journal of Chinese Affairs* 2:1–20.

Meisner, Maurice. 1986. *Mao's China and After: A History of the People's Republic.* New York: Free Press.

———. 1999. *Mao's China and After: A History of the People's Republic.* 3rd ed. New York: Free Press.

Merriam, Alan. 1964. *The Anthropology of Music.* Evanston, IL: Northwestern University Press.

Milewski, Barbara. 2014. "Remembering the Concentration Camps: Aleksander Kulisiewicz and His Concerts of Prisoners' Songs in the Federal Republic of Germany." In *Dislocated Memories: Jews, Music, and Postwar German Culture,* edited by Tina Frühauf and Lily Hirsch, 141–60. New York: Oxford University Press.

Min, Anchee. 1994. *Red Azalea.* New York: Pantheon.

Mittler, Barbara. 2008. "Popular Propaganda? Art and Culture in Revolutionary China." *Proceedings of the American Philosophical Society* 152, no. 4: 466–89.

———. 2010. "'Eight Stage Works for 800 Million People': The Great Proletarian Cultural Revolution in Music—a View from Revolutionary Opera." *Opera Quarterly* 26 (2–3): 377–401.

———. 2012. *A Continuous Revolution: Making Sense of Cultural Revolution Culture.* Cambridge, MA: Harvard University Asia Center.

———. 2016. "Just Beat It! Popular Legacies of Cultural Revolution Music." In *Listening to China's Cultural Revolution: Music, Politics, and Cultural Continuities,* edited by Paul Clark, Laikwan Pang, and Tsan-huang Tsai, 239–68. New York: Palgrave Macmillan.

New China TV. 2017. "The Belt and Road Is How" (music video). YouTube, 10 May 2017. https://youtu.be/MolJc3PMNIg.

Oliver, John. 2018. "Xi Jinping: *Last Week Tonight with John Oliver* (HBO)." YouTube, 17 June 2018. https://youtu.be/OubM8bD9kck.

Pease, Rowan. 2016. "The Dragon River Reaches the Borders: The Rehabilitation of Ethnic Music in a Model Opera." In *Listening to China's Cultural Revolution: Music, Politics, and Cultural Continuities,* edited by Paul Clark, Laikwan Pang, and Tsan-huang Tsai, 167–86. New York: Palgrave Macmillan.

Perris, Arnold. 1983. "Music as Propaganda: Art at the Command of Doctrine in the People's Republic of China." *Ethnomusicology* 27, no. 1: 1–28.

Perry, Elizabeth J. 2012. *Anyuan: Mining China's Revolutionary Tradition.* Berkeley: University of California Press.

Pomfret, John. 2007. *Chinese Lessons: Five Classmates and the Story of the New China.* New York: Holt.

Qiao Jianzhong 乔建中. 1974. "Liaoliang de wuchan jieji zhange—zan *Zhandi xinge* di san ji" 嘹亮的无产阶级战歌—赞《战地新歌》第三集 [Loud and clear proletarian battle songs—in praise of the third volume of *New Songs of the Battlefield*]. *Shandong wenyi* 山东文艺 [Shandong literature monthly magazine] Z1: 103–5.

Quackenbush, Casey, and Aria Hangyu Chen. 2018. "'Tasteless, Vulgar and Obscene.' China Just Banned Hip-Hop Culture and Tattoos from Television." *Time,* 22 January 2018. http://time.com/5112061/china-hip-hop-ban-tattoos-television/.

Qureshi, Regula. 1995. "Music Anthropologies and Music Histories: A Preface and an Agenda." *Journal of the American Musicological Society* 48, no. 3: 331–42.

Ramzy, Austin. 2014. "Xi Jinping Calls for Artists to Spread 'Chinese Values.'" *New York Times: Sinospheres*, 16 October 2014.

Rao, Nancy Yunhwa. 2016. "Sonic Imaginary after the Cultural Revolution." In *Listening to China's Cultural Revolution: Music, Politics, and Cultural Continuities*, edited by Paul Clark, Laikwan Pang, and Tsan-huang Tsai, 213–38. New York: Palgrave Macmillan.

Rees, Helen. 2000. *Echoes of History: Naxi Music in Modern China*. New York: Oxford University Press.

Ren Weixin 任卫新. 2020. "Zheng Nan yu Hainan liang shou geci" 郑南与海南两首歌词 [Zheng Nan and lyrics of two Hainan songs]. *Ci kan* 词刊 [Journal of words] 136:46–54.

Ross, Alex. 2016. "When Music Is Violence" (originally titled "The Sound of Hate"). *New Yorker*, 4 July 2016, 65–69.

Rovit, Rebecca, and Alvin Goldfarb. 1999. *Theatrical Performance during the Holocaust*. Baltimore: Johns Hopkins University Press.

Sant Cassia, Paul. 2000. "Exoticizing Discourses and Extraordinary Experiences: 'Traditional' Music, Modernity and Nostalgia in Malta and other Mediterranean Societies." *Ethnomusicology* 44, no. 2: 299.

Schoenhals, Michael. 1992. *Doing Things with Words in Chinese Politics: Five Studies*. Berkeley: Institute of East Asian Studies, University of California.

Schuman, Howard, and Jacqueline Scott. 1989. "Generations and Collective Memories." *American Sociological Review* 54, no. 3: 359–81.

Spence, Jonathan. 1990. *The Search for Modern China*. New York: W. W. Norton.

———. 1999. *Mao Zedong*. New York: Penguin Putnam.

Storr, Anthony. 1992. *Music and the Mind*. New York: Free Press.

Taking Tiger Mountain by Strategy: The Story of the Modern Peking Opera. 1972. Peking: Foreign Languages Press.

Tang, Xiaobing. 2016. "Socialist Visual Experience as Cultural Identity: On Wang Guangyi and Contemporary Art." In *Red Legacies in China: Cultural Afterlives of the Communist Revolution*, edited by Jie Li and Enhua Zhang, 115–48. Cambridge, MA: Harvard University Asia Center.

Tuohy, Sue. 1999. "The Social Life of Genre: The Dynamics of Folksong in China." *Asian Music* 30, no. 2: 39–86.

———. 2001. "The Sonic Dimensions of Nationalism in Modern China: Musical Representation and Transformation." *Ethnomusicology* 45, no. 1: 107–31.

Turino, Thomas. 2000. *Nationalists, Cosmopolitans, and Popular Music in Zimbabwe*. Chicago: University of Chicago Press.

———. 2008. *Music as Social Life: The Politics of Participation*. Chicago: University of Chicago Press.

Wagner, Vivian. 2001. "Songs of the Red Guards: Keywords Set to Music." University of Heidelberg working paper. http://academics.wellesley.edu/Polisci/wj/China/CRSongs/wagner-redguards_songs.html.

Wang, Ban. 1997. *The Sublime Figure of History: Aesthetics and Politics in Twentieth-Century China*. Stanford: Stanford University Press.

Wang Guixia 王桂霞, Liu Yunyan 刘云燕, and Li Xiaowei 李晓微. 2008. "Buxie de zhuiqiu buxiu de jilu—lishi wutai shang de *Zhandi xinge*" 不懈的追求不朽的记录—历史舞台上的《战地新歌》[Relentless pursuit immortal record—*New Songs of the Battlefield* on the historical stage]. *Dazhong wenyi* 大众文艺 [Popular literature] 12:78–79.

Wang Haiyuan 汪海元. 2011. "'Wenge' shiqi de erhu yinyue chuangzuo" "文革" 时期的二胡音乐创作 [Erhu music creation during the "Cultural Revolution"]. *Renmin yinyue* 人民音乐 [People's music] 6:32–35.

Wang, James C. F. 1998. *Contemporary Chinese Politics: An Introduction*. New Jersey: Prentice Hall.

Wei Jianbin 韦建斌. 2011. "Jian shu 'Wenge' shiqi dizi duzou qu de chuangzuo" 简述 "文革"时期笛子独奏曲的创作 [A brief introduction to the creation of dizi solo during the "Cultural Revolution"]. *Renmin yinyue* 人民音乐 [People's music] 12:30–33.

Wei Jun 魏军. 2000. "*Zhandi xinge* de lishi yuanyuan ji qi pingxi" 《战地新歌》的历史渊源及其评析 [Historical origin of *New Songs of the Battlefield* and analysis of it]. *Ezhou daxue xuebao* 鄂州大学学报 [Journal of Ezhou University] 7, no. 1: 14–17.

———. 2005. "*Zhandi xinge* chutan" 《战地新歌》初探 [Preliminary exploration of *New Songs of the Battlefield*]. *Nanjing yishuxueyuan xuebao* 南京艺术学院学报 [Journal of Nanjing Arts Institute] 4:65–69.

———. 2007. "Zai kan *Zhandi xinge* de lishi yuanyuan" 再看《战地新歌》的历史渊源 [Revisiting the historical origin of *New Songs of the Battlefield*]. *Shidai jiaoyu* 时代教育 [Time education] 29:26.

———. 2009. "*Zhandi xinge*: 'Wenge' yinyue de lishi zhuanxing" 《战地新歌》: "文革"音乐的历史转型 [*New Songs of the Battlefield*: Historical transformation of "Cultural Revolution" music]. *Wuhan yinyue xueyuan xuebao* 武汉音乐学院学报 [Journal of Wuhan Conservatory of Music] 3:111–18.

Wilcox, Emily. 2018. *Revolutionary Bodies: Chinese Dance and the Socialist Legacy*. Oakland: University of California Press.

Wong, Chuen-Fung. 2010. "Representing the Minority Other in Chinese Music." In *Reading Chinese Music and Beyond*, edited by Joys H. Y. Cheung and King Chung Wong, 121–45. Hong Kong: Chinese Civilisation Centre, City University of Hong Kong.

Wong, Isabel K. F. 1984. "Geming Gequ: Songs for the Education of the Masses." In *Popular Chinese Literature and Performing Arts in the People's Republic of China, 1949–1979*, edited by Bonnie S. McDougall, 112–43. Berkeley: University of California Press.

Xi Jinping. 2014. *The Governance of China*. Beijing: Foreign Languages Press.

———. 2017. "Secure a Decisive Victory in Building a Moderately Prosperous Society in All Respects and Strive for the Great Success of Socialism with Chinese Characteristics for a New Era." Delivered at the 19th National Congress of the Communist

Party of China, 18 October 2017. English version accessed at http://www.chinadaily
.com.cn/china/19thcpcnationalcongress/2017–11/04/content_34115212.htm.

Yan, Jiaqi, and Gao Gao. 1996. *Turbulent Decade: A History of the Cultural Revolution.* Honolulu: University of Hawai'i Press, SHAPS Library of Translations.

Yan, Yunxiang. 2009. *The Individualization of Chinese Society.* Oxford: Berg.

Yang, Guobin. 2000. "China's Red Guard Generation: The Ritual Process of Identity Transformation, 1966–1999." PhD diss., New York University.

———. 2003. "China's Zhiqing Generation: Nostalgia, Identity, and Cultural Resistance in the 1990s." *Modern China* 29, no. 3: 267–96.

Yang, Hon-Lun. 2007. "Power, Politics, and Musical Commemoration: Western Musical Figures in the People's Republic of China 1949–1964." *Music and Politics* 1, no. 2: 1–14.

Yano, Christine. 2002. *Tears of Longing: Nostalgia and the Nation in Japanese Popular Song.* Cambridge, MA: Harvard University Asia Center, distributed by Harvard University Press.

Yue, Meng. 1993. "Female Images and National Myth." In *Gender Politics in Modern China: Writing and Feminism,* edited by Tani E. Barlow, 118–36. Durham, NC: Duke University Press.

Yung, Bell. 1984. "Model Opera as Model: From *Shajiabang* to *Sagabong.*" In *Popular Chinese Literature and Performing Arts in the People's Republic of China, 1949–1979,* edited by Bonnie S. McDougall, 144–64. Berkeley: University of California Press.

Zhang Juan 张娟. 2018. "Zhiqing gequ de gainian liding ji qi lishi fenqi" 知青歌曲的概念厘定及其历史分期 [The conceptualization of educated youth songs and its historical stages]. *Renmin yinyue* 人民音乐 [People's music] 8:82–85.

Zhang, Lijia. 2008. *"Socialism Is Great!": A Worker's Memoir of the New China.* New York: Atlas and Co.

Zhengge bianxuan xiaozu 征歌编选小组 [Song Collection Editorial and Selection Committee]. 1977. *Shiyue zhange: Quanguo zhengge xuanji* 《十月战歌: 全国征歌选集 》 [October battle songs: National song collection]. Beijing: Renmin yinyue chubanshe 人民音乐出版社 [People's Music Publishing House].

Zhong, Xueping, Wang Zheng, and Bai Di, eds. 2001. *Some of Us: Chinese Women Growing Up in the Mao Era.* New Brunswick, NJ: Rutgers University Press.

Zhongguo yishu yanjiuyuan 中国艺术研究院 [Chinese Academy of Arts]. 1984. *Zhongguo yinyue cidian* 中国音乐词典 [Chinese music dictionary]. Edited by Miu Tianrui 谬天瑞, Ji Liankang 吉联抗, and Guo Naian 郭乃安. Beijing: Renmin yinyue chubanshe 人民音乐出版社 [People's Music Publishing House].

Zhou Heqing 周河清. 2013. "Wenhua duanceng hou de jixu tansuo—Wang Xilin *Di wu jiaoxiang qu* jiazhi tanxi" 文化断层后的继续探索—王西麟《第五交响曲》价值探析 [Continuing exploration after cultural fault—an analysis of the value of Wang Xilin's *The Fifth Symphony*]. *Renmin yinyue* 人民音乐 [People's music] 11:25–27.

Zhou Yun 周耘. 2012. "Hongge: Teding shidai de lishi jiyi" 红歌: 特定时代的历史记忆 [Hongge (red songs): The historical memory of a particular era]. *Wuhan yinyue xueyuan xuebao* 武汉音乐学院学报 [Journal of Wuhan Conservatory of Music] 2:26–32.

Zou Xia 邹霞. 2015. "Qiantan 20 shiji ertong gequ fazhan xianzhuang" 浅谈20世纪儿童歌曲发展现状 [An overview of the development of children's songs in the 20th century]. *Beifang yinyue* 北方音乐 [Northern music] 11:8.

Zhandi xinge 《战地新歌》 [New songs of the battlefield]

Zhandi xinge: Wuchanjieji wenhuadageming yi lai chuangzuo gequ xuanji 《战地新歌: 无产阶级文化大革命以来创作歌曲选集》 [New songs of the battlefield: An anthology of new song compositions since the Great Proletarian Cultural Revolution]. 1972. Edited by Guowuyuan wenhuazu geming gequ zhengji xiaozu 国务院文化组革命歌曲征集小组编 [Revolutionary Song Collection Task Force, Cultural Affairs Office under the State Council]. Beijing: Renmin wenxue chubanshe 人民文学出版社 [People's Literature Publishing Group].

Zhandi xinge: Xuji 《战地新歌: 续集》 [New songs of the battlefield: A sequel]. 1973. Edited by Guowuyuan wenhuazu geming gequ zhengji xiaozu 国务院文化组革命歌曲征集小组编 [Revolutionary Song Collection Task Force, Cultural Affairs Office under the State Council]. Beijing: Renmin wenxue chubanshe 人民文学出版社 [People's Literature Publishing Group].

Zhandi xinge: Di san ji 《战地新歌: 第三集》 [New songs of the battlefield: Third collection]. 1974. Edited by Guowuyuan wenhuazu wenyi chuangzuo lingdao xiaozu 国务院文化组文艺创作领导小组编 [Literary and Artistic Creation Leadership Task Force, Cultural Affairs Office under the State Council]. Beijing: Renmin wenxue chubanshe 人民文学出版社 [People's Literature Publishing Group].

Zhandi xinge: Di si ji 《战地新歌: 第四集》 [New songs of the battlefield: Fourth collection]. 1975. Edited by *Zhandi xinge* bianxuan xiaozu 战地新歌编选小组 [*New Songs of the Battlefield* Editorial Committee]. Beijing: Renmin wenxue chubanshe 人民文学出版社 [People's Literature Publishing Group].

Zhandi xinge: Di wu ji 《战地新歌: 第五集》 [New songs of the battlefield: Fifth collection]. 1976. Edited by *Zhandi xinge* bianxuan xiaozu 战地新歌编选小组 [*New Songs of the Battlefield* Editorial Committee]. Beijing: Renmin wenxue chubanshe 人民文学出版社 [People's Literature Publishing Group].

Personal Communication

Chen Jiebing. 2015. Personal interview. Saratoga Springs, NY, August.

———. 2018. E-mail correspondence, April.

Chen Xiaojie [pseud.]. 2015. Personal interview. Flushing, NY, January.

Huang [pseud.]. 2003. Personal interview. China, winter.

Jin Laoshi [pseud.]. 2018. Personal interview, United States, January.
———. 2018. E-mail correspondence, October.
Wang Guowei. 2014. Personal interview. Saratoga Springs, NY, March.
———. 2015. Personal interview. Elmhurst, NY, May.
———. 2018. E-mail correspondence, April.
Yang [pseud.]. 2018. Personal interview. United States, October.
Zhang Haihui. 2018. Personal interview. Pittsburgh, PA, January.

Chen, Xiaomei, 12, 117, 118; on *East is Red*, 35; on eight model works, 36

Cheng, Nien, 117, 170n8

Cheng Tan, 52

Chessa, Antonio, 22, 129–30

Chiang Kai-shek, 34

childhood, 18; during Cultural Revolution, 17; generational imprinting of, 1–2; memory of, 152; music and, 76; *New Songs of the Battlefield* and, 12; revolutionary arts and, 109. *See also* children's songs

children's music: "darker side" of, 21, 98; as resting spot, 76, 101, 102

children's songs, 21, 76, 152; action songs, 80, 84–87, 98; dissemination of, 77–78, 173n1; formal elements of, 78–80, 83, 86, 88; ideology and, 99; "little" (*xiao*) songs, 80, 98; Little Red Guards in, 81, 83–84, 136; nation building and, 89; patriotism in, 81, 92; politically explicit songs, 80, 81–84; politicization of, 90–93, 98, 99–102; post-Cultural Revolution, 173n1; propagandizing of, 90–93; socialist realism in, 84; themes of, 85. See also *New Songs of the Battlefield*; *and particular songs*

China, People's Republic of (PRC): capitalism and, 5, 144; censorship in, 4, 40, 77, 119, 146, 149; class in, 125–27, 132–33; economic reform in, 114; ethnic groups of, 31; individual, shift to, 5, 118, 127; nostalgia in, 11, 141; opening of, 98, 117–19, 145; relations with Soviet Union, 155, 156; role of arts in, 22; post-socialist society of, 141; socialism, transformation into, 1, 15–16, 76, 142, 144, 146, 150, 155–56

China's Cultural Revolution in Memories: CR/10, 15, 20, 21, 72–75

Chinese Communist Party (CCP), 7, 169n3; campaigns of, 155–56; capitalism and, 144, 156; censorship and, 146; Central Committee, 24–25; control of arts, 145; cultural policy of, 23; Cultural Revolution, position on, 15–16, 169n7; minority exoticism of, 63; musical nationalism of, 147; revolutionary songs of, 29, 51–52, 57, 66, 67, 68–69; socialist realism and, 84; taking of power, 111

Clark, Paul, 13–14, 35, 109, 155, 171n9, 171n11, 173n8

class: of Chen Jiebing, 96, 100; of Chen Xiaojie, 14, 125–26, 127; in China, 125–27, 132–33; Cultural Revolution and, 14, 96, 100, 123, 132–33, 142–43, 174n10; popularization and, 31–32

Confucius, 27, 68, 82–84; on music as political tool, 28–29

countryside: Cultural Revolution and, 14, 21, 75, 95, 106–7, 109, 123–28, 131, 142; Mao's cultural policies and, 4, 93, 95, 127; popularization of music and, 140; Red Guards in, 38–39; reeducation and, 93; "sent-down" youth and, 93, 106–7, 109, 123–28, 131, 142, 174n3

COVID-19: fieldwork and, 19

Cultural Revolution, 170n2; aesthetics of, 149; agricultural policies and, 27, 53, 143; arts careers during, 106–8; aural experience of, 16–17; bureaucracy of, 9; Central Cultural Revolution Group, 24–25; childhood during, 17; class and, 14, 96, 100, 123, 132–33, 142–43, 174n10; cultural context of, 155–57; education during, 131–34, 142; embodiment of, 17, 139–40, 148–49; end of, 28; gender equity during, 48–49; group identity during, 116; guiding principles of, 24; history of, 23, 24–28; ideology of, 21, 25–26, 33, 36, 99, 117, 138, 142–46; idleness during, 133; indoctrination under, 82, 86–87; language of, 134–35; launching of, 157; loss in, 117; memory and, 72, 74, 103–4, 109, 151; as "mistake," 15–16; music of, 1, 33; nostalgia and, 110–12, 118, 128, 141; political indoctrination in, 82; political slogans of, 68–69, 84, 87, 131–32; principles of, 24–25; reeducation, 93, 126; regressive politics of, 1; revolutionary songs of, 5; rhetoric of, 24, 67–69, 139; stages of, 33–39, 69; storytelling of, 11; trauma of, 22, 109–10, 111, 128, 146, 151, 152; "Up to the Mountains and Down to the Countryside" campaign, 106–8, 116, 142, 174n3; violence of, 22, 25, 73–75, 104, 111, 132–33, 145–46, 150–52; youth participation in, 25, 84, 115

Cultural Revolution generation, 111; music memory and, 111–14, 129–30; nostalgia of, 116, 127–29; "sent-down" youth of, 116, 123, 142, 174n3

dance: 30; *East is Red*, 33–35; performance songs and, 171n19; troupes, 96–97

Daqing (Mao's model in industry), 53

Daughtry, Martin, 11, 21, 71, 147, 150, 151

Daxelmüller, Christoph, 93

Dazhai (Mao's model in agriculture), 51, 53

realm of, 25; mobilization of, 32–33, 35, 44, 67, 130, 132, 142, 147; nationalization and, 31; popularization and, 31–32, 140–41; in preface to *New Songs*, 43–44; songs intended for, 57–58, 66–67

mass songs. *See* revolutionary songs

McDougall, Bonnie S., 12, 13, 30, 31, 76, 109, 170n6

Meisner, Maurice, 16, 142, 143, 155, 156

memory, 2, 18; of childhood, 152; collective, 21–22, 112–13, 114–15, 127; Cultural Revolution and, 72, 74, 103–4, 109, 151; emotion and, 112–16, 128–29, 141, 151–52; as field site, 10–11, 20; generational imprinting, 115, 129; model revolutionary operas and, 122–23; music and, 10, 17–18, 91, 112–16, 128–29; *New Songs of the Battlefield* and, 12, 109–10, 122; nostalgia and, 22, 113–14, 117, 129–30; propaganda music and, 10; reminiscence bump, 129–30; songbooks and, 111, 113; trauma and, 11; violence and, 11; youth, impact of, 114–15, 129–30

Merriam, Alan P., 91, 99

Milewski, Barbara, 18

Min, Anchee, 117, 170n8, 172n25

minzu, 170n7

minzuhua. See nationalization

Mittler, Barbara, 13–14, 16–17, 35, 109, 139; on propaganda art, 101, 148–49, 173n8

model ballets, 33, 109; stagecraft of, 35, 171n15; traditional elements in, 35

model revolutionary operas (*yangbanxi*), 4–5, 13, 33, 74–75, 109, 120; aesthetics of, 17; comprehensive study of, 15; dissemination of, 39; groups, 94; *jinghu* in, 95; memory and, 122–23; stagecraft of, 35, 171n15; *Taking Tiger Mountain by Strategy*, 35–36; traditional elements in, 35

Mongolians: in "Red Guards on the Grasslands," 61–63

Murre, Jaap, 22, 129–30

music: capitalism and, 5; CCP cultural policy and, 23; childhood and, 76; of Cultural Revolution, 1, 33; emotion and, 7–18, 90–93, 109–10, 112–16, 127–30, 151–52; enculturation and, 99, 100–101; exploitation of, 2; functions of, 90–91, 92–93, 139; ideology and, 112, 17, 21, 33, 50, 53, 67–68, 77, 90, 92, 147; identity and, 92; memory and, 10, 17–18, 91, 112–16, 128–29; nation-

alism and, 22, 112, 147; nationalizing of, 31, 98, 140, 141; nostalgia and, 127–29; politicization of, 18, 20, 23–24, 28–32, 44–45, 50, 68, 70, 90–93, 136, 153; popularizing of, 141–42; propagandizing of, 1, 90–93, 143–44; revolutionary, history of, 45; revolutionizing of, 23, 30–31, 44–45, 68, 70, 98, 134–35, 139–40, 149; solidarity and, 12; totalitarianism and, 2, 32, 92, 151–52; as torture, 92–93; trauma and, 149; universalism and, 91–92; violence and, 149; of war, 52; weaponization of, 1–2, 12, 14, 22, 39, 67, 76, 138–39, 149, 151–53. See also *New Songs of the Battlefield*; propaganda music; revolutionary songs

Music Research Institute of the Chinese National Academy of Arts, 3–6, 10

nationalism, musical, 22, 112, 147

Nationalist Party (*Guomindang* / KMT), 35–36, 131

nationalization (*minzuhua*), 33, 98; of the arts, 30–33, 98, 140; the masses and, 31; of music, 31, 98, 140, 141; youth and, 140; 170n7

New Songs of the Battlefield, 3–4, 6, 7; aesthetics of, 40, 66–67, 69–70, 118, 176n27; anonymous composers, 45; arrest of collaborators, 24; basic musical features of, 46–49; categories of, 46, 80, 171n21; CCP classics, 51–52, 57, 66, 67, 68–69; childhood and, 12; children's songs, 58–60, 78–90; collective compositions, 54, 67, 172n27; compilation process of, 8, 9, 21, 24, 39, 41, 43–45, 51, 66; dissemination of, 41; editorial committees, 45–46; ethnic minorities in, 43, 45, 46, 66, 171n21, 172n31; ethnic minority songs, 43, 46, 50, 53, 60–63, 64, 78, 80; generational response to, 7, 128–29; historical context of, 24, 77; ideology and, 4, 77, 81, 86, 99, 130; imprisonment of collaborators, 8; influence on composition, 13; as inspirational, 135–36; instrumentation of, 46, 48, 50–51, 62, 172n24; international relations songs, 64–66, 80; key signatures of, 47–48, 78; Mao poetry songs, 51; memory and, 12, 109–10, 122; musical complexity of, 66–67; newly composed songs, 53–67, 69–70; nostalgia for, 113, 117; notation in, 46–47, 53, 172n23;

LEI X. OUYANG is an associate professor of music at Swarthmore College.

The University of Illinois Press
is a founding member of the
Association of University Presses.

University of Illinois Press
1325 South Oak Street
Champaign, IL 61820-6903
www.press.uillinois.edu